LUXURY LAW

Law Over Borders Comparative Guide 2022

Edited by
Fabrizio Jacobacci, Studio Legale Jacobacci & Associati
& Alan Behr, Phillips Nizer

GLOBAL LEGAL POST

Published in 2022 by:
Global City Media
86-90 Paul Street
London EC2A 4NE
United Kingdom
Telephone: +44 (0) 20 7193 5801
www.globalcitymedia.com
www.globallegalpost.com

Second Edition Copyright © 2022 (First Edition Copyright © 2016) Global City Media Ltd

The moral rights of the authors have been asserted.

While all reasonable care has been taken to ensure the accuracy of the publication, the publishers cannot accept responsibility for any errors or omissions. This publication is protected by international copyright law. All rights reserved. No paragraph or other part of this document may be reproduced or transmitted in any form by any means, including photocopying and recording, without the prior written permission of Global City Media Ltd or as expressly permitted by the provisions of the Copyright Designs and Patents Act 1988 (as amended), by licence or under terms agreed with the appropriate reprographic rights organisation. Such written permission must also be obtained before any paragraph or other part of this publication is stored in a retrieval system of any kind.

This publication does not constitute legal advice and no liability is accepted for use made of opinions or views expressed in the book.

Editor: Fabrizio Jacobacci & Alan Behr
Editorial Director: Mary Heaney
Associate Publisher: Claudia Tan
Editorial and Production Manager: Debbie Knowles
Commercial Director: Maria Sunderland
Digital: Elanganathapillai Sivakanthan

Printed in the UK by:
TJ Books Ltd
Trecerus Industrial Estate
Padstow
Cornwall
PL28 8RW
www.tjbooks.co.uk

ISBN: 978-0-9935776-3-5

CONTENTS

Foreword   5
Nicolas Martin, Hermès & Sheila Henderson, Richemont

Belgium   9
Moana Colaneri, Beyond Law Firm

Brazil   21
Luiz Edgard Montaury Pimenta & Marianna Furtado de Mendonça, Montaury Pimenta, Machado & Vieira de Mello

China   37
Yunze LIAN & Rebecca LIU, Jadong IP Law Firm

Cyprus   51
Maria Hinni, George Tashev, Nasos Kafantaris & Ioanna Martidi, A.G. Paphitis & Co

Czechia   65
Michal Havlík & Michael Feuerstein, Všetečka Zelený Švorčík & Partners

France   81
Sophie Marc, Santarelli

Germany   95
Dr. Wiebke Baars, Taylor Wessing

India   109
Pravin Anand, Dhruv Anand, Udita M. Patro, Kavya Mammen & Sampurnaa Sanyal, Anand and Anand

Italy   125
Fabrizio Jacobacci, Studio Legale Jacobacci & Associati

Japan   141
Koichi Nakatani, Momo-o, Matsuo & Namba

Netherlands   153
Tjeerd Overdijk, Herwin Roerdink & Nadine Reijnders-Wiersma, Vondst Advocaten

South Korea   165
Dae Hyun Seo & Won Joong Kim, Kim & Chang

Spain   179
Rubén Canales, Eleonora Carrillo, Carolina Montero, Fernando Ortega & Ignacio Temiño, Jacobacci Abril Abogados

Taiwan   195
Crystal J Chen & Nick J.C. Lan, Tsai, Lee & Chen

Turkey   207
Özlem Futman & Yasemin Aktas, Ofo Ventura

United Kingdom   223
Rosie Burbidge, Gunnercooke

United States   237
Alan Behr & Tod Melgar, Phillips Nizer

Contact details   251

FOREWORD

Nicolas Martin
Hermès

Sheila Henderson
Richemont

FOREWORD

The recent months of global pandemic have shown us that the Luxury Goods business has true resilience, flexibility and enduring appeal to its ever growing client base. Traditional routes to market have quietly coexisted alongside the ever dynamic e-commerce business model and supported by the explosion in social media platforms and offerings. Are we different to any other business sector? As an insider, the answer must be yes, we thrive on the personal interactions, we love to share our artisanal skills with our customers and we strive to bring the customer experience to the pinnacle of experiential interaction. A global pandemic with restrictions on travel, boutique closures and limitations on customer gatherings all conspire to challenge the prerequisites of our business model. However, as the business results show, we can adapt and continue to delight our customers with our precious creations.

The legal landscape constantly challenges the possibilities of protecting our artistic expressions through restrictions on protecting 3D trademarks globally, limiting the scope of copyright protection and jurisdictional complexities around online enforcement. Are we different? We beg to answer yes, our creations are designed to delight and endure for generations, not just a couple of years like the average consumer product. We must find ways to bridge those rights with limited lives such as designs and copyright with more strategic protection plans that can endure.

Now we can exist in a metaverse, how do our products and our rights translate into this new world of NFT's and digitally downloadable clothing and accessories? We are on the cusp of answering that. Will the trademark regime give the necessary protection and flexibility? While our *maisons* aim to fulfil desires, surprise and excite with their beautiful craftsmanship, we wait to see how this translates into the metaverse and the nature of the inevitable copies. There is no decrease in the volume and sophistication of those seeking to steal our creativity and short circuit our craftsmanship, and there is no decrease in those willing to pay for a poor substitute. Can we change the thinking and cut off the demand side of the equation? Perhaps the increasing awareness of sustainability and CSR more generally will lead people to appreciate the value of intellectual property and its role in protecting true craftsmanship.

This book offers a one stop shop to the curious reader eager to navigate the cross border nature of our dilemma. No one legal tool provides the 'silver bullet' and this book provides the armoury needed.

 **Nicolas Martin** is Group General Counsel at Hermès International.

 **Sheila Henderson** is Chief Intellectual Property Counsel at Richemont International Ltd.

BELGIUM

Moana Colaneri
Beyond Law Firm

1. TRADEMARK

1.1 Sources of law

Belgium is part of the Benelux trademark system (along with Luxembourg and The Netherlands), regulated by the Benelux Convention on Intellectual Property (trademarks and designs) (BCIP).

Belgium also takes part in European instruments adopted to support uniformization and harmonization efforts in respect of trademarks, including:

- Regulation (EU) 2017/1001 of 14 June 2017 on the European Union trademark.
- Directive (EU) 2015/2436 of 16 December 2015 to approximate the laws of the Member States relating to trademarks.
- Regulation (EU) 608/2013 of 12 June 2013 concerning customs enforcement of intellectual property rights (repealing Council Regulation (EC) 1383/2003).
- Directive 2004/48/EC of 29 April 2004 on the enforcement of intellectual property rights.

Belgium is also a member to several international instruments, notably:

- The Paris Convention for the Protection of Industrial Property of 20 March 1883 (as revised and amended).
- The Madrid Agreement of 14 April 1891 concerning the international registration of mark and Protocol relating to the Madrid Agreement of 27 June 1989 (as revised and amended).
- The Nice Agreement of 15 June 1957 concerning the International Classification of Goods and Services for the Purposes of the Registration of Marks (as revised and amended).
- The Agreement on Trade-Related Aspects of Intellectual Property Rights of 15 April 1994 (TRIPS Agreement).

When a conflict arises, international and EU treaties ratified by the competent Belgian authorities take precedence over the Belgian legislation. Case law is not considered a formal source of law; it is, however, an important interpretational instrument.

1.2 Substantive law

Use is not considered a source of trademark rights. Protection is only granted through registration, or when the trademark is well-known.

(Registered) trademarks with a reputation are distinguished from (unregistered) well-known trademarks. Trademarks with a reputation have been defined by the European Court of Justice (CJEU) as trademarks "known by a significant part of the public concerned by the products or services covered by that trademark" (CJEU, 14 September 1999, General Motors, C-375/97). Unlike trademarks without reputation, the protection of trademarks with a reputation extends to dissimilar goods and services, provided that the earlier trademark is reputed and the use of the later trademark without due cause would take unfair advantage of, or be detrimental to, the distinctive character or the repute of the earlier trademark. Proof of likelihood of confusion is not necessary, unlike for unregistered well-known trademarks. These well-known trademarks "must be well known throughout the territory of the Member State of registration or in a substantial part of it" (CJEU, 22 November 2007, Nieto Nuño, C-328/06). As per Article 6bis of the Paris Convention, the broader protection only extends to the categories of goods and services for which these trademarks are well-known.

No specific legal provisions ensure a broader range of protection for trademarks belonging to the luxury industry. However, an "aura of luxury" may make it easier to argue that the use of a sign takes unfair advantage of, or is detrimental to, the distinctive character or the repute of a trademark (see above, and C-375/97, General Motors).

1.3 Enforcement

To assess broader protection, consideration is given to all the relevant facts of the case, in particular the market share held by the trademark, the intensity, geographical extent and duration of its use, and the size of the investment made by the undertaking in promoting it (see Section 1.2 Trademark: Substantive law and C-375/97, General Motors). This can be proven through all legal means (including oral testimony, affidavit or expert evidence).

A trademark can be enforced against a domain or trade name used in the course of trade. Trademarks can also be successfully enforced against metatags, provided the use is liable to affect the functions of the trademark (CJEU, 23 March 2010, Google France and Google, C-236/08 to C-238/08).

Trademarks can also be enforced against their unauthorized use in social media, provided it occurs in the course of trade. Outside a commercial context, enforcement requires that the use be without due cause and would take unfair advantage of, or be detrimental to, the distinctive character or the repute of a Benelux trademark. In some instances, social media platform operators may also be held accountable.

The owner can enforce their trademark against use in comparative advertising where the advertising takes unfair advantage of, or is detrimental to, the distinctive character or the reputation of a Benelux trademark.

There is no specific parody exception in trademark law. Yet, unauthorized use of a trademark in parody does not go unpunished, provided such use takes unfair advantage of, or is detrimental to, the distinctive character or the reputation of a Benelux trademark. A trademark considered a copyrightable work can be enforced against its unauthorized use in parody, provided the latter fails to meet its essential conditions under copyright law.

A trademark owner cannot take action claiming both trademark infringement and unfair competition for the same set of facts. The owner will only be able to rely on unfair competition in parallel or separate proceedings provided the use of such sign can be considered abusive.

Luxury brands are particularly vulnerable to (online) piracy, stressing the importance of using continually evolving technology to protect and enforce their IP rights. In addition to the measures and actions set up on their own, luxury brands are, for example, increasingly collaborating with online marketplaces, imposing tougher sanctions and setting up monitoring systems.

2. COPYRIGHT

2.1 Sources of law

Copyright protection is regulated by Belgian law; copyright provisions have been included in the Belgian Economic Code (BEC) (Art. XI.164 to XI.293).

Belgium also takes part in European instruments adopted to support copyright harmonization efforts, including:
- Directive (EU) 2019/790 of 17 April 2019 on copyright and related rights in the Digital Single Market (amending Directives 96/9/EC and 2001/29/EC).
- Regulation (EU) 2017/1563 and Directive (EU) 2017/1564 of 13 September 2017 (amending Directive 2001/29/EC).
- Directive 2001/29/EC of 22 May 2001 on the harmonisation of certain aspects of copyright and related rights in the information society.
- Regulation (EU) 608/2013 of 12 June 2013 and Directive 2004/48/EC of 29 April 2004 (see Section 1.1 Trademark: Sources of law).

Belgium is also a member to international instruments dealing with copyright, notably:
- The Berne Convention for the Protection of Literary and Artistic Works (as revised and amended on 28 September 1979).
- The Rome Convention for the Protection of Performers, Producers of Phonograms and Broadcasting Organizations of 26 October 1961.
- The TRIPS Agreement.

Should a conflict arise between these instruments, the conflict rules mentioned above shall apply (see Section 1.1 Trademark: Sources of law).

2.2 Substantive law

Copyright protects all artistic and literary works, as long as they are original and expressed in tangible form, in line with the case law of the CJEU. An infinite number of protectable works may exist, as long as they satisfy these two requirements.

Objects of industrial, fashion or accessory design are copyrightable when considered as original creations, that is when they are the author's own intellectual creation, resulting from the author's own creative choices (CJEU, 16 July 2009, *Infopaq International*, C-5/08). This will not be the case if the design of the object is merely dictated by technical or functional characteristics.

Copyright covers two types of rights. Economic assignable and transferable rights, namely the author's reproduction right and right of communication to the public. Moral rights include the right for the author to decide (when) to disclose their work, a "paternity right", and the right to integrity of the work.

The copyright holder is the natural person-creator of the work. Legal entities may however claim authorship of works created by their employees, consultants, shareholders, directors, or suppliers, through an agreement. Usually, a provision will be added in this respect in the employment or services agreement. A presumption exists that the author is the person whose name is fixed to the work.

Assignments shall always be proven in writing and shall be interpreted restrictively. For transfers involving the author-natural person, additional requirements apply:
- The remuneration of the author, extent and duration of the assignment must be specified for each form of exploitation, which shall be consistent with honest practices.
- The assignment cannot cover unknown forms of exploitation.

- Assignment relating to future works is valid only for a limited time, provided the genres are specified.
- When the object incorporating a work is assigned, this does not automatically entail the right to exploit it; the author must be guaranteed continued access to their work.

Less stringent formalities apply for assignments in the framework of an employment contract and for works made for hire.

Moral rights are inalienable; their exercise may however be waived, although undisputably (e.g. in writing) and only regarding a specific work.

Copyright protection expires 70 years after the death of the (last) author. The term of protection is calculated from the 1 January of the year following the event that triggers the protection period.

2.3 Enforcement

Copyright protection is not subject to any registration formality.

Actual copying is not necessary for the assessment of copyright infringement. One will look at the *overall impression* the original and allegedly infringing work produce.

Copyright can be enforced against a trademark, a design, a patent, a domain or trade name and a pseudonym.

Copyright can also be enforced against its unauthorized use in social media.

Copyright can be enforced against its unauthorized use in comparative advertising, provided the infringing work reproduces the elements of an original work.

The author may not prohibit parody of a lawfully published work since it is considered as an appropriate way to express an opinion, unless the parody fails to meet its essential characteristics (i.e. evoke an existing work while being noticeably different from it and constitute an expression of humour and mockery).

The alleged infringer can rely on the typical defences under procedural law. They could also challenge the claimant's authorship or the original character of their work. They could demonstrate that the allegedly infringing work does not reproduce the original elements of the work. The alleged infringer could also challenge the existence or seek reduction of damages sought by the claimant. There is no "fair use" doctrine in Belgium since the legislator has provided for a closed list of copyright exceptions, which can also be relied on as defences.

In case of dual protection under copyright and trademark law, a copyright may be declared unenforceable if the copyright holder tolerated its use for 5 years. In any case, a copyright may be declared unenforceable if the copyright holder abuses their right to institute proceedings.

The time limit for bringing a copyright infringement action is governed by the general rules of the Belgian Civil or Criminal Code, depending on the type of claim. The prescription period can vary from 5, 10 to 30 years. In addition, the BEC provides for specific time limits, which shall take precedence over the general rules concerning prescription periods in criminal and civil law.

3. DESIGN

3.1 Sources of law

There is no Belgian design law. At Benelux level, designs are regulated by the BCIP.

At European level, designs are regulated by Council Regulation (EC) 6/2002 of 12 December 2001 on Community designs (Community designs Regulation), providing for a uniform design protection in all EU Member States. This Regulation covers (un)registered Community designs.

Belgium is also a member country to international instruments, notably the Paris Convention and the TRIPS Agreement.

Should a conflict arise between these instruments, the conflict rules mentioned above (see Section 1.1 Trademark: Sources of law) shall apply.

3.2 Substantive law

Various types of products are protectable by way of (un)registered design in Belgium. This includes any industrial or handicraft item, including *inter alia* parts intended to be assembled into a complex product, packaging, get-up, graphic symbols, and typographic typefaces. Computer programs fall outside the scope of protection.

As a rule, designs must be registered to enjoy protection under design law, with the exception of unregistered designs. They can benefit from a protection under the Community designs Regulation. Two requirements must be met to obtain a valid (un)registered design: novelty and individual character. Moreover, the design must not be expressly excluded from the scope of protection (designs dictated by their technical function, designs of interconnection, or contrary to public policy or morality).

The right to the design shall vest in the designer. Assignments must be in writing and basic rules of contract law remain entirely applicable.

When drafting a design assignment agreement, attention should be paid to the dual protection under copyright and design law. Under design law for employment contracts and works made for hire, the employer or commissioning party is presumed to be the holder of the right to the design (contrary to copyright law). It has thus been legally provided that when an original design is created by an employee, the copyright relating to the (un)registered design shall belong to the employer. As a matter of precaution, it is recommended to incorporate a copyright assignment clause in favour of the employer or commissioning party in the agreement.

There are no moral rights on designs, although the designer is entitled to the right to be cited.

Registered designs shall be protected for 5 years as from the date of the filing of the application. The term of protection may be renewed for one or more periods of 5 years each, up to a total term of 25 years. Unregistered designs shall be protected for 3 years as from the date on which the design was first made available to the public within the EU.

3.3 Enforcement

The design holder shall have the right to oppose the use of any design which produces a different overall impression on the informed user (EU General

Court, 6 October 2011, *Industrias Francisco Ivars v. OHMI – Motive*, T-246/10). For unregistered designs, actual copying is necessary to assess design infringement.

A design can be enforced against a copyright (provided the design is original), a trademark (provided the design has a distinctive character), a patent (when features of appearance of a product are not solely dictated by its technical function), as well as a domain or trade name.

A design can furthermore be enforced against its unauthorized use on social media.

A design can also be enforced against its unauthorized use in comparative advertising. The design holder will however not be entitled to oppose their design against non-commercial or experimental uses, nor against uses for illustrative or teaching purposes.

There is no specific parody exception in design law. A design could however be enforced against its unauthorized use in parody, provided the latter fails to meet its essential conditions under copyright law (see Section 2.2 Copyright: Substantive law).

The alleged infringer can rely on the typical defences under procedural law. They could also object to the novelty or individual character of the design or demonstrate that the allegedly infringing elements of their design are actually dictated by their technical function. The alleged infringer could object to the existence or seek reduction of damages sought by the claimant. The alleged infringer can also rely on the repair clause as a defence, provided they respect a threefold duty of care (CJEU, 20 December 2017, Acacia, C-397/16, §§ 86 to 88).

A design may be declared unenforceable on the same grounds as those mentioned above (see Section 2.3 Copyright: Enforcement). The time limit for bringing a design infringement action is governed by the general rules concerning prescription periods in the Belgian Civil and Criminal Code. Consequently, a similar reasoning as outlined in Section 2.3 applies to proceedings brought by the design holder.

A design holder can take action claiming both design and copyright infringement for the same set of facts. A design holder cannot, however, take action claiming both design infringement and unfair competition. Reliance on unfair competition in parallel or separate proceedings requires that the use of such design be considered abusive.

4. RIGHT OF PRIVACY, PUBLICITY AND PERSONAL ENDORSEMENT

4.1 Sources of law

Individuals are entitled to control (i.e. consent to) the commercial use of their name, image, likeness, or other unequivocal aspects of their identity (*image*).

The foundation of the right of publicity stems from Article XI.174 BEC, as well as the right of privacy. It has essentially been developed in case law and doctrine.

4.2 Substantive law

The right of publicity is universal. Any individual is a right holder owing to the simple fact that they are a living human being. No further conditions (e.g. capacity) are required under Belgian law. The individual must however be distinguishable (recognizable) to rely on the right of publicity.

The right of publicity survives the death of the individual. It can then be exercised by the heirs of the deceased individual against an unauthorized use of the individual's image, for a maximum period of twenty years following the death of that individual. Pursuant to Belgian case law, the heirs also have a right to the protection of the memory (intimacy) of the deceased. This right is considered as the heirs' own personality right, independent from the right of publicity. It can be opposed as a ground against any use of the image of the deceased which would violate their memory.

As a rule, the (exercise of the) right of publicity cannot be assigned or licensed by way of an agreement. In practice however, an individual can authorize the use of their image (reproduction, communication, exhibition, etc.), under certain conditions. Such authorization is not equivalent to an assignment. It must moreover be specific to the intended use and cannot be granted in unrestricted terms.

The user will only be granted an authorization to use the licensor's image through a(n) (non) exclusive license. The license does not entail a waiver of the (exercise of the) right of publicity in itself, but of the right holder's right to prohibit certain uses of their image. Following the death of the licensor, the license will not be transferred to the heirs, unless the terms of the license state otherwise.

Belgian law does not impose specific requirements with respect to the granted license. All basic rules of contract law remain applicable. Although a written contract is not required, it is highly recommended to facilitate the burden of proof. Pursuant to Belgian case law, such authorization can be granted tacitly, provided it is certain and unequivocal. Tacit evidence will usually be based on a series of presumptions (surrounding circumstances, no objection, etc.), subject to restrictive interpretation.

As a rule, a licensor may withdraw their consent at all times (only for the future). Contractual authorization with respect to a certain use of an image does not prevent such withdrawal. The right holder may however have to refund any remuneration which has been paid by the user to the right holder or be required to pay damages, provided they demonstrate the existence and extent of it.

4.3 Enforcement

In Belgium, the right of publicity can be enforced against any unauthorized use (be it commercial or not) of an individual's image.

Since any individual has a right of publicity, it is not necessary to prove that the individual's image has commercial value to contest the unauthorized use of their image. However, when an individual's image becomes a source of income, proof of the commercial value of their image may facilitate the grant of an injunction or other remedies.

The right of publicity can be enforced against anyone making or using an individual's image. This does not mean that the scope of enforcement of this right is unrestricted. Among the defences available to the alleged infringer, the latter could rely on the right to freedom of expression, which comprises the public's right to information. This right is, however, not absolute and the act of disclosure must notably be weighed in against the contribution to a debate of public interest and the relevance of such disclosure for the public. The alleged infringer may also claim (by providing all relevant evidence) that authorization has been granted for the use in question. In the event a third party was responsible for gathering such authorization but failed to do so, the alleged infringer may also pursue remedies against them.

To add more value to their brand's image, luxury brands rely on celebrities and online influencers. The latter could however decide to stop collaborating with a brand and claim damages (e.g. should the brand be confronted with scandals or unethical practices), or pressure the brand to change certain policies (e.g. being fur-free).

5. PRODUCT PLACEMENT

Pursuant to Article 11 of the AMS directive (Directive 2010/13/EU of 10 March 2010 on the coordination of certain provisions laid down by law, regulation or administrative action in Member States concerning the provision of audiovisual media services, as amended by Directive (EU) 2018/1808 of 14 November 2018), product placement is allowed as a rule, subject to certain exceptions. Due to Belgium's particular institutional framework, the provisions relating to product placement have been transposed in three separate media decrees for the country's French Community (Decree of 4 February 2021), Flemish Community (Decree of 19 March 2021 amending the Decree of 27 March 2009), and German-speaking Community (Decree of 1st March 2021).

The requirements laid down in the respective decrees in relation to product placement are the same as those provided for in Article 11, § 3 of the AMS directive. The last requirement, which provides that the viewer be clearly informed of the existence of product placement, only applies to programmes that have been produced or commissioned by a media service provider or by a company affiliated with that media service provider. Product placement for tobacco and medicinal products and treatments is prohibited. Under the French Community's decree, there is no limitation as such for medicinal products, although publicity surrounding it is subject to additional requirements.

As provided under Article 11, § 2 of the AMS directive, product placement is expressly prohibited in news and current affairs programmes, consumer affairs programmes, religious and children's programmes. The decree enacted by the French Community also extends the prohibition to non-confessional philosophical programmes.

No specific remedies are provided to the brand owner in the event the other party fails to perform the agreement. The brand owner could however always initiate civil proceedings to repair the harm suffered as a consequence of the contractual breach.

6. PROTECTION OF CORPORATE IMAGE AND REPUTATION

The right of publicity does not extend to legal entities or corporations. However, corporations may rely on the protection of their image and reputation *vis-à-vis* (non-)competitors and customers. Counterfeiting, unfair competition, denigration and defamation have been recognized in Belgian case law as acts that may adversely affect the image and reputation of a corporation.

Corporations may to a certain extent also rely on their right to privacy (e.g. in respect of violation of trade secrets).

Corporations may protect their image by relying on specific clauses included in selective distribution agreements. These agreements however fall outside the scope of the European Block Exemption Regulation (BER) (Commission Regulation (EU) 330/2010 of 20 April 2010) when they contain clauses qualifying as hardcore or excluded restrictions.

Selective distribution agreements may typically include clauses prohibiting retailers to sell the corporation's products to re-sellers whose image is below a defined standard.

The prohibition to sell below a certain price is equivalent to the establishment of a fixed or minimum resale price or a fixed or minimum price level. Such clause would be prohibited as it includes a hardcore restriction infringing EU competition law (Article 4, (a) BER).

In the same vein, a clause providing that a retailer be prohibited from buying non-original (but otherwise legitimate) spare parts and components would also be prohibited (Article 4, (b), (iv) BER).

Liquidated damages or stipulated fines clauses for breach by a party of any provisions protecting reputation or corporate image may legitimately be included in selective distribution agreements. Judges are however entitled to reduce the damages claimed or the fines stipulated should such amounts be considered excessive.

Luxury brands have always considered the resale market as a threat to their image. However, since the secondary luxury market is expected to grow even faster than the primary one, luxury brands are forced to reconsider and adapt their strategy, depending on what they want to achieve (control of their brand image, sustainability, and so on).

AUTHOR BIOGRAPHY

Moana Colaneri

Moana Colaneri is a partner at Beyond Law Firm in Brussels. Moana is an experienced IP lawyer and specializes in both contentious and non-contentious matters in relation to Intellectual Property law (IP), ICT law, Data Protection, advertising and media.

Her practice spans the full spectrum of IP services, ranging from initial strategy, clearance searches to IP litigation, exploitation, and licensing work, with the development, review and implementation of IP enforcement and protection strategies throughout.

Moana's areas of expertise include the production and distribution of media content and software as well as doing business on the Internet such as e-commerce, online media, and digital marketing. In addition, she assists clients in data protection and privacy matters.

Besides having worked in a Belgian and international law firm, both market leaders in her areas of expertise (Koan Law Firm and Olswang), Moana has also gained experience as an in-house counsel, which is reflected in her proactive and solution-minded approach.

BRAZIL

**Luiz Edgard Montaury Pimenta
& Marianna Furtado de Mendonça**
Montaury Pimenta, Machado & Vieira de Mello

1. TRADEMARK

1.1 Sources of law

The main source of law relating to trademarks in Brazil is the Brazilian Industrial Property Law. Moreover, the Brazilian Constitution is also an important source of law, since it guarantees trademark ownership in its main chapter of "Fundamental Rights and Guarantees". Furthermore, Brazil has been an original signatory of the Paris Convention for the Protection of Industrial Property since 1883 and a signatory of the Madrid Protocol. In addition, there are also some regulations of the Brazilian Patent and Trademark Office (BPTO) that are significant sources of law.

Although the Brazilian Industrial Property Law considers as a rule that the trademark property is acquired by a validly granted registration, the law also determines that any person who, in good faith, has been using the trademark for at least six months can claim preferential right to registration.

1.2 Substantive law

Brazilian law distinguishes between well-known trademarks and highly-reputed trademarks.

Generally, the trademark registration procedure in Brazil observes the principles of territoriality and specialty. The Principle of Territoriality grants exclusive use of the registered trademark in the national territory, in other words, throughout Brazil. Whereas, the Principle of Specialty refers to the fact that the protection granted to a trademark is limited to the specific products or services identified by the trademark, that is, to the products or services related to the class in which the trademark is registered. However, there are exceptions to these principles, which are the well-known mark and highly reputed trademark. The well-known mark is an exception to the Principle of Territoriality, pursuant to Article 6-bis of the Paris Convention.

There is no broader range of protection for brands in the "luxury industry".

1.3 Enforcement

To determine that a trademark is highly reputed and, therefore, entitled to special protection, the Brazilian Patent and Trademark Office (BPTO) presents, in Resolution No. 107 of August 19, 2013, some instructions regarding the necessary evidence. At first, it is important to emphasize that all evidence presented must be linked to three fundamental requirements, such as:
- recognition of the mark by a large portion of the general public;
- quality, reputation, and prestige that the public associates with the mark and the products or services marked by it; and
- degree of distinctiveness and exclusivity of the trademark in question.

A trademark can be enforced against a domain name as well as against a trade name, in such a way that third parties cannot register a domain name or a trade name that contains a trademark registered by another person. Besides that, there is no specific provision in Brazilian Law regarding the use of trademarks in metatags. In this view, it is understood that this use is allowed, so that it cannot be enforced. However, depending on the situation, the trademark owner may be able to enforce against this use through other provisions, such as unfair competition.

The Brazilian Industrial Property Law grants to the registrant of a trademark, or an applicant for a mark, the guaranteed right to exclusive use of the mark throughout the national territory, and also having the right to care for its material integrity or reputation. In this way, any misuse and/or unauthorized use, including on social media, can and should be opposed by the trademark owner. It is important to emphasize that the Brazilian Industrial Property Law presents some limitations to the owner's exclusive use of the trademark. For example, the law prohibits the owner from preventing accessory manufacturers from using the mark to indicate the use of the product, provided they obey fair competition practices and prevent the mention of the mark in speeches, scientific or literary works or in any other type of publication, provided that it is without any commercial connotation and without prejudice to its distinctive character.

As a rule, comparative advertising using a third party's trademark is allowed in Brazil, as long as the comparisons make use of objective facts or data that can be proven and, further, that they do not create a risk of confusion and do not violate the reputation of the third party's trademark. The Brazilian Superior Court expressed its opinion on this matter in a famous case, in which the battery trademark *Rayovac* used the competing trademark *Duracell* in an advertisement, claiming that both had the same life span. The Brazilian Court held that the advertisement was promoted in accordance with what is allowed by the advertising market, pointing out that the right of the trademark holder is not absolute and unrestricted.

Brazilian legislation does not specifically set the limits of trademark use in parodies. Thus, in some cases, the Brazilian Copyright Law is subsidiarily applied, since it better determines the limits of parody, clarifying that parodies that are not true reproductions of the original work, nor that discredit it, are permitted. But, as a rule, the Brazilian courts understand that such use is seen as trademark infringement, making a broad interpretation that assures the owner of the trademark to care for its reputation.

A trademark owner can take action claiming both trademark infringement and unfair competition for the same set of facts, as well as for parasitism claims.

The piracy industry is mainly online.

The lack of regulation of position marks in Brazil is also an issue to be overcome, particularly for luxury brands. Such regulation is extremely necessary and welcome, as there are several cases of position marks that are not granted by the Brazilian Trademark Office (BTO) due to lack of regulation and, in these cases, the consequences are harmful to their holders, since third parties in bad faith can take advantage and make use of them freely.

2. COPYRIGHT
2.1 Sources of law
The main source of law governing copyright is Brazil's Copyright Act (LDA, Law No. 9.610/1998).

It should be noted that although Brazil's main source of law is indeed Law No. 9.610/1998, which regulates copyright and related rights (performers, artists, phonographic producers and broadcasting companies), other specific and complementary legislation is still in force in Brazil in connection with copyright, which has not been expressly or tacitly revoked by Law. 9.610/1998. In this regard, a variation of other specific legislations, as well as Brazil's Civil Code (Law No. 10.406/2002) are still in force.

In addition, although Brazil's current Copyright Act (LDA) was revised and updated in 2013 by Law 12.853, said revision focused on changing the regulation related to management of collective copyrights.

Copyright protection is also guaranteed by the Brazilian Constitution, in subsections XXVII and XXVIII of section 5.

Copyright is also subject to supranational provisions contained mainly in International Treaties regarding copyright to which Brazil is a contracting party, such as the Berne Convention.

When in conflict the order of priority of relevant sources is specific regulations to general regulations, such as the Brazilian Copyright Act and the Brazilian Constitution.

2.2 Substantive law

The following are protected under copyright: the texts of literary, artistic or scientific works, lectures, addresses, sermons and other works of the same kind; dramatic and dramatic-musical works; choreographic and mimed works whose stage performance is set down in writing or otherwise; musical compositions with or without words; audio-visual works, with or without accompanying sounds, including cinematographic works; photographic works and other works produced by a process analogous to photography; drawings, paintings, engravings, sculptures, lithographs and works of kinetic art; illustrations, maps and other works of the same kind; drafts, mock-ups and three-dimensional works relating to geography, engineering, topography, architecture, park and garden planning, stage scenery and science; adaptations, translations and other transformations of original works, presented as new intellectual creations; computer programs; collections or compilations, anthologies, encyclopedias, dictionaries, databases and other works which, by virtue of the selection, coordination or arrangement of the subject matter, constitute intellectual creations. Said lists of copyrighted works is open and not thorough.

Fashion and accessory design may be copyrightable in Brazil as they can be considered as an "artistic expression". However, such will only be considered as copyrightable if they are invested with a great deal of creativity and originality.

Regarding the requirements for originality and creativity, we emphasize that these are met as long as the object contains "the creator's personal brand". The so-called "creator's personal brand" can occur even in the event of the use of elements already known to the public, provided that, with these elements, a new, individualized work is created, which is not confused with those existing ones on the market.

In this respect, to meet the basic requirement of originality, the object must have its "own contours, in terms of expression and composition" so that the work is protected by copyright.

The so-called "creator's personal brand" can occur even in the event of the use of elements already known to the public, provided that, with these elements, a new, individualized work is created, which is not confused with those existing ones on the market.

In this regard, to meet the basic requirement of originality, the object must have its "own contours, in terms of expression and composition" so that the work is protected by copyright.

In Brazil, copyright is recognizable through author's material (economic) and moral rights. The author's material rights encompass the right to use the literary, artistic, or scientific work, to profit of such and to dispose of it. The author's material rights include the authorization for partial or complete reproduction, adaptation, translation, incorporation into a phonogram or audio-visual work, distribution rights.

The author's moral rights include the right to claim authorship of the work at any time, to have their name, pseudonym or conventional sign to appear or be announced as being the author's when the work is used, to keep the work unpublished; to ensure the integrity of the work by objecting to any modification or any act liable in any way to have an adverse effect on the work or to be prejudicial to their reputation or honour as author; to amend the work either before or after it has been used; to withdraw the work from circulation or to suspend any kind of use that has already been authorized where the circulation or the use of the work is likely to have an adverse effect on the author's reputation or image; to have access to the sole or a rare copy of the work that is lawfully in a third party's possession with a view to preserving the memory thereof by means of a photographic process or similar or an audio-visual process, in such a way that the least possible inconvenience is caused to its possessor who shall in any event be indemnified for any damage or prejudice suffered.

The author of copyrightable work is the natural person who created it, that is, the individual.

Despite that, LDA has excepted the creations resulting from "work for hire" relationships. It is important to note that such a relationship must be established within a written contract. Moreover, the Law also accepts the authorship of legal entities in regard to the "collective works", that is, the works of the mind created under the initiative, instructions and responsibility of a legal entity, who publishes it under its name or mark, and consists of contributions by two or more authors whose work is merged into a self-contained creation.

With regard to its employees, legal entities shall acquire the rights to the works created by the employee under the expressed provision to be included in the employment contract. It should be noted that said provision shall be explicit regarding the scope of use of the copyrightable work. In case the employee is hired to create a specific work, the legal entity shall have the rights related to such within the scope of the employment contract. It is important to emphasize that the employee's moral rights will always remain with the employee, as these cannot be waived or assigned. The same applies to the creations of the legal entities' consultants, shareholders, directors and suppliers.

The copyright assignment shall be written, otherwise it will not be valid. Moreover, the assignment agreement must be executed through a marginal note within the registration of the copyrightable work or, when the work is not registered among the appropriate entities, the assignment must be registered in a Registry of Deeds and Documents. Important provisions regarding the assignment of economic rights of copyrightable work are those in which the assignment, when not explicit, is presumed to be onerous, as well as that the assignment of both the author's work, as well as of their future work, shall not exceed more than five years.

Moral rights are inalienable and irrevocable. However, upon the author's death, their moral rights are transferred to their successors.

Material rights over copyrightable works last 70 years, counted from 1 January of the year following the author's death. Then, the work enters the public domain. It should be noted that regarding copyrightable works by anonymous or pseudonymous authors, the material rights shall be exercised by the person who publishes, and within 60 years counted from 1 January of the year following the work's first publication. Regarding moral rights, these never expire and are indefeasible. Upon the death of the author, they are transferred to their successors. In addition, the Brazilian Copyright Act prescribes that it is also the State's obligation to safeguard and protect the integrity and authorship of a work that has fallen into the public domain.

2.3 Enforcement

The Brazilian Legal system does not require the registration of copyrightable works for them to be protected or enforced. The only legal requirement that authors must comply with in order to be granted protection over their artistic, literary or scientific work is that it be a result of the author's mind, expressed by any means.

Although not required, registration of a copyrightable work is highly recommended as it does contribute to the enforcement of such rights. In Brazil, copyrightable works may be registered among the following: Brazil's National Library; School of Music at the Federal University of Rio de Janeiro; School of Fine Arts of the Federal University of Rio de Janeiro; or at the Federal Council of Engineering, Architecture and Agronomy.

The protection of industrial design objects through copyright is a very controversial subject in Brazil as it was not prescribed by any regulation. In that regard, intellectual property in Brazil has long been divided whether an intellectual work can be protected under more than one institute, the so-called "overlapping of rights or overlapping protection", with some arguing that allowing copyright protection in industrial design objects would be prejudicial to competition as this extends the duration of the protected work.

However, others consider that, if industrial design objects, because of their aesthetic form, are subject to being contemplated as art objects, they will indeed by entitled to protection under copyright in Brazil.

In this regard, it is important to note that Brazilian Courts have already recognized the possibility of copyright protection over industrial design objects.

Copyright infringement can be total or partial. Under the Brazilian legal system, it is not necessary to evidence the exact copy of the work, rather to evidence the substantial similarity thereof and the unauthorized use by the infringer.

A trademark reproduces a copyrightable work, it may not be registered according to Brazilian Industrial Property Law. Likewise, copyright can indeed be enforced against the misuse of a mark that reproduces or imitates a copyrightable work.

Copyright can be enforced against a registered design/design patent, patent, domain name, trade name, a pseudonym and other IP rights.

Although the Brazilian Internet Bill of Rights (Law. No. 12.965/2014) has established that the providers of internet applications, such as social media, are only liable when they do not comply with a court order to remove unauthorized content, said provision was excepted by the very same regulation with regard to copyright infringement, which was supposed to be regulated under a specific regulation which, however, was never edited.

In this regard, in light of the absence of the specific regulation on copyright infringement through social media, the enforcement of copyright is made through cease-and-desist letters and application providers shall be considered liable if, after duly notified by the right owner, they failed to remove the infringing content, in spite of specific court order to do so.

Copyright may also be enforced against unauthorized comparative advertising through the filing of an infringement lawsuit, on the grounds of copyright infringement (potentially coupled with practice of unfair competition) as well as through the filing of a complaint before the Conselho Nacional de Autorregulamentação Publicitária (CONAR), Brazil's National Advertising Self-Regulation Council, which is responsible for supervising and regulating advertisement in Brazil.

In accordance with art. 47 of the LDA, paraphrases and parodies shall not be considered as copyright infringement as long as they are not actual reproductions of the original work and are not in any way derogatory to it. In this regard, it is important to state that the LDA has not conditioned parodies concerning its commercial use or not, the Brazilian legislator having chosen to privilege the constitutional principle of free speech.

There are some exceptions to Copyrightable works as established in article 46 of the Brazilian Copyright Law.

In Brazil, the doctrine of fair use does not exist, as the Brazilian Copyright Law has adopted the French doctrine with regard to copyright, in which the rights protected are related to the author and not the work itself. However, the situations prescribed by the LDA as non-infringement of copyrights indicate that Brazil does indeed except copyright with regard to the right of information and cultural access, as long as the use of the copyrightable work does not detrimentally affect the author or their regular exploitation of the work.

Considering that Brazil acknowledges both moral and economic rights of copyrightable work, it is important to note that the author's moral rights are always enforceable as they do not expire, ever. Although enforceable, the right to obtain compensation over said infringement of the author's moral rights expires 3 years after the violation, considering that the statute of limitations applicable to compensation related to copyright infringement is the one prescribed by Brazil's Civil Code, as the Copyright Law did not establish said deadline.

With regard to the economic rights, if the violation is due to breach of contract, the statute of limitations is of 5 years. If the violation does not result from breach of contract, the statute of limitations is of 10 years. Compensation over the violation of economic rights also expires within 3 years of the violation.

The main issue faced by luxury brands related to copyright protection of its products is regarding the fact that clothing apparel in general is deemed as too utilitarian and of industrial application to be recognizable as copyright protected. Although some courts have already recognized copyright protection on luxury handbags, the great controversy lies in whether luxury products that might be granted copyright protection are perceived, not as a contemplation object, but rather a utilitarian object, with a functional/practical character. In this regard, copyright claims over luxury items shall focus on the aesthetic aspect of the product and whether it has achieved the "contemplation" aspect.

3. DESIGN
3.1 Sources of law

Although design protection was acknowledged by the Brazilian Constitution, the main source of law that regulates design in Brazil is Title II of the Brazilian Industrial Property Law, which establishes general provisions on registration requisites, registration procedure as well as nullity procedure, and scope of protection.

International Treaties such as the Paris Convention for the Protection of Industrial Property and Agreement on Trade-Related Aspects of Intellectual Property Rights also regulate designs in Brazil.

When in conflict, the different applicable sources are prioritized as follows: the LPI and ratified international treaties in their scope of application.

3.2 Substantive law

In Brazil, design protection shall be granted over products that bear new and original ornamental plastic form or over the ornamental arrangement of lines and colours of a product, resulting in a new and original visual external configuration, with industrial appliance. It is important to emphasise that in Brazil designs must be registered in order to be granted protection and be enforceable.

In order to be granted protection, the design must be new and original.

With regard to the new/novelty requisite, the LPI clarifies that designs shall be considered new whenever they are not encompassed by the so-called "state of the art", which consists of everything made available to the public prior to the filing date of the application, in Brazil or abroad, by use or by any other means, with the exception of the "grace period", that is, if the disclosure of the design was made 180 days prior to the filing of the design in the BPTO either by (i) the inventor; (ii) the BPTO; or (iii) by third parties, based on information obtained directly or indirectly from the inventor or as a consequence of actions taken by him.

The originality requisite shall be considered fulfilled whenever the design results in a distinctive visual configuration, in connection to other prior objects.

In this regard, it should be noted that it is irrelevant whether the design results from a combination of a known element.

Rights to designs created by employees can be acquired by legal entities through express provisions in the employment contract.

Similarly, legal entities can acquire the rights to designs created by consultants, shareholders, directors and suppliers through contract.

In order to be valid, the assignment agreement must indicate the valid registration number of the design and such assignment must be registered before the BPTO. The payment shall also be made through a fixed fee, agreed between the parties.

It is important to include crucial clauses when drafting a design assignment agreement such as:
- a confidentiality clause regarding determined information that employees, consultants, shareholders, directors and suppliers will obtain regarding such design;
- exceptions to the assignment, if any; and
- conflicting employment and non-competition covenants.

In Brazil, designers are not entitled to "moral rights".

The protection on industrial design registrations lasts for a period of 10 (ten) years from the date of filing, being extendable for 3 (three) successive periods of 5 (five) years each. In this connection, industrial designs may be enforceable for 25 years from the filing of the design in the BPTO.

Unregistered designs are not granted protection/are not enforceable in Brazil.

3.3 Enforcement

In Brazil, design infringement does not require the design to be identical to the registered design, but that the design has substantially the same design/format as the registered design. In this regard, the level of novelty of the registered design - how substantially similar is the protected design to the so-called "state of the art" - is taken into account as well as the existence of similar registrations. That is because if there are two similar designs registered, sufficient novelty is presumed in said designs that might prevent the finding for infringement regarding the new design that is just as similar.

A design can be enforced against a trademark (in case a trademark misuses the registered design, it may enforced), a registered design/design patent, a patent and other IP rights.

In case there is an unauthorized reproduction of a registered design on social media, such use is considered infringement and the holder of the rights may send cease and desist letters requesting the takedown of the infringing content. In accordance with the Brazil's Internet Bill of Rights, application providers are, however, only liable if, after court order to do so, the application providers do not remove the infringing content of the social media. It is important to note that the court order shall indicate the URL containing the infringing content for the takedown.

A design may be enforced against unauthorized comparative advertising through the filing of an infringement lawsuit, on the grounds of copyright infringement (potentially coupled with practice of unfair competition) as well as through the filing of a complaint before CONAR, which is responsible for supervising and regulating advertisement in Brazil.

In principle, a design can be enforced against its unauthorized use in parody. Likewise, regarding comparative advertising, it should be assessed in each specific case whether the use in parody is damaging to the holder and is within the scope of freedom of speech.

A design may not be enforced against third parties that use it in an experimental or private manner, without commercial use/gain. Designs are also not enforceable if used on a product manufactured in accordance with a product that was introduced to the domestic market directly by the holder with his consent.

The BIPL also recognizes the unenforceability of the design registration by the prior *bona fide* users who were using the design in good faith prior to registration. In this case, *bona fide* users are entitled to continue to use the design in the same manner and under the same conditions as the design was being used before, without any burden to the prior *bona fide* user.

In addition, the Brazilian Industrial Property law allows arguing the nullity of the industrial design as a defence in infringement actions. In this regard, the defendant in a design infringement action is allowed to argue that the design registration being enforced is null as it does not fulfil the legal requisites for registration and thus, cannot be enforced. In this regard, it is important to emphasize that the decision in an infringement action that finds for the unenforceability of the design, since it does not meet the legal requirements, does not implicate in the nullity, *erga omnes*, of the design registration, but rather recognizes that in that specific case, the design cannot be enforced against the infringer.

The "repair clause" doctrine does not exist in Brazil.

Designs are not enforceable in the situations listed above prior *bona fide* user, private/experimental non-commercial use or when the design does not meet the legal requisites prescribed by the BIPL. Design is also not enforceable after the registration, having entered the public domain. In this regard, designs may be enforceable for 25 years from the filing of the design with the BPTO.

It is possible for a design holder to take action claiming both design as well as copyright infringement for the same set of facts. However, the multi protection of an object, such as industrial design and copyright is still a controversial subject for specialists and the courts. The Courts, however, recognized the overlapping protection of an object protected as both under copyright and industrial design. With this connection, claim of unfair competition is also possible and usual in relation to industrial design claims.

The current issue luxury brands face in expanding their design refers to the registration of new designs, as multiple registration of similar designs may diminish their protection, considering that the more registrations made with a small variation, the more incorporated into the "state of the art" the design becomes. This allows competitors to imitate it.

In addition, recently, the Brazilian Trademark Office (BTO) started a Public Consultation on the examination of applications for registration of Position Marks, enabling interested parties to contribute with criticism and suggestions regarding the regulation of the subject.

BRAZIL

Such regulation is extremely necessary and welcome, as there are several cases of position marks that are not granted by the BTO due to lack of regulation and, in these cases, the consequences are harmful to their holders, since third parties in bad faith can take advantage of make use of them freely.

Fortunately, the public consultation carried out has the objective of hearing the opinion of specialists and those interested in the subject, so that clear rules can be created to officially regulate the matter in Brazil, thus modernizing the Brazilian Trademark system. Once the final version of the Technical Note has been approved, it will apply to applications already filed before its publication, which are pending examination by the INPI and which qualify as position marks.

It is estimated that the regulation of the subject is scheduled to come into force in 2021, although the implementation date has not been scheduled.

4. RIGHT OF PRIVACY, PUBLICITY AND PERSONAL ENDORSEMENT

4.1 Sources of law

An individual has the right to control the use of their own name, image and any other private information. In this regard, the Brazilian Constitution determines, in its chapter on Fundamental Rights and Guarantees, that the privacy, private life, honor and image of a person are inviolable. Also, the Brazilian Civil Code determines, regarding the Personality Rights, that a person's name cannot be used in commercial advertising without his or her authorization.

Brazilian law does not contain specific provisions for what is called "Right of Publicity", but rather for "Personality Rights", which are considered Fundamental Rights, and for personal data. The main sources of law for these matters are the Brazilian Constitution, the Brazilian Civil Code (Law No. 10.406, 2002), the Brazilian Internet Bill of Rights (Law No. 12.965, 2014) and the Brazilian General Data Protection Law (Law No. 13.709, 2018).

4.2 Substantive law

Any human being has the right of personality, that is, the right to have inviolable privacy, name, private life, honor and image. Always bear in mind that if the personality rights of a deceased person are being violated, the spouse, ascendants, or descendants are legitimate parties to protect these rights.

In Brazil, the existence of a natural person ends with death. However, the Brazilian Civil Code understands that it is possible for a deceased person to suffer violation of personality rights, such as violation of name, intimacy, honor, and private life. Therefore, the spouse or any relative in a direct line, or collateral to the fourth grade is allowed to demand an end to such violations. Furthermore, the Brazilian Civil Code also authorizes these relatives to prohibit the disclosure of writings, the transmission of words, or the publication, the exhibition or use of the deceased's image, to their request and without prejudice to any compensation that may be due, if affects their honor, good name or respectability, or if it is intended for commercial purposes. Besides that, the Brazilian General Data Protection Law also strengthens the legitimacy of a relative/spouse to request the non-disclosure and or the end of the processing of a deceased relative's data, since this new law makes it clear that personal data is any information "related to an identified or identifiable natural person", so that some information of the deceased may help to identify the spouse or some relative of the deceased.

An individual can assign their right of publicity in whole or in part and it shall be inserted in the assignment agreement.

An individual can license their right of publicity and such license can be exclusive or non-exclusive. Such provision must be inserted in the assignment agreement.

To be valid, according to Brazilian Law, an agreement for the assignment/license of the right of publicity should be a typical contract, having its own unique requirements. It presents as main elements the parties, the object and written form. It can be free or onerous and, thus, respectively, it will be a unilateral or bilateral contract. The assignment/license can be partial or total.

In case of contractual breach, the licensor may withdraw consent to use the licensing object.

In the event that the licensor dies while the license agreement is still in force, his rights and obligations are transferred to his successors. This will only not occur in the event that it is specifically provided for in the contract, since the agreement binds the successors.

The same occurs in the case of the death of the Assignor: his rights and obligations are transferred to his successors.

The heirs must comply with the requirements and clauses of this contract until its termination.

If the right of publicity is related to the image of the transferor / licensor, then 70 years, counting from 1 January in the year following the death of the transferor / licensor.

4.3 Enforcement

The privacy, private life, honor and image of a person are inviolable, and can be enforced against commercial use and use that affects a person's honor, good name or respectability.

The misuse of a person's personal information can be countered regardless of who that person is and/or whether that personal data has any commercial value.

Regarding the processing of personal data, the Brazilian General Data Protection Law determines in Article 7 the "legal bases", that is, the legal grounds that can be used to justify the processing of personal data.

One of the main issues luxury brands should be concerned with when working with celebrities relates to the end of the authorized period of use, so what has been agreed should be checked. Often this agreed period is ignored and future use, without a new authorization, can be an issue.

5. PRODUCT PLACEMENT

Despite there being no current legislation/specific regulation, product placement is common in Brazil. The only regulation is provided by Brazil's National Advertising Self-Regulation Council that imposes that any advertisement, including product placement, shall be identified/informed to the public, as advertisement.

In this regard, we cite as general provisions the obligation of a true representation of the product as well as that the ad/placement must be carried out in such a way as not to abuse the consumers' trust, not exploit their lack of experience or knowledge, and not benefit from their trust.

If a party fails to perform an agreed product placement the remedy for the brand owner shall depend on the clauses of the agreement. In case the agreement provides that the other party may cease the communication, such shall be possible. If not, damages are available.

The main concern with regard to product placement is that such is done in a manner that it does not overexpose the product or the brand, so it does not lose the "aura of luxury".

6. PROTECTION OF CORPORATE IMAGE AND REPUTATION

In Brazil, right of privacy/image/reputation is encompassed as "personality rights", with constitutional protection. Although there is some controversy among Brazilian specialists that consider the right of privacy/image as an extremely personal right, only applicable to the natural persons, the right of privacy/protection of reputation/ image of legal entities and corporations is indeed recognized by the Brazilian Courts, Brazil's Superior Court of Justice even having recognized the possibility of moral damages to be awarded to legal entities/corporations due to violation of their reputation/image.

With regard specifically to data/privacy, Brazil has only recently edited Law No. 13.709/2018, Brazil's General Law of Data Protection (LGPD) which aims to regulate and protect the collection, treatment, and use, by individuals, legal entities and/or corporations, of the personal data of individuals.

The law has specifically prescribed that the data protected under said regulation is only of natural persons and its scope is not limited to the data collected online, but rather any and all personal data, including sensitive data.

Currently, there is no equivalent regulation about the protection of data of legal entities/ corporations in Brazil. In this regard, the data of legal entities and corporations are most likely to be protected under trade secret and provisions on unfair competition.

The Brazilian legislation has not specifically provided for requisites for the protection of corporate image/reputation of legal entities/corporations. However, precedents have established that said protection shall consider the fame/notoriety of the corporation.

Moreover, the provisions on unfair competition practice of article 195, II of BIPL also aim to protect corporations' reputation/image, such as when a competitor discloses false information on the legal entity/corporation.

It is generally possible to include specific clauses in agreements aimed at protecting the corporate image/reputation of one of the parties. With regard specifically to luxury products, it is very common and recommended that legal entities and corporations should include in distribution agreements a set of high standard requirements with regard to point of sales in order to preserve the image of luxury brands associated with the goods. Other provisions allowed in the Brazilian legal system that may be included in agreements aimed at protecting the corporate image/reputation of luxury brands are:

- Prohibition to sell the products to resellers whose image is below a certain defined standard.
- Prohibition to sell below a certain price or to do so outside of specific time periods.
- Prohibition to buy non original – but otherwise legitimate – spare parts and components.

The stipulated fine shall not be fixed at an abusive amount, that is, when obviously excessive or derisory. In this case, the Trial Court Judge may lower the amount to a sum that he considers fair.

Resale is one of the biggest concerns for luxury brands in the secondary market. That is because the resale may allow the depreciation and prestige of the luxury goods.

AUTHOR BIOGRAPHIES

Luiz Edgard Montaury Pimenta
Senior Partner at Montaury Pimenta, Machado & Vieira de Mello
Luiz Edgard Montaury Pimenta is a trial lawyer and the president of ABPI (Brazilian Association of Intellectual Property) since 2018. Luiz leads the IP litigation team of Montaury Pimenta, Machado & Vieira de Mello and has been representing national and international clients for over 30 years in a wide range of IP disputes covering various technologies and areas in the Federal and State Courts of Brazil.
Recognized by the most important international rankings, Luiz is an active speaker at IP events in Brazil, USA, Latin America and Europe and is the author of numerous publications in his area of expertise.

Marianna Furtado de Mendonça
Partner at Montaury Pimenta, Machado & Vieira de Mello
Marianna has been working with Intellectual Property since 2000 is one of the heads of Montaury Pimenta, Machado & Vieira de Mello´s litigation department. Marianna's experience covers all aspects of IP with special emphasis on civil litigation involving trademarks, copyright, industrial designs, domain names and unfair competition & trade dress, as well as in the development and enforcement of strategies for protecting these rights. She has been representing and advising clients in said fields at several Federal and State Courts across the country. In addition to participating in international conferences and seminars as a speaker or moderator, Marianna is constantly recognized for her practice in the most renowned rankings in the area.

CHINA

Yunze LIAN & Rebecca LIU
Jadong IP Law Firm

1. TRADEMARK

1.1 Sources of law

The principal sources of national law and regulation relating to trademarks include the Trademark Law of the People's Republic of China (PRC) (last amended in 2019), the Implementing Regulations of the Trademark Law of the PRC (last amended in 2014) and other laws, regulations, administrative rules, judicial interpretations, administrative interpretations, as well as local regulations, judicial replies, administrative replies, and so on. There are also several international treaties related to trademarks, such as the Paris Convention, the Agreement on Trade-Related Aspects of Intellectual Property Rights (TRIPS), the Madrid Agreement and the Madrid Protocol, the Nice Agreement concerning the International Classification of Goods and Services, and the Trademark Law Treaty (TLT).

In the event of a conflict, the provision of the international treaty prevails over the national laws, except those on which the PRC has announced reservation; the law in force supersedes the regulations, rules, judicial interpretations and administrative interpretations. Judicial and administrative interpretations are of parallel legal force, but implemented by the courts and administrations respectively.

Although PRC practices first-to-file principle, well-known unregistered trademarks and unregistered trademarks with certain impact are also protected.

1.2 Substantive law

The Trademark Law of the PRC distinguishes well-known trademarks and trademarks with a reputation. The term "famous trademarks" is not a legally recognized term in PRC.

For the proprietor of a registered trademark with a reputation, the protection scope is almost the same as that of a common registered trademark, but when determining whether or not two marks have constituted similar marks on similar goods or services, the Chinese authorities will consider the reputation of the mark seeking protection and tend to give a slightly broader protection.

For the proprietor of a well-known trademark that has been registered in the PRC, it could prohibit third parties from registering or using a trademark which is a replication, an imitation or a translation of the well-known mark, in relation to non-identical or non-similar goods or services.

For the unregistered well-known trademarks, the proprietor could prohibit third parties from registering or using a trademark, which is a replication, imitation or translation of the well-known trademark, in respect of identical or similar goods or services.

In the PRC the trademarks belonging to the "luxury industry" do not enjoy a broader range of protection than other trademarks and there is no rule protecting the "aura of luxury" surrounding them in a way that differs from that of a trademark with a reputation belonging to another industry.

1.3 Enforcement

The proprietor of a trademark which is well known by the relevant public may request protection of a well-known trademark when it is of the view that its rights are infringed upon. The request for well-known trademark recognition could be filed together with the relevant petition before the National Intellectual Property Administration of the PRC (CNIPA), the relevant courts and the relevant Administration for Market Regulation.

The fame of the mark must be established in order to have it recognized as a well-known trademark. The following factors will be taken into account for recognizing a well-known mark:
- the extent of the relevant public's familiarity with the said trademark;
- the duration of continued use of the said trademark;
- the duration, extent and geographical scope of any promotional campaign for the said trademark;
- the record of the said trademark being protected as a well-known trademark; and
- any other factors for the said trademark's fame.

The proprietor should provide as much evidence as possible proving that the mark is well known by a substantial portion of the relevant public in the PRC, and the following is usually required and helpful to prove reputation:
- Statistics demonstrating the general sales, revenue, income, net profit, tax amount, sales area, market share, and advertising expenditure for at least 5 years preceding the petition or prior to the application date of the disputed/opposed trademark, preferably issued or published by authoritative organization or guild. Normally, auditing reports concerning advertisements and sales of the products bearing the trademark and market share data issued by local authoritative organization or guild would be very helpful.
- Sales materials including contracts, invoices, packing lists, certificates of origin, bills of lading, certificates of quarantine, customs clearance document, order list, etc.
- Promotional materials including contracts, invoices, payment documents and so on, as agreed with local advertisement companies as well as copies of the advertisements and promotional materials (TV programs, newspapers, periodicals, internet, outdoor signboards, posters, brochures, advertising leaflets, and so on).
- Documents and materials relating to promotional or sponsored events and activities.
- Official support such as official decisions, court judgments and the like indicating that the mark has been protected as a well-known mark, and report on assessment of the value of the mark as an intangible asset issued by qualified assessment organization in the PRC.
- Honors and awards the trademark has obtained in the PRC.

Oral testimony, affidavit or expert evidences do not have high probative force in comparison with the above evidences.

When there is a conflict between different types of right like trademark right, domain name right and trade name right, the basic principle is to protect the prior right. And the protection of a trademark is usually stronger than any other rights such as domain name right and trade name right.

A registered trademark can be enforced against a domain name on condition that the domain name is identical or similar to the registered trademark, which is likely to cause misidentification among the relevant public, and that the owner of the domain name does not enjoy any rights over the domain name or the distinctive part of the domain name, but has bad faith in registering or using the domain name.

Pursuant to Article 58 of the Trademark Law of the PRC, use of others' registered trademark or an unregistered well-known trademark as an enterprise name to mislead the public which constitutes unfair competition shall be dealt with pursuant to the Anti-Unfair Competition Law of the PRC.

There are no specific regulations regarding whether or not a trademark could be enforced against its unauthorized use in social media. However, if such use has constituted use of the trademark in respect of identical or similar goods or services or such use has caused confusion or harmed the interests of the owner of the trademark, the owner of the registered trademark or well-known unregistered trademark could stop such use based on the Trademark Law of the PRC.

There are no specific regulations regarding whether or not a trademark could be enforced against its unauthorized use in comparative advertising. However, if the comparative advertising does not reflect the facts or it has constituted an unfair completion deed, the owner of the registered trademark or well-known unregistered trademark could stop such use according to the Advertising Law and Anti Unfair Competition Law of the PRC.

There are no specific provisions clearly indicating whether or not a trademark could be enforced against its unauthorized use in parody. But if such parody is made by the competitors, the owner of the trademark could stop such use according to Anti Unfair Competition Law of the PRC.

A trademark owner is entitled to choose taking action claiming either trademark infringement or unfair competition for the same set of facts, but not both.

2. COPYRIGHT

2.1 Sources of law

The principal sources of copyright related law and regulation include the Copyright Law of the PRC, the Implementing Regulations of the Copyright Law of the PRC and other laws, regulations, administrative rules, judicial interpretations, administrative interpretations, as well as local regulations, judicial replies, administrative replies, and so on. The PRC is also member country of several international treaties such as the Berne Convention for the Protection of Literary and Artistic Works, Universal Copyright Convention, the International Convention for the Protection of Performers, Producers or Phonograms and Broadcasting Organizations, the WIPO Copyright Treaty and the WIPO Performances and Phonograms Treaty.

In the event of a conflict, the provision of the international treaty prevails over the national laws except those on which the PRC has announced reservation; and the law in force supersedes the regulations, rules, judicial interpretations and administrative interpretations. Judicial and administrative interpretations are of parallel legal force, but implemented by the courts and administrations respectively.

2.2 Substantive law

An open list of the copyrightable works is provided, which includes written works, oral works, musical, dramatic, *quyi* (ancient Chinese performing art), choreographic and acrobatic works, works of fine art and architecture, photographic works, audiovisual works, graphic works and model works such as engineering design drawings, product design drawings, maps and schematic diagrams, computer software, other intellectual achievements that conform to the characteristics of the work.

Objects of industrial design are copyrightable if they meet the requirements of copyrightable works on original, reproducible, and artistic characters, such as works of applied art.

The rights covered by copyright include both personal rights (or moral rights) and property rights, which include the rights of publication, authorship, alteration, integrity, reproduction, distribution, lease, exhibition, performance, projection, broadcast, information network dissemination, production, adaptation, translation, compilation and other rights which shall be enjoyed by the copyright owner. Among these rights, moral rights include the rights of publication, authorship, alteration and integrity.

Regarding the work created in the course of employment, the copyright shall be enjoyed by the author, but the legal entity or other organization shall have the right to give priority to the use within the scope of its business. But the following situations are exceptions, and in such case, the author shall enjoy the right of authorship, and other rights of copyright shall be enjoyed by the legal entity or other organization:

- A work created by mainly using the material and technical conditions of a legal entity or other organization and for which the legal entity or other organization is responsible.
- A work created by staff of newspapers, periodicals, news agencies, radio stations and television stations.
- A work created in the course of duty for which the copyright is enjoyed by a legal entity or other organization as stipulated in laws, administrative regulations or contracts.

As to other kinds of works excluding the works created in the course of employment as mentioned above, the copyright belongs to the author, which could be a citizen who creates the work, or a legal entity or other organization, if the work is created under its auspices, on behalf of its will, and with the said legal entity or other organization assuming the responsibility.

The ownership of copyright in a commissioned work shall be agreed upon by the principal and the trustee through a contract. If there is no explicit agreement or contract, the copyright belongs to the trustee.

The copyright owner can assign in whole or in part the rights except for the moral rights and the parties should sign an assignment agreement in writing. The author cannot transfer or waive their moral rights.

No time limit is set on the term of protection for an author's rights of authorship, alteration and the right to protect the integrity of the work.

In respect of a work of a citizen, the term of protection of the right of publication and the rights of reproduction and other rights to be enjoyed by the copyright owner is the lifetime of the author and 50 years after their death, expiring on 31 December of the 50th year after their death. In the case of a work of joint authorship, the term shall expire on 31 December of the 50th year after the death of the last surviving author.

As for a work of a legal entity or other organization, or a work created in the course of duty, whose copyright (except the right of authorship) is owned by a legal entity or other organization, the term of protection of the right of publication and the right of reproduction and other rights to be enjoyed by the copyright owner shall be 50 years, expiring on 31 December of the 50th year after the first publication of such work. However, any such work that has not been published within 50 years after the completion of its creation shall no longer be protected by the Copyright Law of the PRC.

As for audio-visual works, the term of protection of the right of publication is 50 years, ending on 31 December of the 50th year after the completion of the creation of the works; The term of protection of the rights except for moral rights shall be 50 years, ending on 31 December of the 50th year after the first publication of the work. However, if the work has not been published within 50 years after the completion of the creation, it shall no longer be protected by the Copyright Law of the PRC.

2.3 Enforcement

It is not compulsory to do copyright registration in the PRC, but it is possible and normally recommended to do so as early as possible. A Copyright Registration Certificate is considered as *prima facie* evidence to prove ownership of copyright. Further solid evidence may also be required to prove the creation date, publication date, and so on, especially if the copyright registration date is later than the contested objective or if the ownership of copyright is questioned by the contested party, and normally such solid evidence occurring outside China should be notarized and legalized. Neither copyright deposit nor notice is required.

To have industrial designs protected by copyright, it should be proven that the industrial designs belong to works under the Copyright Law of the PRC, which means that the industrial designs should be original and artistic. Evidence such as judgment and a copyright registration certificate proving the industrial designs have already been protected as copyrighted works in other member countries of the Berne Convention is helpful. Acceptance of oral testimony, affidavit, and expert evidence is at the judge's discretion.

Substantial similarity and contacts are necessary and sufficient to establish copyright infringement.

Copyright can be enforced against a trademark, domain name, trade name, registered design patent, and other distinctive signs.

Copyright can be enforced against its unauthorized use in social media, comparative advertising, and parody unless the use could be considered as "fair use" according to the law.

The defenses available to an alleged infringer are fair use, expiration of term of protection, and statutory license.

The following ways of use are considered as "fair use", however, the name of the author or the name of the work shall be specified, and the normal use of

the work shall not be affected, nor shall the legitimate rights and interests of the copyright owner be reasonably damaged:
- use of others' published works for the purpose of the user's own personal study, research or appreciation;
- appropriate quotation from others' published works in one's own work for the purpose of introducing or commenting on a work or explaining an issue;
- inevitable reappearance or quotation of published works in newspapers, periodicals, radio stations, television stations or other media for the purpose of reporting news;
- republishing or rebroadcasting by newspapers, periodicals, radio stations, television stations and other media, of the current event articles on political, economic and religious issues, which have been published by other newspapers, periodicals, radio stations, television stations or other media, unless the copyright owner declares that they are not allowed to publish or broadcast;
- publishing or broadcasting by newspapers, periodicals, radio stations, television stations and other media, of speeches delivered at public gatherings, unless the author declares that publication or broadcasting is not permitted;
- adapting, compiling, broadcasting or reproducing in a small quantity of published works for classroom teaching or scientific research in schools, for the use of teaching or scientific researchers, but publishing or distribution is not allowed;
- use of published works by State organs within a reasonable range in order to perform their official duties;
- reproduction of works collected by libraries, archives, memorial halls, museums and cultural centers for the purpose of displaying or preserving versions;
- performance of published works free of charge, which is not charged to the public, nor paid to the performers, and is not for profit;
- copying, painting, photographing and video recording of works of art set up or displayed in public places;
- translation of works created in the national common language published by Chinese citizens, legal entities or organizations into works in the language of ethnic minorities for publication and distribution in China;
- providing published works to dyslexics in an accessible way that they can perceive; and
- other circumstances stipulated by laws and administrative regulations.

In addition, in compiling and publishing textbooks for the implementation of compulsory education and the national education plan, a person may, without the permission of the copyright owner, compile in the textbooks fragments of published works or short written works, musical works, or single artistic works, photographic works and graphic works, but shall pay remuneration to the copyright owner in accordance with regulations, indicating the name of the author and the name of the work, and shall not infringe upon other rights enjoyed by the copyright owner in accordance with the Copyright Law of the PRC.

In respect of computer software, the prescriptions on "fair use" include:
- The owner of legal duplicated copy of the software has the rights to load the software into a device with information processing capability such as a computer according to the needs of use; make a backup copy to prevent damage to the duplicated copy, but these backup copies shall not be provided to others for use in any way, and the backup copies should be destroyed when the owner loses the ownership of the legal copies; make necessary modifications in order to use the software in the actual computer application environment or improve its function and performance. However, unless otherwise agreed in the contract, the modified software shall not be provided to any third party without the permission of the software copyright owner.
- Use of the software by means of installing, displaying, transmitting or storing the software for the purpose of learning and studying the design ideas and principles contained in the software.

A valid copyright that is unenforceable is mainly due to the following reasons:
- a work with weak original creation; or
- other fair uses of such work as mentioned above.

For the same set of facts, a copyright holder is not allowed to take action claiming both copyright infringement and design infringement and/or unfair competition. The copyright holder is entitled to choose either copyright infringement or design patent infringement or unfair competition claim.

3. DESIGN

3.1 Sources of law

The principal sources of law relating to designs include the Patent Law of the PRC, which sets out the requirements for patent prosecution, rights and legal remedies; the Implementing Rules of the Patent Law of the PRC and the Guidelines for Patent Examination, which provide detailed requirements and procedures on patent litigation proceedings.

The PRC is member country to some international treaties relating to patents and patent litigation such as WIPO Paris Convention for the Protection of Industrial Property 1883 (Paris Convention); Patent Cooperation Treaty 1970; and WTO Agreement on Trade-Related Aspects of Intellectual Property Rights 1994.

In the event of a conflict, the provision of the international treaty prevails over the national laws except those on which the PRC has announced reservation; and the law in force supersedes the regulations, rules, judicial interpretations and administrative interpretations. Judicial and administrative interpretations are of parallel legal force, but implemented by the courts and administrations respectively.

3.2 Substantive law

All industrial products, as long as its appearance is a new design, could be protected by way of registered design in the PRC. An unregistered design is not protected under Chinese law.

To be granted for patent design, the design shall not belong to the existing design, no entity or individual has filed an application with the CNIPA for the same design before the application date and recorded it in the patent documents announced after the application date; the design shall be obviously different from the existing design or the combination of existing design features; the design should not conflict with the legal rights already obtained by others before the date of application.

To file an application for a patent for design, besides a written request, pictures or photographs of the design as well as a brief description of the design shall be submitted. The relevant pictures or photographs submitted by the applicant shall clearly show the design of the product.

Regarding designs created by employees, shareholders or directors in the course of performing a duty or by using the material and technical resources of an entity employer, the right to apply for a design patent registration belongs to the entity. After the application is approved, the entity shall be the patentee.

As for designs which are not created in the performance of the task of any entity, the right to apply for a design patent registration belongs to the inventor or designer. After the application is approved, the inventor or designer shall be the patentee.

For designs created by employees, shareholders or directors by using the material and technical resources of an entity employer, if the entity has entered into an agreement with the inventor or designer on the right to apply for a design patent registration and the ownership of the patent right, such agreement shall prevail.

If a design is completed jointly by two or more entities or individuals, or by an entity or individual entrusted by another unit or individual, unless otherwise agreed, the right to apply for a design patent registration and the ownership of the patent right shall belong to the entity or individual who completed or jointly completed the design.

The patent assignment agreement will be effective once it is signed by both parties, but the assignment shall take effect only after the assignment request is registered before the CNIPA.

To exploit others' patent, an exploitation license contract should be signed with the patentee. The licensee has no right to allow any entity or individual other than those specified in the contract to exploit the patent.

The designer could waive their moral rights in the designs. The term of the patent right for design is 15 years, which shall be calculated from the application date of the design.

3.3 Enforcement

The scope of protection of the patent right for design shall be subject to the design of the patented product shown in the pictures or photos. The brief description of the design and its major design features, the patentee's opinion statement in the invalidation procedure and the litigation procedure, etc. can be used to understand the scope of protection of the patent right for design.

The overall comparison principle is adopted. When determining the scope of protection of a design, comprehensive consideration shall be given to the complete design content composed of all design elements such as the shape, pattern and color displayed in the picture or photograph representing the design in the grant publication, and all design features displayed in each view in the picture or photograph shall be taken into account, you cannot consider only some design features and ignore others.

To establish design infringement, first of all, the alleged infringing product and the design product should belong to the same or similar types of products, and to determine whether the types of products are the same or similar, comparison should be made based on the function, purpose and use environment of the design product.

Meanwhile, to establish design infringement, the designs should be the same or similar, while it is not necessary for confusion or misunderstanding. Whether designs are the same or similar shall be judged according to the overall visual effect in the eyes of the general consumers with general knowledge and cognitive ability, rather than the observation ability of the general designer of the design product or the actual buyer of the product. And the design features determined by the product function shall not be considered when judging two designs are the same or similar.

A registered design patent can be enforced against a trademark, a registered design patent could be basis to oppose a trademark application, invalidate a trademark registration, and to invalidate a later registered design patent.

The common defenses available to an alleged infringer are non-infringement, that the design patent should be invalidated, prior use and prior art. Infringement proceedings must be brought within three years of the date on which a patentee knew or should have known of the infringement.

For the same set of acts, a design holder is not allowed to take action claiming design infringement and copyright infringement and/or unfair competition. The design holder is entitled to choose design infringement or copyright infringement or unfair competition claim.

4. RIGHT OF PRIVACY, PUBLICITY AND PERSONAL ENDORSEMENT

The right of publicity is not recognized by Chinese law. In practice, the similar rights should be the right of personal name, right to portrait, right of reputation, copyright, trademark, right of commercialization, and so on.

The Anti-Unfair Competition Law of the PRC prohibits unauthorized use of enterprise names (including abbreviations, brand names, etc.), social organization names (including abbreviations, etc.), names (including pen names, stage names, translated names, etc.) that have certain influence on others by a business operator to mislead people into believing that it is another person's commodity or has a specific connection with another person.

Pursuant to Trademark Law of the PRC, the application for trademark registration shall not prejudice the prior rights of others. And personal name, right to portrait, copyright, trademark, right of commercialization, etc. all could be a kind of prior right.

Therefore, for a person who is a celebrity or is of some distinction, they could protect their name right and right to portrait pursuant to Trademark Law of the PRC or Anti Unfair Competition Law of the PRC.

CHINA

5. PRODUCT PLACEMENT

There are no laws or regulations prohibiting product placement in the PRC. In practice, it is common to have product placement in TV drama or movies. Product placement is considered as a kind of advertisement which should be applied to Advertisement Law of the PRC.

According to Measures for the Administration of Radio and Television Advertising Broadcasting issued by the State Administration of Radio, Film and Television and amended in 2011, the following radio and television advertisements are prohibited:
- advertisements published in the form of news reports;
- advertising of tobacco products;
- prescription drug advertising;
- drugs, food, medical devices and medical advertisements for treating malignant tumors, liver diseases, sexually transmitted diseases or improving sexual function;
- name analysis, travel analysis, fate test, making friends and chatting and other audio service advertisements;
- dairy advertisements with the term "breast milk substitutes"; and
- other advertisements prohibited from broadcasting by laws, administrative regulations and relevant provisions of the state.

6. PROTECTION OF CORPORATE IMAGE AND REPUTATION

There is no law regarding right of publicity and/or privacy for legal entities or corporations. However, according to the Civil Code of the PRC promulgated in 2020, civil subjects (including legal entities and corporations) enjoy the right of reputation. No organization or individual may infringe upon another person's right of reputation by insulting or slandering.

In general, for the purposes of protecting the corporate image and reputation, it is allowed to include specific clauses in an agreement aimed at protecting the corporate image or reputation of one of the parties, for example, prohibition to sell the products to re-sellers whose image is below a certain defined standard, prohibition to sell below a certain price or to do so outside of specific time periods, prohibition to buy non original – but otherwise legitimate - spare parts and components.

There are no liquidated damages or stipulated fines clauses for breach by a part of any provisions protecting the reputation or corporate image of the other party permissible in the PRC.

However, the parties signing such agreements should avoid violating Articles 13 and 14 of the Anti-monopoly Law of the PRC, which prohibits competitive operators from concluding the following monopoly agreements: on fixing or changing commodity prices; limiting the production or sales quantity of commodities; splitting the sales market or raw material procurement market; restricting the purchase of new technologies and equipment or the development of new technologies and products; or boycott deal; and prohibits an operator and its trading counterparty from concluding the monopoly agreements on fixing the prices of commodities resold to a third party, or limiting the minimum prices for commodities resold to a third party.

AUTHOR BIOGRAPHIES

Yunze LIAN

Yunze LIAN is founder and head of Jadong IP Law Firm. He started his legal practice in 1982 and worked for 14 years with CCPIT. He has practiced in the IP field for 36 years and is recognized as an IP expert both by the international brand owners he represents and by the IP community in general. He is a frequent speaker at many international conferences and a panelist for several domain name dispute resolution centers. He is a committee member of the INTA Internet Committee, ECTA Internet Committee, MARQUES China Team and Trademark Committee of AIPPI China Group. He regularly receives awards from a variety of legal publications, like MIP, WTR, Chambers Asia-Pacific, Asia Law, Asia IP, Expert Guides. He writes extensively in many international publications circulated in European countries.

Rebecca LIU

Rebecca is a Partner and Trademark Attorney at Jadong IP Law Firm. She is the Head of the Trademark Team. Prior to joining Jadong, she has been Head of the Trademark Team of another big law firm.

Rebecca specializes in trademark prosecution and enforcement. She has been practicing in this area for 16 years and has extensive experience. Her areas of practice include trademark strategic planning, advising on trademark availability, trademark search and monitoring, assignment, licensing, renewal, opposition, invalidation, cancellation, etc., taking actions against counterfeiting and IP infringements, negotiating for trademark acquisition and license, dealing with domain name registration and disputes, copyright and unfair competition matters. Rebecca has represented many well-known brand owners from both domestic and abroad in developing their branding strategies and protecting their trademark rights in China and internationally.

CYPRUS

**Maria Hinni, George Tashev,
Nasos Kafantaris & Ioanna Martidi**
A.G. Paphitis & Co

CYPRUS

1. TRADEMARK

1.1 Sources of law

The principal sources of law and regulation governing the registration and protection of trademarks in Cyprus are the Cyprus Trademarks Law, Cap. 268 and the Trademarks Regulations, as amended.

On June 2020, the Cyprus Parliament passed the new trademarks law incorporating the EU Trademarks Directive (Directive (EU) 2015/2436) into national law, which, as a result, simplifies the procedures pertaining to the registration, administration and handling of a trademark.

The following additional laws are also relevant to trademarks legislation:

- The Control of Movement of Goods Infringing Intellectual Property Rights Law No. 61(I)/2018. The authority responsible for this is the Customs Department. This legislation confers exclusive competence in the handling of goods infringing intellectual property rights, especially when there is a *prima facie* suspicion that the goods infringe trademarks and/or any other intellectual property right.
- The Trademark Law Treaty Ratifying Law No. 12(III)/1996 is the main treaty which aims to standardize the procedure for registering a trademark in multiple jurisdictions.
- The Madrid Agreement as well as the Madrid Protocol - their aim is to provide a cost-effective system for obtaining and maintaining trademark registrations across 122 countries.
- The Nice Agreement. Under this treaty each of the countries party to this Agreement has classified the goods or services for which the trademarks are registered.

Following the new amendments to the Trademarks Law, use as a source of trademark rights is recognized. Cyprus has harmonized its law with article 6(2) of the Trademark Directive about earlier rights. Earlier rights may be established even if a trademark is not registered but an application for it has at least been filed.

The main difference between the non-registered and registered trademarks is that the owners of the non-registered trademarks have no right to file an infringement action.

However, owners of unregistered marks are free to bring a passing-off action against any party which passes off its goods as those of the rights holder and to claim damages in respect thereof.

1.2 Substantive law

Cypriot law does not distinguish between famous trademarks, well-known trademarks and trademarks with a reputation. All trademarks are treated the same and there is not a broader range for protection for a specific "luxury industry" in Cyprus.

1.3 Enforcement

A trademark can be enforced against a domain name.

Trade names are protected under different legislation, namely the Partnerships and Business Names Law.

To date, the IP Department in Cyprus has not examined a case against the unauthorized use in social media. However, if a trademark is being used by a third party on social media without consent, the question for the brand owner is whether it actually presents a real problem to the owner.

The owner should think twice as to whether to proceed with any actions against those who use the trademark in social media since it will be very difficult to identify who is behind the infringing material as social media accounts can be set up anonymously.

An unauthorized use of a mark in comparative advertising would be liable for trademark infringement. However, the law recognizes the benefit of competition in several laws and regulations within EU member-states. Those provide an exemption for use of a third party's trademark in lawful comparative advertising. A comparative advertisement should:
- not be misleading;
- compare goods or services meeting the same needs or intended for the same purpose;
- objectively compare one or more material, relevant, verifiable and representative features of those goods and services, which may include price;
- not discredit or denigrate the competitor or its trademarks;
- for products with designation of origin, relate in each case to products with the same designation;
- not take unfair advantage of the reputation of the competitor's trademark;
- not present goods or services as imitations or replicas; and
- not create confusion among traders, between the advertiser and a competitor, or between the advertiser's trademarks, trade names, other distinguishing marks, goods or services and those of a competitor.

2. COPYRIGHT

2.1 Sources of law

In Cyprus, copyrights are governed by the Intellectual Property Rights Law No. 59/76 as amended, the Berne Convention, Geneva Convention, Paris Convention, Rome Convention, the Agreement on Trade-Related Aspects of Intellectual Property Rights (TRIPS), Directive 2014/26/EU of the European Parliament and of the Council of 26 February 2014 on collective management of copyright and related rights and multi-territorial licensing of rights in musical works for online use in the internal market.

Apart for the provisions of EU Law, national laws and international treaties governing Intellectual Property rights, precedents from case law are of equal importance. Cases and the decisions by the competent court in the Republic of Cyprus and in the European Union in general provide the guidance for lawyers in intellectual property practice to navigate throughout the relevant concepts and legal doctrines of the copyright laws. Case law shows how right holders are enforcing their intellectual property in the EU. This information is crucial for practitioners, judges and law-makers and provide clear interpretations adopted by the competent courts of Member States and of the Republic of Cyprus in particular and how these legal principles should apply in real life business, commercial, industrial, artistic and educational aspects of society. Furthermore, these judgments relate to the application of enforcement-related measures or procedures in IP rights infringement cases, and are considered to be key when they provide a new trend or development in jurisprudence.

In the event where a conflict between the relevant sources of laws arises, the European Law will preside over the national law of the Republic of Cyprus since the latter is a member state of the European Union.

2.2 Substantive law

Copyright protects the following types of works:
- **Scientific works.** They are works of scientific nature irrespective of their value or standard as scientific works.
- **Literary works.** Irrespective of its literary value or standard, literary works include fiction, novels, poems, plays, stage directions, scenarios for cinematography films, broadcasts, treatises, historical works, biographies, essays, articles, encyclopedias, dictionaries, correspondence, memoranda, lectures, speeches, computer software.
- **Musical works.** Copyright protects a musical work irrespective of its musical value or standard.
- **Artistic works.** Irrespective of their artistic value or standard, artistic works are paintings, drawings, works of metallography, lithographs, wood engravings, engravings, printing works, geographical maps, sketches, graphs, sculptural works, photographs, works of architecture.
- **Cinematography.** Films, audiovisual productions, motion pictures, with or without sound.
- **Databases.** Organized collections of works, data or independent elements.
- **Sound recordings.**
- **Radio and television broadcasts**.
- **Publishing of previously unpublished works**.

When copyright expires the individual who legally published a previously unpublished work becomes holder of the copyright and is thus entitled to all the intellectual property rights and benefits of the creator.

There are two approaches when it comes to copyrights: the open list and closed list. The Republic of Cyprus, in terms of copyrights, offers a closed list approach. By closed list, jurisdictions like United Kingdom, Australia, India and Cyprus attempt to elaborately outline the contours of different categories of subject-matter protectable under its copyright regime (for example literary works, artistic works, musical works, and so on), by legislation that exhaustively lists categories of works which cumulatively designates what can be afforded copyright protection.

For an object of industrial, fashion or accessory design to be eligible for protection, it generally needs to be both "new" and to have an "individual character". Law 4(I)/2002 specifies the following requirements:
- **Novelty.** Section 4(2) provides that a design is considered to be new if, up to the filing or priority date, no identical design or sample has been disclosed to the public. "Identical" designs or samples are those whose characteristics differ only in minor details.

- **Individual character.** Section 4(3) provides that a design or sample has individual character if the overall impression it makes on the informed user differs from that made by a design or sample which is disclosed to the public before the filing or priority date. In order to appraise the individual character of a design or sample, consideration is given to the degree of free will of its creator at the time of its creation.
- **Disclosure to the public.** Section 4(4) provides the definition of disclosure to the public. A design or sample is considered to have been disclosed if it has been:
    - published, through its filing or by any other means; or
    - exposed; or
    - used in commerce; or
    - disclosed in any other way, however, disclosure will prevent a design from receiving protection only when it is used during normal business practice in the area concerned by professionals who operate either within Cyprus or the European Union, before the filing date of the application or the priority date.

Additionally, a design or sample is not disclosed to the public when it is disclosed to someone under an explicit or implicit term. When the design has been disclosed by its creator, beneficiary or a third party acting on their behalf, within the twelve-month period before the filing or priority date, this does not invalidate novelty, according to section 4(5)(a). This also applies when the disclosure has taken place as a result of abusive misconduct against the creator or the beneficiary.

Copyright protects two types of rights:
- Economic rights allow right owners to derive financial reward from the use of their works by others.
- Moral rights allow authors and creators to take certain actions to preserve and protect their link with their work.

The Berne Convention, in Article 6, requires its members to grant authors the following rights:
- the right to claim authorship of a work (sometimes called the right of paternity or the right of attribution); and
- the right to object to any distortion or modification of a work, or other derogatory action in relation to a work, which would be prejudicial to the author's honor or reputation (sometimes called the right of integrity). Unlike economic rights, the moral rights stay with the author and cannot be waiver or assigned.

Copyright can be transferred by assignment as movable property. An assignment can be limited to some of the acts the copyright owner has the exclusive right to control, to part of the period for which the copyright is to subsist, or to a specified country or other geographical area. An assignment can be effectively made in relation to a future work, or an existing work in which copyright does not yet subsist. Copyright can only be assigned by waiver or by will. Waiving of copyright under a private agreement cannot be valid. An assignment of copyright can only be valid if it is in written format (Article 12(6)).

In contrast to the economic rights under copyright, moral rights cannot be sold or assigned to another person (moral rights are the right to be identified as the author of the work or to object to derogatory treatment or to a distortion or mutilation of the work, to protect the personality and reputation of authors).

The duration of protection is determined by reference to the nature of the author as well as the type of work under protection. For example, copyright protection over a literary work created by a natural person subsists for 70 years from the end of the calendar year of the author's death (see *www.thelawreviews. co.uk/title/the-intellectual-property-review/cyprus#footnote-019*). If the author of the work is a legal person, protection subsists for 70 years from the end of the calendar year of the time the work was first published. Broadcasts are protected for 50 years from the date of the broadcast.

2.3 Enforcement

Registration of copyrights is not required to enforce a copyright, although it is highly recommended. Having the copyrights registered enables the owner to bring an action for copyright infringement. If the copyright is not registered and it is infringed, the owner must first register the copyright to be able to bring a Court action, since its registration satisfies the requested level of proof that the work is validly protected. Registration also provides notice to the public that the work is protected by copyright, and if they wish to 'borrow' the work, they must first receive permission from the owner, creating a 'license to use'.

Industrial designs are protected by Law 4(I)/2002, the Paris Convention and the Agreement on Trade-Related Aspects of Intellectual Property Rights (TRIPS). For an industrial design to be eligible for protection, the design must be new and present individuality in such a way that the informed user will not consider the design as similar to a design that is already known to the public.

Protection may be renewed for a period of 25 years upon payment of the relevant fee.

EU copyright law does not (expressly) provide a defence for copyright infringement. Advertisers that use competitors' logos are therefore at risk of infringing the rights in those logos.

Following recent developments in copyright law, which have arguably extended the scope of copyright protection to works that previously would not have benefitted from copyright protection, including images of products, could also carry risk.

Since copyright law prohibits the substantial use of a copyrighted work without permission of the copyright owner, and because such permission is highly unlikely when the use is to create a parody, it may be necessary for the parodist to rely on the fair-use defense to forestall any liability for copyright infringement. However, the fair-use defense, if successful, will only be successful when the newly created work that purports itself to be parody is a valid parody.

Fair Use is a limitation in copyright protection. Fair use allows people to use a protected work without the owner's permission, for purposes of criticism, news, teaching, research and more.

In the fashion and luxury space, the cut or shape of garments, accessories and furniture (all of which are categorised as useful articles) are not protected by copyright and as a result the floodgates for imitations and faux products bearing identical useful articles can open and easily flood the market of luxury branding. However, certain useful articles may contain features that may qualify for copyright (and even patent) protection.

3. DESIGN

3.1 Sources of law

The Law on the Legal Protection of Industrial Designs 2002, which was implemented for the purposes of harmonizing with the European Community Act entitled "Directive 98/71 / EC of the European Parliament and of the Council of 13 October 1998 on the legal protection of designs" (OJ L 289, 28.10.1998, p. 28).

Chrysostomou v. Chalkousi & Sons (1978) 1 CLR 10 (assignment of rights can be defended by law).

3.2 Substantive law

A registered design protects the overall visual appearance of a product or a part of a product.

The protection is given to the way the product looks and the design may be two or three dimensional. The appearance of the product may result from a combination of elements such as shapes, colours and materials.

Design protection guarantees you the exclusive **right** (the holder or holders of the IP can exclude anyone else from using the IP in question) to use a design, which includes making, offering, putting on the market, importing, exporting or using the product in which your design is incorporated or to which it is applied.

For an industrial design to be eligible for protection, the design must be new and present individuality in such a way that the informed user will not consider the design as similar to a design that is already known to the public.

A design is protected by a right on a design, in accordance with the provisions of this Law, provided that:
- it is new;
- shows individuality; and
- has been registered in accordance with the provisions of this Law.

Natural or legal persons are entitled to registration of a design. A claim for registration of a design and rights from a registered design, in accordance with this Law, are provided:
- to natural persons who are nationals of the Republic of Cyprus or a Member State of the European Union or have their habitual residence in Cyprus or in the territory of a Member State of the European Union; and
- to companies and other legal entities having an actual industrial or commercial establishment in Cyprus or in the territory of a Member State of the European Union.

The creator of the design has the right to protect it, subject to the provisions of Articles 8 to 11. Whoever submits, in accordance with articles 10 and 14 the application for registration of a design, is considered its creator, subject to the provisions of article 22 of this Law.

Transfer can take place through written agreement submitted in the Register.

When designs are created in the context of the author's employment relationship, the design rights are granted to the creator's employer, who for the purposes of this Law is considered the creator, unless the relevant contract or working conditions provide the opposite.

When the designs are created under a contract other than a contract or employment relationship, the design rights shall be granted to the contracting party that ordered the design, unless the relevant contract provides otherwise.

Cyprus law has no express provision of requirements which must be satisfied in order to assign rights of a contract, however, equity law and case law have provided guidance on the matter providing requirements and considerations. The assignee has a legal right in action whereby the assignee can autonomously claim an action in law for defending their rights, if the following apply:
- the assignment must be absolute;
- the assignment is not considered as an agent relationship; and
- consideration is not a requirement.

The right to register a design and the rights from the registered design enjoyed by the persons referred to in Articles 7, 8, and 9 may be transferred by written agreement or inherited.

Upon registration, a design which meets the requirements of Article 4 shall be protected for a period of one or more periods of five years from the date of filing of the application for registration with the Registrar. The beneficiary may, if he pays the relevant fees in accordance with the terms of Article 26, renew the term of protection for one or more periods of five years, up to a maximum of twenty-five years from the date of filing of the application.

Unregistered Design has no protection.

3.3 Enforcement

The test to assess design infringement is still a simple visual comparison between the appearances of the two designs, whether the design is so similar that it will cause confusion to the extent that one product is mistaken for the other.

The protection of an industrial design or sample grants to its proprietor the exclusive right to use the design or sample, and prohibits others from using it without his consent. The law itself defines the term "use" as including manufacture, offer, marketing, import and export and use or possession for these purposes of a product incorporating or applying the said design or sample. The above rights are not infringed by:
- private acts done for non-commercial purposes;
- acts done for experimental purposes; and
- acts done to reproduce the design or sample for educational reasons.

The above claims are barred after five years after the holder of the certificate became aware of either the infringement or the damage and the person liable to be compensated, and certainly after twenty years from the infringement.

Many sophisticated fakes are being produced with serious design infringement. It is often difficult to find the source of manufacture therefore it is difficult to take action against the source of production. Action is taken against sellers who knowingly sell products which infringe design rights however this is not enough to offer significant protection.

4. RIGHT OF PRIVACY, PUBLICITY AND PERSONAL ENDORSEMENT
4.1 Sources of law
The law in Cyprus does recognize the right of an individual to control the commercial use of his or her name, image, likeness, or other unequivocal aspects of one's identity.

The principal sources of law relating to the right of publicity are:
- Cyprus Constitution Article 15.
- ECHR Law – European Convention on Human Rights Article 8.
- General Data Protection Regulation (GDPR) law.
- Case law of ECHR Court – V*on Hannover v. Germany* 59320/00 ECHR 2004-VI.

4.2 Substantive law
Other than being a living human no other conditions exist for an individual to own a right of publicity.

In legal terms, the General Data Protection Regulation (GDPR) and the Data Protection Act no longer apply to identifiable data that relate to a person once they have died. However any duty of confidence established prior to death does extend beyond death.

The non-commercial elements are not transmissible *mortis causa*. However, the deceased remains protected against infringements of their human dignity and serious infringements of their honour or distortion of their image. The relatives of the deceased (and not the heirs) are entitled to claim for injunctive relief and revocation. Claims for damage compensation are excluded.

4.3 Enforcement
According to article 15 of the constitution of Cyprus everyone has the right to private life therefore commercial use doesn't have to be proved. Only that consent was not given to make use of the said publicity.

As per the case against studio ENA in Nicosia, Cyprus, it was held that the claimants were entitled to an injunction in case the infringer hasn't ceased use of the content and damages.

Celebrities can sign exclusive agreements with a certain luxury brand barring them from being associated to another brand. Thus having to be very cautious when publicizing any kind of content so as to not breach the agreement.

5. PRODUCT PLACEMENT
As a general rule, product placement in Cyprus is prohibited pursuant to Article 30 Z (1) of the Law on Radio and Television Organizations of 1998 (7 (I) / 1998). There are, however, two exceptions:

- where the product placement is used in cinematographic works, films and serials for audiovisual media services, sports programs, and light entertainment programs; and
- where there is no payment but only the free provision of certain products or services, such as production facilities or awards, for the purpose of being included in a program.

In general, programmes containing product placement should meet all the following requirements:
- The content and, in the case of television broadcasts, scheduling, should under no circumstances be affected in such a way to hinder the responsibility and editorial independence of the audio-visual media service provider.
- There should be no direct encouragement to purchase or rent goods or services, particularly by making special promotional references to those goods or services.
- There should be no undue display of these products, including any close-up or prolonged display.
- The audience should be clearly informed of the existence of product placement.

There are certain types of products which are overall prohibited to be included in any broadcasts. Such products include:
- Tobacco or cigarette products.
- Specific medicinal products or therapies available in the Republic only by prescription.
- Children's toys (subject to some exceptions).
- Any other product, commodity or service, the advertising of which is not permitted under the Law.

Available remedies to brand owners in case of a breach of any relevant agreement include:
- Repudiation.
- Damages.
- Specific Performance.

It is common knowledge that luxury fashion brands are not accessible for mass consumption due to their high-price position. Nevertheless, they still develop new strategies to accumulate their profits.

The consumer world can be further analyzed by creating two sections that show the differentiation between the buyers and the need for these luxury brands to broaden their marketing strategies. On the one side, we have the leader group which consists of the *'crème de la crème'*, the elite consumers who have the means to afford luxury brands. On the other side, we have the following group which is comprised of most people. Luxury brands use their marketing tactics to effectively cover the gap between the two groups, by using proper advertising without over exceeding their limited advertising budget.

In the current merchandizing world, product placement is the main form of strategy to reach their audience without the use of traditional advertising. Movies, TV, and especially social media are being bombarded with embedded marketing, which is another term for concealed marketing.

It is of extreme importance for luxury brands to track down more interactive activities between their brands and their audience through different social media platforms. Recognizing the preferences of their customers, for instance, which social media platform they use more regularly is of vital importance. However, this should be handled with caution to keep the character and standards of the brand to cater for the different standards and expectations of the two groups.

6. PROTECTION OF CORPORATE IMAGE AND REPUTATION

According to articles 1, 2 and 3 of GDPR, data protection rules only apply to personal data of natural persons; hence, data protection rules do not apply to data of legal persons such as companies or any other legal entities.

Nevertheless, information in relation to one-person companies may be subject to personal data laws where, for example, any information of such companies leads to the identification of a natural person. The rules also apply to all personal data relating to natural persons during a professional activity.

Under the Contract Law and The Law of Unfair Clauses in Consumer Contracts of 1996 (Law 93 (I) / 1996) there is no general prohibition applicable to clauses aimed at protecting the corporate image/reputation of one of the parties. If any such clauses are articulated in a manner not infringing any other laws applicable to the circumstances of a contract, then such clauses would not be in any way prohibited under Cyprus law.

Nonetheless, some EU manufacturers (especially those using SDSs to distribute their products), seek to prevent retailers from selling via online marketplaces either absolutely (marketplace or platform bans) or where those marketplaces do not fulfil certain quality criteria. Although it is arguable that these types of restraint could be used as mechanisms to reduce (rather than prohibit) cross-border trade or to limit price transparency and price competition, manufacturers frequently justify marketplace restrictions on the basis that they are necessary to:

- protect their brand image and reputation;
- combat the sale of counterfeit products;
- ensure the provision of enough pre-sale's services by retailers (including brick and mortar shops) and to prevent free riding on them; or
- protect direct customer relationships.

Brick and mortar requirements, pure online players and quality are criteria for online selling. In some cases, manufacturers wish to ensure that retailers have a brick and mortar store for the provision of pre- and post-sales services and/or to create an appropriate selling environment for their products/brands. Such a requirement will, of course, exclude pure online players from the distribution system, although a brick and mortar retailer may also sell online. A manufacturer may also wish to ensure that its retailers, whether selling off- or online, adhere to requirements, for example, encouraging the provision of dealer services or the projection of an appropriate image for its product. In some cases, therefore, restrictions may be imposed on selling online via channels which do not adhere to specified criteria.

Cyprus does not belong to the countries having restrictions on sales below cost in their legal systems. However, it is stated in the Protection of Competition Law of 2008 and 2014, Article 5 (1) that the Council of Ministers can issue Orders which are then published in the Official Gazette of the Republic. A recent example of such orders are the Orders issued during the pandemic fixing the lowest and highest prices of products related to COVID-19, such as antiseptics and masks.

Pursuant to Antitrust/Commission Regulation (EC) No 1475/95, the Regulation opens the market for independent suppliers of spare parts and resellers. The supply of contract goods (Article 10(4)) to resellers may not be prohibited where they belong to the same distribution system (Article 3(10)(a)), or where the purchase of spare parts is for their own use in effecting repairs or maintenance (Article 3(10)(b)).

The manufacturer will automatically lose the benefit of the group exemption, if he directly or indirectly restricts:

- the freedom of spare-part suppliers to supply such products of matching quality to resellers of their choice, including those which are undertakings within the distribution system (Article 6(1) (10)); and/or
- the spare-part manufacturers are hindered from affixing effectively and in an easily visible manner their trademark or logo on the spare parts bought by the manufacturer or supplied to the network (Article 6(1) (11)).

Cypriot law protects an individual's reputation under Defamation law, which is a civil wrong. It is distinct in two types, libel and slander, with the latter requiring the claimant to prove any special damages sustained. Subsequently, the law provides that defamation consist of 'publication by any person any printed matter, writing, painting, effigy, gestures, spoken words or other sounds or any other means, including broadcasting by wireless telegraphy, of any matter' which imputes crime to a person or misconduct in a public office. Additionally, it applies where it naturally injures or prejudices the reputation of a person or is likely to expose any person to general hatred, contempt or ridicule or likely to cause another person to be shunned or avoided upon by other persons. Nevertheless, there must be a harmonization of laws consisting the Freedom of Expression and the protection of honors and rights of third parties, under the Cyprus Constitution. Consequently, in order to succeed a defamation claim, the plaintiff must prove that there was a publication, the publication referred to the plaintiff and that the publication was defamatory in nature. In the case where there is a slander, the plaintiff must prove that he/she sustained special damage.

Luxury brands and secondary market or resale are not usually associated together. Mostly because luxury brands are often seen as unattainable for the majority masses. In addition, every time a non-mainstream brand is being seen on a person that does not have the ability to purchase a luxury brand item at its full price and relies on obtaining it through a secondary market it reduces that brands value and status. To conclude, secondary market, resale and third-party providers are damaging and could be considered detrimental to a brand's value and reputation.

AUTHOR BIOGRAPHIES

Maria Hinni
Admitted to the Cyprus Bar in 2011. Joined AGP in 2019 as Senior Associate - Commercial & Corporate Department. Maria worked as a lawyer at the Office of the Attorney General of Cyprus and thereafter worked as corporate and commercial lawyer at a prestigious law firm, where she was involved in litigation and corporate matters. Maria has in-depth knowledge and expertise in corporate and commercial law, liquidation proceedings, intellectual property, data protection matters negotiating and drafting of various corporate and commercial agreements, setting up/management of corporate structures and appearing in court for company petitions and requirements.

George Tashev
Joined AGP in early 2021 as an Associate Lawyer after having worked at his own practice for 5 years. George has the diverse role of not only advising on legal issues but also being involved in the front end of the firm's dealings. This involves communicating proficiently with clients and ensuring smooth completion of all cases. As a practicing lawyer, George established his own business dealing with clients from all around the world in a variety of matters, mostly, but not limited to the Corporate and Banking sector. This invaluable experience gave him the necessary skillset to become an agile legal professional able to handle different types of matters for clients with different backgrounds, effectively.

Nasos Kafantaris
Admitted to the Cyprus Bar Association in 2016. Joined AGP in 2021 as an associate - Corporate Department. Currently undertaking his LPC as well as LLM on International Legal Practice. Nasos has previously worked at a prestigious forex company as a Legal and Compliance Consultant, also at a boutique corporate law firm as an associate. Traineeship at Nicos Chr. Anastasiadis and Partners LLC. Throughout the years Nasos has evolved as a lawyer having been involved in several regulatory and corporate matters, thus he gained valuable expertise in different areas of the law. Nasos handles various legal matters that include research, drafting, reviewing all sort of agreements and contracts; assisting on legal opinions; reviews, drafts and prepares corporate documents; handles the incorporation of companies in various jurisdictions.

Ioanna Martidi
Ioanna graduated law from Democretus University of Thrace, in Greece and has obtained her Master's degree on International Commercial Law at the University of Leicester, in the UK. Joined AGP & Co in 2020 as a trainee lawyer and after passing her Bar exams, has become an Associate lawyer - Litigation Department. During her trainee program Ioanna worked in all practice areas in order to gain the necessary experience and knowledge for her bar exams and future career. She has shown excellent commitment and always strives for excellence.

CZECHIA

Michal Havlík & Michael Feuerstein
Všetečka Zelený Švorčík & Partners

CZECHIA

1. TRADEMARK

1.1 Sources of law

The principal sources of trademark law are as follows.

National sources:
- Act No. 441/2003 Coll., on Trademarks (TA). It provides complex rules on trademarks. It contains both substantive law and procedural law.
- Act No. 221/2006 Coll., on Enforcement of Industrial Property Rights. It contains provisions regulating enforcement of trademarks.
- Act No. 89/2012 Coll., the Civil Code (CC). It contains provisions governing license agreements.
- Act No. 355/2014 on Competence of Customs in Intellectual Property Enforcement. It established framework for customs seizures of counterfeits on the Czech internal market.

International sources:
- Paris Convention for the Protection of Industrial Property of 20 March 1883.
- Madrid Agreement Concerning the International Registration of Marks of 14 April 1891.
- Protocol relating to the Madrid Agreement Concerning the International Registration of Marks of 27 June 1989 (with effect from 25 September 1996).
- Nice Agreement Concerning the International Classification of Goods and Services for the Purposes of the Registration of Marks of 15 June 1957.
- Trademark Law Treaty of 27 October 1994.
- Agreement on Trade-Related Aspects of Intellectual Property Rights (TRIPS) of 15 April 1994.

European Union sources:
- Directive (EU) 2015/2436 of 16 December 2015 to approximate the laws of the Member States relating to trademarks.
- Regulation (EU) 2017/1001 of 14 June 2017 on the European Union trademark.
- Directive 2004/48/EC of 29 April 2004 on the enforcement of intellectual property rights.
- Regulation (EU) No 608/2013 of 12 June 2013 concerning customs enforcement of intellectual property rights.

Court decisions:

Czech law does not expressly recognize the concept of binding precedents. However, it requires that court decisions are foreseeable meaning that a case should be decided similarly to other legal cases that have already been decided and that coincide in essential aspects with the case to be decided. Uniformity of decision-making practice is secured by the decisions of the courts of higher instances. The courts of the lower instances thus in practice generally follow the decisions of the courts of higher instances.

Furthermore, since the TA implements to a great extent the Trademark Directive, the Czech courts shall comply with the decisions of the Court of Justice of the European Union regarding the interpretation of the TA.

The use of a non-registered sign in the course of trade may constitute an opposition ground against a trademark application. In order for a non-registered sign to constitute the opposition ground, it is required that its user acquired rights to it prior to the filing or priority date of the opposed trademark application (i.e. the user has been using the said sign before the aforesaid date) and that there is a likelihood of confusion on the part of the public due to the identity or similarity of the respective signs and the relevant goods or services.

Non-registered signs may be protected under unfair competition. The difference between trademarks and non-registered signs consists particularly in the fact that the burden of proof in relation to infringement of a non-registered sign is more challenging, as the claimant needs to prove that it has been using the non-registered sign for relevant goods and / or services earlier than the defendant. On the other hand, in the case of trademarks, the registration is sufficient evidence of the existence of the complainant's rights, whereas it is presumed that the trademark, if registered, is valid.

1.2 Substantive law

Czech law recognizes well-known trademarks and trademarks with reputation. Legal concept of famous trademarks is not recognized under Czech law.

Under the TA, a well-known trademark is a trademark which is well-known in the territory of Czechia in accordance with Article 6bis of the Paris Convention and Article 16 of the TRIPS Agreement. A well-known trademark does not need to be registered in the Czech Trademark Register in order for it to confer rights on its owner in Czechia. The rights conferred by a well-known trademark in Czechia are identical as rights conferred by other types of trademarks recognized by the TA.

Trademarks with reputation enjoy a broader scope of protection. The scope of their protection extends to goods and services which are dissimilar to those for which such trademark is registered. Furthermore, the likelihood of confusion is no requirement to assume an infringement. Such trademarks are protected against later identical or similar signs provided that the use of the later sign takes without due cause unfair advantage of, or is detrimental to, the distinctive character or the reputation of the trademark.

The "aura of luxury" of a trademark is a supportive argument in order to prove that the use of the later sign takes unfair advantage of, or is detrimental to, the reputation of the trademark.

1.3 Enforcement

The TA does not define the concept of the "reputation". According to the case-law, the reputation implies a certain degree of knowledge of the earlier trademark among the public. It is required that the trademark is known by a significant part of the public although there is no fixed threshold of recognition.

When assessing whether a trademark has reputation, all the relevant facts of the case shall be taken into account (particularly, the market share held by the trademark, the intensity, geographical extent and duration of its use, and the size of the investment made by the undertaking in promoting).

Czech law does not provide for an exhaustive list of means of evidence which may be used for proving reputation of a trademark. Any means from which the status of the matter may be found may be used. Typically, catalogues, offering letters, leaflets, evidence of advertising activities, media presentations, sponsorship of cultural and sports events, information and printouts from websites, orders, invoices, delivery notes and surveys are used for the purpose of proving reputation. The evidence shall contain the trademark in question, have connection with the relevant territory and the relevant goods and services. Oral testimony is also possible although it is not commonly used in these matters. Affidavits claiming certain degree of use of the trademark are commonly used.

A trademark may be enforced against a domain name either by means of civil court litigation or alternative dispute resolution (ADR) proceedings. A trademark may be successfully enforced by means of civil court litigation in case the conditions for trademark infringement or unfair competition are fulfilled. In order to succeed, the disputed domain name needs to be used in the course of trade. If the disputed domain name is not actively used, its registration may still amount to unfair competition.

ADR proceedings are in practice independent of the trademark or unfair competition law. In order to succeed in .cz ADR proceedings, the trademark owner needs to prove, apart from the confusing similarity between the disputed domain name and the trademark, that either:
- the disputed domain name has been registered or acquired by its holder without rights in the disputed domain name or a protected sign (such as trademark or tradename); or
- the disputed domain name has been registered, acquired or is being used in bad faith.

A trademark may be enforced against a domain name in .cz ADR proceedings regardless of whether the domain name is actively used or not.

A trademark may be enforced against a trade name. However, the business activity of the entity having a conflicting trade name needs to be taken into account so that it can be assessed whether the trade name is used in relation to goods or services which are identical or similar to those for which the enforced trademark is registered.

The protection of a trademark against the use of other identical or similar distinctive signs depends on their kind. Generally, in case such signs are used in order to designate origin of goods or services, a trademark may be enforced against them.

Provided that the conditions of trademark infringement are fulfilled, a trademark may be enforced against metatags.

A trademark may be enforced against its unauthorized use in social media in the same way as against its any other unauthorized use.

A trademark may be enforced against its unauthorized use in comparative advertising if its use is in conflict with other laws (particularly the CC which provides for the conditions for admissibility of comparative advertising) and particularly if the comparative advertising unfairly benefits from the trademark or if it offers goods or services as an imitation or copy of goods or services identified by the trademark. A trademark may be enforced against comparative advertising not only if it harms its essential function but also if it harms any its other functions.

Czech law does not provide for a limitation on trademark rights which would allow use of a trademark in parody. However, this does not mean that a trademark owner may prohibit any unauthorized use of the trademark in parody as the fundamental right to property and freedom of speech are weighed against each other. Generally, the fundamental right to property would prevail in the case of a trademark being used in parody predominantly for a commercial purpose, or in case the use of the trademark in parody would unfairly benefit from the trademark´s reputation or cause a likelihood of confusion as to the origin.

It is possible to claim both trademark infringement and unfair competition for the same set of facts and to bring parallel trademark infringement and unfair competition proceedings.

Probably the most significant issue, particularly for luxury brands, is counterfeiting. There are cases where infringers offer a mix of genuine goods and counterfeits (particularly on online stores or through closed social media groups). As a consequence, the enforcement of trademarks by means of customs seizures and destruction is more challenging.

2. COPYRIGHT

2.1 Sources of law

The principal sources of copyright law are as follows.

National sources:
- Act No. 121/2000 Coll., on Copyright and Rights Related to Copyright ("CA"). It provides complex regulation of copyright and rights related to copyright including collective management of these rights. It lays down the conditions the work needs to fulfil in order to be protected by copyright. It also stipulates the rights arising from copyright and rights related to copyright, exceptions and limitation thereto, their duration and the provisions on its enforcement.

International sources:
- Berne Convention for the Protection of Literary and Artistic Works of 9 September 1886.
- World Intellectual Property Organization Copyright Treaty of 20 December 1996.
- Agreement on Trade-Related Aspects of Intellectual Property Rights (TRIPS) of 15 April 1994.

European Union sources:
- Directive 2001/29/EC of 22 May 2001 on the harmonisation of certain aspects of copyright and related rights in the information society.
- Directive 2004/48/EC of 29 April 2004 on the enforcement of intellectual property rights.
- Certain specific subject matters relating to copyright (such as computer programs, databases, performance´s rights and broadcasters´ rights) are regulated by further specific European Union Directives.

The Czech courts shall comply with the decisions of the Court of Justice of the European Union regarding the interpretation of the CA as far as its provisions implementing European Union law are concerned.

Generally, the European Union law takes precedence over Czech law. Regulations have immediate effect in Czechia. Directives need to be implemented into Czech law. In case a Directive is not implemented into Czech law within the prescribed time-limit, the Czech law shall be interpreted in accordance with the Directive and the Directive may even, under certain conditions, gain immediate effect in Czechia.

International treaties to the ratification of which the Czech Parliament has given its consent and by which Czechia is bound take precedence over Czech national law.

2.2 Substantive law

The subject matter of copyright may be a literary work or any other work of art or a scientific work. The CA does not provide for a closed list of copyrightable works. It merely mentions types of works which may be protected by copyright.

In theory, objects of industrial, fashion or accessory designs are capable of protection by copyright. However, the Czech practice tends to impose a rather high threshold of originality and creative activity required for application of copyright protection to such works of applied arts (it needs to go beyond an average level of industrial design).

Copyright consists of economic and moral rights. The moral rights consist of:
- the right to decide about making the work public;
- the right to claim authorship, including the right to decide whether, and in what way, the authorship is to be indicated when the work is made public and further used, provided that the indication of authorship is normal in such use; and
- the right to the inviolability of the work.

The economic rights cover:
- the right to use the work in its initial form or in a form adapted by another person or otherwise modified, whether separately or in a collection or connection with any other work or elements, and to grant authorisation on a contractual basis to any other person to exercise that right;
- resale right (*Droit de suite*); and
- the right to remuneration in connection with reproduction of work for personal use and for legal person's own internal use.

Unless otherwise agreed, the author's economic rights to a work created by the author in fulfilling their duties arising from the employment contract shall be exercised by the employer in their own name and on their own account. The employer may only assign the exercise of the right pursuant to this paragraph to a third party with the author's consent, unless this occurs when an undertaking or any part thereof is being sold. The author's moral rights to an employee work remain unaffected.

As to non-employees, if a work is created by the author on the basis of a contract for work, unless otherwise agreed, it shall be deemed that the author has granted a licence for the purpose following the contract. If the work is not created on the basis of a contract for work, or in case the principal wishes to use the work for the purpose which goes beyond the contract for work, the principal needs to obtain a license for such a use.

Both moral and economic rights cannot be assigned. The economic rights may be only licensed. The license agreement does not need to be in writing, unless the license is exclusive. The author cannot transfer or waive their moral rights.

The economic rights generally last for the life of the author and 70 years after their death. The moral rights shall become extinct on the death of the author. After the death of the author no one may arrogate authorship of the work; the work may only be used in a way which shall not detract from its value and, unless the work is an anonymous work, the name of the author must be indicated, provided that such shall be a normal practice.

2.3 Enforcement

Under the CA, copyright arises once the work is expressed in any objectively perceivable manner including electronic form. No copyright registration, deposit or notice is required for enforcing copyright.

Actual copying is not necessary to establish infringement of copyright. The copyright protection extends not only to copyrighted work in its initial form but also to form adopted by another person (including translation) or otherwise modified.

Copyright can be enforced against any infringing use of the copyrighted work regardless of whether the copyrighted work is unauthorized use as a protected IP right or as a part of it. As to the trademarks, the copyright constitutes an opposition and invalidity ground in case the use of the sign applied for may infringe on the copyright. There is no provision precluding enforceability against patents, however, it is difficult to imagine a situation in which a patent would use copyrighted work.

Copyright can be enforced against unauthorized use of a copyrighted work in social media under the same conditions as in case of any other unauthorized use.

Czech law does not provide for any explicit limitation of when it would not be possible to enforce copyright in comparative advertising. On the other hand, the likely conclusion would be that copyright cannot be enforced against the use of copyrighted work in permissible comparative advertising if the use of the copyrighted work is necessary for the legitimate comparative advertising. Such enforcement would not be deemed as legitimate or compliant with honest business practices.

A person who uses the copyrighted work for the purpose of cartoons or parody does not infringe copyright. The parody needs to humorously adapt the work or its features which may themselves be a copyrighted work. At the same time, the use of a work shall not conflict with the normal exploitation of the work and shall not unreasonably prejudice the legitimate interests of the author. The parody does not comply with the normal exploitation of the work if, for example, the work is used for the purpose of advertisement. The decision on whether the use of the copyrighted work falls within the parody statutory limitation will always require the comparison of the fundamental right to property and freedom of speech.

The CA provides statutory exceptions and limitations to copyright. These are applied only if the use of a work is not in conflict with its normal exploitation and it does not unreasonably prejudice the legitimate interests of the author. Probably the most significant exception is a free use of a work. Under this exception, the use of a copyrighted work for personal needs by a natural person without seeking to achieve direct or indirect economic benefit generally does not amount to copyright infringement. This exception also covers making a fixation, reproduction or imitation of a copyrighted work for personal use. The other statutory exceptions and limitations are, for example, quotation, use of a work located in public place or use of a work in periodical press or broadcasting.

The copyright is not subject to statute limitation except for the financial claims arising from copyright infringement (damages, immaterial harm, unjust enrichment) which are subject to limitation. The limitation period amounts to 3 years and commences from the date on which the copyright owner became aware of the damage / immaterial harm / unjust enrichment and the person liable to provide the compensation. In any case, such financial claims becomes time-barred no later than ten years after the date the damage / immaterial harm / unjust enrichment was incurred (15 years where it was caused wilfully).

There are no particular issues for luxury brands, mainly because copyright is not the primary legal instrument for IP protection of luxury brands. Trademark and design protection are easier to enforce for the reasons stated above.

3. DESIGN
3.1 Sources of law
The principal sources of design law are as follows.

National sources:
- Act No. 207/2000 Coll., on the Protection of Designs and the Amendment to Act No. 527/1990 on Inventions, Designs and Rationalization Proposals (DA). It provides complex rules on designs and contains both substantive law and procedural law.
- Act No. 221/2006 Coll., on Enforcement of Industrial Property Rights. It contains provisions regulating enforcement of designs.
- Act No. 89/2012 Coll., the Civil Code (CC). It contains provisions governing license agreements.
- Act No. 355/2014 on Competence of Customs in Intellectual Property Enforcement. It established a framework for customs seizures of counterfeits on the Czech internal market.

International sources:
- Paris Convention for the Protection of Industrial Property of 20 March 1883.
- Agreement on Trade-Related Aspects of Intellectual Property Rights (TRIPS) of 15 April 1994.

European Union sources:
- Directive 98/71/EC of 13 October 1998 on the legal protection of designs.
- Regulation (EC) 6/2002 of 12 December 2001 on Community Designs.
- Directive 2004/48/EC of 29 April 2004 on the enforcement of intellectual property rights.
- Regulation (EU) No 608/2013 of 12 June 2013 concerning customs enforcement of intellectual property rights.

  For information on the precedence of the European Union law and international law over Czech law, see Section 2.1 Copyright: Sources of law.

3.2 Substantive law

A design is the appearance of the whole or a part of a product consisting in the features of, in particular, the lines, contours, colours, shape, texture and/or materials of the product itself and/or its ornamentation. A product means any industrial or handicraft item, including *inter alia* parts intended to be assembled into a complex product, packaging, get-up, graphic symbols and typographic typefaces, but excluding computer programs. These types of products are thus protectable by way of registered design in Czechia. The DA does not recognize national unregistered designs, but enforcement of Community unregistered designs is available.

In order for a design to obtain a registration, the design needs to be new and have an individual character. A design shall be considered new if no identical design has been made available to the public before the application or priority date. Designs shall be deemed identical if their features differ only in immaterial details.

A design shall be considered to have individual character if the overall impression it produces on the informed user differs from the overall impression produced on such a user by any design which has been made available to the public before the application or priority date. In assessing individual character, the degree of freedom of the designer in developing the design shall be taken into consideration.

The right to the design belongs to the author or their successor in title. Where an author has created a design as part of their duties deriving from an employment relationship, by reason of the fact that he is a member of an organisation or of any other similar relationship, the right to the design shall pass to the person who assigned the task of creating the design ("the principal"), unless otherwise laid down by contract. In such a case, the author shall be required to notify the fact without delay, in writing, to the principal and to hand over documents required for assessing the design. Where the principal does not claim the right to the design within a period of three months as from receipt of the communication referred to above; the right shall revert to the author.

The above-mentioned process applies to employees and directors. As to consultants, shareholders and suppliers, the right to the design may be acquired only by means of an assignment.

Assignment of a design must be executed in writing, otherwise it is null and void. The assignment must be recorded in the Register of Designs of the Czech IPO in order to become effective. If the rights to a design pertain to two or more persons, the consent of all co-proprietors is required. A co-proprietor may assign their co-proprietorship interest to another co-proprietor without the consent of the others. A co-proprietorship interest may only be assigned to a third party if none of the other co-proprietors has accepted an assignment offer made in writing within one month.

No legalization or notarization of the deed of assignment is required.

In the case of an assignment agreement with consultants, shareholders and suppliers, it is prudent to stipulate that the rights to the designs created within a particular activity shall be assigned to the principal at the time of their creation and that these persons will make any declarations necessary in order to enable the registration of the design in the name of the principal.

The employment contracts and the contracts entered into with directors should contain acknowledgement of the fact that the right to the design shall pass to the employer / principal and that the employee / director shall notify the creation of a design without delay and in writing.

Moral rights cannot be waived or transferred.

Czech national registered designs as well as Community designs can be protected for five years from the filing date, extendible four times for a period of five years, up to total term of protection of twenty-five years

The DA does not protect national unregistered designs. However, unregistered Community designs enjoy protection of 3 years as from the date on which the design was first made available to the public with the European Union.

3.3 Enforcement

The scope of protection is determined by the representation of the design as registered. The protection extends to identical designs and to designs that do not produce a different overall impression on the informed user. Protection does not extend to the features dictated by the technical function of the design or to features which must necessarily be reproduced in exact form and dimensions in order to allow the product in which the design is incorporated or to which it is applied to be mechanically connected to or placed in, around or against another product so that each of the products may perform its function. When assessing the scope of protection, the degree of freedom of the designer in developing the design shall be taken into consideration.

A design may be enforced against a trademark as the fact that a design or its 2D reproduction is used as (a part) of a trademark does not deprive the design from the possibility of being enforced. A design may thus be invoked as an opposition and invalidity ground. A design may be also enforced against a younger registered design. An enforcement of a design against patents, domain names, trade names and other similar IP rights is not precluded by Czech law, however, in practice an actual enforcement of a design against these rights seems to be merely theoretical.

A design may be enforced against its unauthorized use in social media under the same conditions as in the case of any other form of its unauthorized use.

It would be possible to enforce a design against its unauthorized use in comparative advertising only in the case that the conditions for permissible comparative advertising are not fulfilled (particularly if the comparative advertising unfairly benefits from the design or if it offers goods or services as an imitation or copy of goods or services impersonating the design).

Generally, a design can be enforced against its unauthorized use in parody. However, the freedom of speech would be weighed against the fundamental right to property. In case the freedom of speech is found to be stronger in a particular case, the use of the design in parody would be permissible.

Primarily, the alleged infringer may claim that the attacked sign produces a different overall impression and thus does not fall within the scope of the protection of the registered design.

Furthermore, the alleged infringer may argue that their act falls within one of the following limitations: acts committed for a) non-commercial purposes only; b) for experimental purposes; c) for the purpose of quotation or education, provided that such acts are in accordance with fair commercial practices and do not cause prejudice to the normal exploitation of the design and the source is quoted.

The alleged infringer may also argue that the design rights have been exhausted. The rights conferred by a design do not extend to acts relating to a product incorporating the design or to which the design has been applied, which has been entered on the market in the European Economic Area by or with the consent of the design proprietor.

The alleged infringer may also raise the "prior user rights" defense. The rights conferred by a design are not enforceable against third persons who can prove that before the filing or priority date, they have commenced or have undertaken serious preparations to use a design falling in the scope of protection of the design registration, if such used design has been created independently of the enforced design. Those persons are authorized to use the industrial design for their business activity, in which the prior use has been made or prepared.

The alleged infringer may also file an application for cancellation of the enforced design. Such applications are heard exclusively by the Czech IPO. The alleged infringer may afterwards request the court to suspend the infringement proceedings until the decision on the application is issued by the Czech IPO. However, since rights conferred by a design are time-limited, the Czech courts tend not to suspend the infringement proceedings in such cases.

The repair clause is not recognized by Czech law for Czech national designs and there is no comparable limitation.

The rights conferred by the design are not subject to statute limitation except for the financial claims arising from design infringement (damages, immaterial harm, unjust enrichment) which are statute limited identically to the financial claims arising from copyright infringement (see Section 2.3 Copyright: Enforcement).

Furthermore, it follows from Czech case-law that longer-term acquiescence in the use of an infringing sign weakens the design proprietor´s claim as the court is not likely to consider the claim as urgent and serious since the design holder has not taken the appropriate legal steps earlier.

The protection under copyright law, civil law or trademark law remains unaffected. Therefore, a claim may be based on design infringement and copyright infringement and/or unfair competition law in the same proceedings.

The most significant issue is probably counterfeiting. For more information, see Section 1.3 Trademark: Enforcement.

4. RIGHT OF PRIVACY, PUBLICITY AND PERSONAL ENDORSEMENT
4.1 Sources of law
Czech law recognizes certain individual's rights such as the right to one's name, the right to one´s image, the right to one's dignity, honour, privacy, expressions of personal nature. When the scope of protection of these rights is assessed, these rights are compared to other fundamental rights such as freedom to speech.

The principal law relating to the right of publicity is the Act No. 89/2012 Coll., the Civil Code (CC). The CC provides for personality rights of an individual including protection of individual´s image and privacy.

4.2 Substantive law

Each living human has a right of publicity. No other conditions need to be satisfied.

The CC does not expressly stipulate that the right of publicity is transmissible *mortis causa*. Generally, in the event of the death of an individual, the personality rights of that individual cease to exist and do not transfer to their heirs. On the other hand, the protection of personality rights of a deceased individual may be claimed by any of their close persons. The entitlement of the aforesaid persons covers the protection of the personality rights. There is no case-law addressing whether the aforesaid persons may grant consent to the use of individual's name, image, likeness, or other unequivocal aspects of their identity. However, since such personality rights are generally closely connected with the individual, it may be argued that the aforesaid persons do not have right to grant such a consent.

The right of publicity cannot be assigned in whole or in part. The individual may only grant the authorization to use a certain element of their right of publicity.

Under the CC, capturing the image of an individual in any way that would allow their identity to be determined is only possible with their consent. Furthermore, the image of an individual may only be distributed with their consent. Therefore, generally, an image of an individual may be captured and distributed only with the individual´s consent regardless of whether the image is used for a commercial or non-commercial purpose. Strictly speaking, the consent to capturing and distributing individual´s image cannot be considered as a license as according to the CC, the license means consent to the use of intellectual property within which the rights of personality do not fall. There is no case-law on whether the consent to capturing and distributing of individual´s image may be granted on an exclusive basis.

Czech law does not prescribe any form for the consent to capturing and distributing of individual´s image. The consent may be also granted implicitly.

A person who consented to the use of documents of a personal nature, portraits or audio or video recordings relating to an individual or their expressions of a personal nature may withdraw their consent, even if granted for a definite period. Such a person is thus generally not limited in withdrawing the consent and he/she does not need any reason for doing so. However, if consent granted for a definite period is withdrawn without it being justified by a substantial change in circumstances or any other reasonable cause, the withdrawing person shall compensate the person to whom he granted the consent to the resulting damage.

The CC does not expressly address the death of the licensor. As mentioned above, an individual may grant consent to the use of certain aspects of their individuality. Such consent, however, cannot be considered as license within the meaning of the CC. On the other hand, it can be argued that the consent remains valid and effective even after the death of the individual granting the consent and that the consent binds the successors.

The close persons of a deceased individual may claim the protection of their personality rights. On the other hand, since it can be argued that consent to the use of certain aspects of individuality remains valid and effective even after the death of the individual and binds the successors, it is probable that the close persons of a deceased individual shall respect the granted consent and cannot claim protection against the use which falls within the granted consent.

The right of publicity is not transmissible *mortis causa*. The right of the close persons of the deceased individual to claim protection of the personality rights of the deceased individual is not time-limited.

4.3 Enforcement

The right of publicity may be enforced against any use (i.e. not only against a commercial use) provided that such use does not fall within any statutory limitation.

It is not necessary to prove that the individual's name, image, likeness, or other unequivocal aspects of one's identity have a commercial value to obtain an injunction or other remedies for the unauthorized use. On the other hand, in practice, the amount of immaterial harm incurred by the individual will depend on the commercial value of the above-mentioned aspects.

The infringer may claim the following statutory limitations:
- **Exercise or protection of other rights.** The image, or audio or video recording capturing an individual is made or used to exercise or protect other rights or legally protected interests of others.
- **Official purpose.** The image, document of a personal nature or audio or video recording is made or used by means of a statute for official purposes.
- **Public act in matters of public interest.** The image, document of a personal nature or audio or video recording is made or used where someone performs a public act in matters of public interest (e.g. public speech).
- **Scientific or artistic purposes.** The image or audio or video recording is reasonably made or used for scientific or artistic purposes.
- **Print, radio, television or similar coverage.** The image, or audio or video recording is reasonably made or used for print, radio, television or similar coverage.

The above-mentioned limitations may not be used unreasonably in conflict with the legitimate interests of the individual.

The images of celebrities are commonly misused in online advertisements where these images are used as a part of promotion of certain dubious products or services without their authorization. Another issue is the advertising made by celebrities in collaboration with brand owners on social media. In case celebrities promote any product within social medias for the consideration received from the brands owner and do not disclose the collaboration (which commonly happens), such an activity may be considered as illicit advertising and thus unfair commercial practice.

5. PRODUCT PLACEMENT

Product placement is permitted provided that the statutory conditions are fulfilled. Product placement is permitted only in cinematography works, movies and series created for television broadcast or for on-demand audio-visual media services, and in sport and entertainment programmes except for programmes for children. It is also allowed in case there is no payment but only the provision of certain goods or services free of charge, such as production props and prizes, with a view to their inclusion in a programme.

The programmes containing product placement shall fulfil the following conditions:
- their content and, in the case of television broadcasting, their scheduling shall not be influenced in such a way as to affect the responsibility and editorial independence of the provider of on-demand audio-visual media services or of the broadcaster;
- they shall not directly encourage the purchase or rental of goods or services, in particular by making special promotional references to those goods or services; and
- they shall not give undue prominence to the product in question.

The product placement is not allowed in relation to cigarettes, other tobacco products, electronic cigarettes and their cartridges, or in relation to products of a person whose main business activity consists in manufacture or sale of the above-mentioned products and in relation to medical products or medical processes which are available only on prescription in Czechia.

The programmes containing product placement shall generally be clearly marked as such at their beginning, end and in case of their interruption by advertisement or teleshopping, also after the end of the termination. This is usually done by the sign "PP" depicted within the program.

In case the other party fails to perform the agreement, the particular possibilities available to the brand owner will depend on the content of the contract. Generally, the brand owner would be entitled to damages. Furthermore, in case the breach of the contract is fundamental, the other party may withdraw from it without undue delay. If a contract obliges to provide continuous or recurrent activities or provide a progressive partial performance, it is possible to withdraw from the contract only with effect from that moment onward. Withdrawal from a contract does not affect the right to be paid a contractual penalty or default interest if already due and the right to be compensated for damage resulting from a breach of a contractual duty.

Based on the content of the contract, the other stipulated remedies may be available. In case the brand owner withdraws from the contract, or the contract is terminated in any other way and the placing party continues in product placing, it is probable that the brand owner is entitled to demand termination of such placing (although there exists no case-law confirming the aforesaid).

Luxury brand owners should pay particular attention to the way in which the product is presented within the product placement. Fines for undue prominence of a product within product placement have already been imposed on broadcasters several times by regulatory authorities.

6. PROTECTION OF CORPORATE IMAGE AND REPUTATION

Czech law protects right to name of legal entities and their reputation and privacy.

The legal entities do not have to fulfil any certain conditions in order to enjoy the right of publicity and privacy. It is presumed that a legal entity has reputation until it is proved to the contrary. The reputation is assessed on a conduct of the legal entity in commercial relationships.

It is possible to include specific clauses in agreements aimed at protecting the corporate image and reputation provided that these clauses comply with antitrust law.

Generally, a system of selective distribution is permissible provided that it complies with the following conditions:
- the nature of the goods requires system of selective distribution;
- the sellers shall be chosen on the basis of objective criteria of qualitative nature which is identical for all potential sellers and which is not applied in a discriminatory way; and
- the criteria shall be strictly necessary.

Generally, a provision setting a certain (minimum) price or prohibiting purchase of non-original but otherwise legitimate spare parts and components are considered as anticompetitive and thus forbidden.

A provision setting out a contractual penalty for breach by a party of any provisions protecting reputation or corporate image of the other party is generally not forbidden, but it must be assessed as to compliance with antitrust law.

Luxury brands face the issue of sale of their products outside the system of selective distribution, particularly in outlets and online. As to third-party providers, the owners of luxury brands (particularly car brands) face the issue of unauthorized providers of repair and maintenance services using the owner´s trademarks in a way causing a false impression as to the commercial relationship between the providers and the owners of luxury brands.

AUTHOR BIOGRAPHIES

Michal Havlík
Michal Havlík is an attorney at law and partner at the firm. He studied law at the School of Law of the Charles University in Prague and Cardiff Law School. He represents clients in intellectual property matters including anti-counterfeiting and unfair competition. Michal currently serves as the president of the Czech National Group AIPPI.

Michael Feuerstein
Michael Feuerstein is an attorney-at-law at the firm where he particularly focuses on the enforcement of intellectual property rights including the domain disputes. He graduated from the School of Law of the Charles University in Prague in 2017. In 2018, he graduated in Intellectual Property Law from the Uppsala University, Sweden, where he obtained a degree of Master of Laws (LL.M.). He is a member of the Czech Bar Association.

FRANCE

Sophie Marc
Santarelli

FRANCE

1. TRADEMARK

1.1 Sources of law

The principal source of law is the Intellectual Property Code (CPI), Book VII, with the latest amendment of the Plan d'Action pour la Croissance et la Transformation des Entreprises (PACTE Law) of 22 May 2019.

As a Member State of the European Union, France has transposed various European legal acts, notably:
- Directive (EU) 2015/2436 of 16 December 2015 replacing EC Directive no. 2008/95/EC.
- Regulation (EU) 2015/2424 of 16 December 2015 (amending EC Regulation no. 207/2009).
- EC Directive 2004/48/EC of 29 April 2004.

France is party to a number of International Treaties concerning trademarks:
- Paris Convention for the Protection of Industrial Property of 20 March 1883.
- Madrid Agreement of 14 April 1891 and Madrid Protocol of 27 June 1989 regarding the International Registration of Marks.
- Nice Agreement of 15 June 1957 concerning the International Classification of Goods and Services.
- Marrakech Agreement on Trade-Related Aspects of Intellectual Property Rights (TRIPS) of 15 April 1994.

The hierarchy of sources of law in France is as follows:
- French Constitution.
- International Treaties and European law.
- French laws.
- Regulatory acts.

Case law is not binding in France.

French law does not recognize use as a source of trademark rights, they are exclusively acquired through registration. Some defense mechanisms can be activated on the basis of non-registered well-known trademarks according to the Article 6bis of the Paris Union Convention.

1.2 Substantive law

Well-known registered trademarks benefit from a broader protection against goods and services not covered by the scope of the registration, if the use made by the third party, without due cause, takes unfair advantage of the distinctive character or the reputation of the mark, or is detrimental to it (Article L.713-3 CPI).

Famous non-registered trademarks corresponding to the criteria of Article 6bis of the Paris Convention are protected for goods and services, which are not similar to those for which the mark is known, in the same conditions as above.

To benefit from this broader protection, well-known/famous trademarks must be "known by a significant part of the relevant public for the products and services it designates".

No specific protection is granted to the luxury industry trademarks but their "aura of luxury" can help to establish their reputation.

1.3 Enforcement

The well-known character of the trademark can be evidenced by "all means", through a combination of objective elements showing that the trademark owns a power of attraction independent from the goods and services covered.

This evidence must show the intensity (commercial success), geographical scope and duration of use in commerce, notably through the market share occupied by the trademark, sales volumes, advertising/promotional investments, press articles, and so on (CJEU, *General Motors* 14 September 1999, CJCE, 14 sept. 1998, aff. C-375/97).

Consumer surveys can be used to show the degree of recognition of the mark amongst the public (in combination with other evidence). The methodology of the survey must be exposed, its results being submitted to the appreciation of the judges.

Oral testimonies, affidavits (if supported by factual evidence) or expert evidence can be used to support the claim. However, the "objective" types of evidence detailed above will be considered as more convincing to the judges.

A trademark can be enforced against a domain name, a trade name and other distinctive signs.

The trademark can be enforced only against uses made "in the course of trade" (CJEU *Arsenal*, 12 November 2002, no. C-206/01). The use of the trademark as a keyword or metatag is usually not considered as a use in the course of trade (CJEU, 23 March 2010, *Google v. Louis Vuitton*, C236/08 to C238-08). However, this use can be considered as infringing if it suggests a link between the trademark owner and the third party, or undermines the function of origin of the mark (Paris, pole 5, 1st ch., June 13, 2017, Merck: PIBD 2018, 1090, III, 204).

In case of well-known marks, such use can be sanctioned if likely to dilute or tarnish the prior famous mark (CJUE, 1re ch., 22 September 2011, aff. C-323/09, *Interflora Inc. c/ Marks & Spencer plc*).

A trademark can be enforced against its unauthorized use in social media in case of counterfeiting, denigration or parasitism, if the use is made in the course of trade. Particular attention must be brought to the potential "bad publicity" which could result in attacking social media users.

Use of a trademark is allowed in comparative advertising, provided that the comparison is "unbiased". It can be sanctioned if this use takes unfair advantage of the reputation of the mark, discredits or denigrates it, creates a risk of confusion or if the goods or services are presented like an imitation or reproduction of the ones protected by the mark.

The use of a trademark in parody is lawful since it is considered as being outside the course of trade (unless this use is made to attract commercial gain by selling products, for instance).

The same set of facts cannot be used to take action claiming trademark infringement and unfair competition (*Cass.com.*, 23 mars 2010, no. 09-66.522). Both grounds can be used in the same action if "distinct facts" constituting unfair practices or aggravating the infringement can be demonstrated.

Luxury brands must be aware of the bad publicity that can result from attacking certain types of infringements on new medias, mainly on social media.

2. COPYRIGHT

2.1 Sources of law

The main national source of law is the Intellectual Property Code (CPI), Books I, II and III, incorporating the provisions of the laws of 1957 and 1985.

France has transposed some European directives with regard to copyright:
- Directive 93/98/EEC of 29 October 1993 for harmonizing the term of protection of copyright and certain related rights.
- Directive 2001/29/EC of 22 May 2001 on the harmonization of certain aspects of copyright and related rights in the information society.

France is also a contracting party to a number of International Treaties:
- Berne Convention of 9 September 1886 for the Protection of Literary and Artistic Works.
- Universal Copyright Convention of 6 September 1952.
- Rome Convention of 26 October 1961 for the Protection of Performers, Producers of Phonograms and Broadcasting Organizations.
- Marrakech Agreement on Trade-Related Aspects of Intellectual Property Rights (TRIPS) of 15 April 1994.
- WIPO Copyright Treaty of 20 December 1996.

The hierarchy of sources of law is as stated above in Trademarks, Section 1.1.

2.2 Substantive law

French copyright law protects "the rights of authors in all intellectual works, whatever their genre, form of expression, merit or destination" (Article L112-1 CPI), provided that they are formalized (and not mere ideas) and that they are sufficiently "original" (bearing the imprint of their author's personality).

The CPI provides a non-exhaustive list of the works which can be copyrightable (Article L112-2 CPI), notably:
- "1 ° Books, brochures and other literary, artistic and scientific writings; (…)
- 5 ° Musical compositions with or without words;
- 6 ° (…) Audiovisual works;
- 7 ° Works of drawing, painting, architecture, sculpture, engraving, lithography;
- 8 ° Graphic and typographical works;
- 9 ° Photographic works and those produced using techniques similar to photography;
- 10 ° Works of applied art; (…)
- 14 ° Creations of seasonal clothing and adornment industries. Industries which, owing to the demands of fashion, frequently renew the form of their products, and in particular the making of clothing, fur, lingerie, embroidery, fashion, footwear, gloves, leather goods, the manufacture of high-novelty or special haute couture fabrics, the productions of dressmakers and shoemakers and upholstery factories."

Objects of industrial, fashion or accessory design are copyrightable. As with other works of the mind, they must be "original", which indeed excludes all works in which their creation has been dictated by purely functional purposes.

Copyright encompasses proprietary (economic) and moral rights.

Proprietary rights include the exclusive right to authorize or forbid the reproduction and representation (communication to the public) of the work.

Moral rights include the right of disclosure (exclusive right to disclose the work to the public and manage the conditions of disclosure, or to forbid it), the right of withdrawal or reconsideration (to amend the work or withdraw it after its first disclosure), the right of integrity (to prevent or control any alteration or modification of the work) and the right of paternity (to be identified as the author of the work).

The right of paternity is limited in the case of works of applied arts if the use of the sector or the object itself makes it difficult for the name of the author to be mentioned on the work (on the body of a car or a perfume bottle, for instance: CA Paris, 4e ch., 22 nov. 1983; CA Paris, pôle 5, 1re ch., 31 oct. 2012, no. 10/21777).

The author is the physical person who created the work. The person under whose name the work is disclosed is presumed to be the author (individual or legal entity).

Employment contracts do not operate a transfer of ownership of the author rights (even if a specific provision states the transfer), since the assignment of future works is prohibited in France. A specific assignment of the author rights must be established for a legal entity to acquire the author rights of any of its employees, consultants, shareholders, directors or suppliers.

As an exception, a legal entity publishing and disclosing a work can be the initial owner of the author rights in the case of a collective work created on its initiative, in which the personal contributions of the authors participating in its elaboration merge together so that it is impossible to grant them each a distinct right on the work as a whole (article L113-2 of the CPI).

The author rights are automatically transferred to the legal entity in some specific cases, as for contracts binding the producer to the authors of an audiovisual work, or commission contracts for advertising.

To be valid, copyright assignment must very precisely determine the object of the assignment, i.e. detailing each of the assigned rights and the scope of the use, limiting its extent and destination, its geographical scope and duration (L131-3 CPI).

Any global assignment of future works is prohibited.

The moral rights are inalienable and imprescriptible. They cannot be waived by the author.

Proprietary rights last for 70 years after the death of the author (starting on the 1 January following the author's death). Collective works as well as anonymous works, or works disclosed under a pseudonym are protected for 70 years from the 1 of January following the disclosure of the work.

Moral rights are perpetual.

2.3 Enforcement

There is no copyright registration system in France. Works are protected from their creation, if they meet the conditions as explained above.

It is highly recommended to keep evidence of the date of creation of the work and of the paternity of the author.

Objects of industrial designs are capable of protection by copyright, provided that they are original and "bear the imprint of the personality of their author".

Copyright infringement can be constituted by the "slavish" copy of the work or by a sufficient imitation. The assessment is made on the resemblances and not on the differences between the works.

Copyright be enforced against a trademark, a registered design/design patent, a patent a domain name a trade name, a pseudonym and other IP rights. With regards patent, in practice, a patent being purely functional, its object rarely collides with the object of protection of a copyright.

Copyright can be enforced against its unauthorized use in social media under the same conditions as in other media.

Comparative advertising does not apply to copyright by law.

The use of the artwork as a parody is one of the exceptions established by French law, based on the freedom of speech. The parody must be made with a humorous intention and should not create a risk of confusion with the work itself.

In terms of defences, the limitations are enumerated by law (article L.122-5 CPI), notably:
- Private and free performances performed exclusively in a family circle.
- Copies or reproductions made from a lawful source and strictly reserved for the private use of the copyist and not intended for collective use.
- Provided that the name of the author and the source are clearly indicated:
- Analyses and short quotes justified by the critical, controversial, educational, scientific or informational nature of the work in which they are incorporated.
- Press reviews.
  (…)
- Reproductions, in whole or in part, of graphic or plastic works of art intended to appear in the catalog of a judicial sale.
- Representation or reproduction of extracts from works for the exclusive purposes of illustration in the context of teaching and research.
- Parody, pastiche and caricature.
  (…)
- The reproduction or representation, in whole or in part, of a graphic, plastic or architectural work of art, by written, audiovisual or online press, for the exclusive purpose of immediate information and in direct relation to this last, subject to clearly indicating the name of the author.
  (…).

The exceptions listed above shall not prejudice the normal exploitation of the work or cause unjustified prejudice to the legitimate interests of the author.

No "fair use" or "fair dealing" can be claimed outside these limitations.

The most common defence against an infringement claim is to challenge the originality of the copyright, the ownership of the author rights, or the existence of a confusing similarity.

An otherwise valid copyright can be deemed unenforceable if its owner has abused its right to act against the infringement (for instance the abuse of the right of disclosure by the heirs after the death of the author).

The prescription period is of five years "starting from the day on which the right owner knew or should have known the last fact enabling him to exercise the action" according to the new "PACTE" law of 2019.

For luxury brands looking to expand and protect their rights in copyright the utmost attention must be given to obtaining specific and lawful assignments from the authors when they are still in contract with the company in order to avoid future difficulties (in addition to employment contracts).

3. DESIGN

3.1 Sources of law

Designs are mainly governed by Book V of the Intellectual Property Code (CPI), notably transposing EC Directive 98/71/EC of 13 October 1998.

Regulation no. 6/2002 of 12 December 2001 applies to Community designs (CDR).

France is a contracting party to a number of International Treaties concerning designs:
- Paris Convention for the Protection of Industrial Property of 20 March 1883.
- Hague Agreement of 1925 concerning the International Registration of Industrial Designs (1960 and 1999 Acts).
- Locarno Agreement of 1968 amended in 1979, establishing an International Classification for Industrial Designs.

The hierarchy of sources of law is as stated above in Section 1.1.

3.2 Substantive law

According to article L. 511-1 CPI, to be protected as a design "the appearance of a product, or part of a product characterized by its lines, contours, colors, shape, texture or materials (…). These characteristics may be those of the product itself or of its ornamentation". This comprises "any industrial or artisanal object, in particular parts designed to be assembled into a complex product, packaging, presentations, etc".

A product protected as a design can be cumulatively protected by copyright in France if it also fulfils the conditions of this protection.

National designs must be registered at the French Industrial Property Office (INPI) and European designs can be either registered at the EUIPO or unregistered.

To be valid, a design must be new, meaning that no identical design has been made available to the public before its date of filing (for registered designs) or before its disclosure (for unregistered designs) and have an individual character, meaning that its overall impression must differ from the one produced by the prior designs.

Design protection excludes shapes which are purely functional.

Design rights are owned by their creator. If the design is disclosed or registered in the name of a legal entity, it will automatically be considered as the owner of the design rights (unless proved otherwise). According to article 14.3 of the CDR "where a design is developed by an employee in the execution of his duties or following the instructions given by his employer, the right to the Community design shall vest in the employer, unless otherwise agreed or specified under national law". The French CPI does not address this point. Recent case law tends to apply article 14.3 of the CDR but it is not unanimous.

Design assignment is governed by contract law. To be valid it needs to be written and published on the register to be opposable to third parties.

If the object of the design is also protectable under copyright law, the rules of copyright assignment also apply.

Designs do not create moral rights (unless the object of the protection is also eligible for a protection under author rights). Designers still keep the right to have their name cited before the Office and in the register.

Registered designs are valid for five years from the date of filing and can be renewed for five years periods to a maximum of 25 years.

Unregistered design protection lasts 3 years from the date of disclosure within the territory of the European Union (not renewable).

3.3 Enforcement

The protection conferred by a design includes any design which does not produce a different overall impression on the informed user. The CDR mentions that "In assessing the scope of protection, the degree of freedom of the designer in developing his design shall be taken into consideration" (this notion does not appear in the French law).

Unregistered European designs give their owner the right to forbid the above acts, if the contested use results from a copy of the protected design.

A design can be enforced against a trademark, a registered design/design patent, a patent (although the scope of the protection should be different), a domain name, a trade name and other IP rights.

A design can be enforced against its unauthorized use in social media under the same conditions as on any other media.

Although French law does not specifically apply comparative advertising to designs, it should be allowed if the comparison is objective.

The notion of parody does not exist in design law, however, this exception is lawful for copyrights. Therefore, should the object of the right be protectable by copyright, it could be parodied. As for trademarks, the parody needs to be made outside of the course of trade.

The most common defence is to challenge the validity of the design (novelty and individual character / ownership of the rights) or the comparison of the designs to show that the secondary design produces a different overall impression.

The repair clause is included in article 8.2 of the CDR and L.511-8 CPI: "Community design shall not subsist in features of appearance of a product which must necessarily be reproduced in their exact form and dimensions in order to permit the product in which the design is incorporated or to which it is applied to be mechanically connected to or placed in, around or against another product so that either product may perform its function".

A valid design could be unenforceable if it has been integrated in a third party trademark and its use has been tolerated for 5 years.

Abusive infringement actions are sanctioned through damages according to the law.

The time limit for bringing an infringement action is 5 years.

The right owner can claim design and copyright infringement in the same action.

The unfair competition claim must be based on a distinct set of facts (in which case both grounds can be claimed in an infringement and unfair competition action).

Fashion items are not always protectable as designs as they may be inspired from previous works and may not benefit from a sufficient individual character. Selecting the works to be filed as designs and ensuring that they can be enforced against third parties can be a challenging mission.

4. RIGHT OF PRIVACY, PUBLICITY AND PERSONAL ENDORSEMENT

4.1 Sources of law

The right of publicity, or more likely in France the right to one's "image" is not specifically consecrated in positive law. It is derived from several dispositions, notably, as personality rights from article 9 of the Civil Code which states "Each individual has a right to the respect of his private life" (or article 226-1 of the Penal Code).

The "patrimonial" aspect of the image right is not consecrated by law but tends to be recognized by case law.

4.2 Substantive law

Individuals have the right to prevent unauthorized use of their name or image to sell products. No specific condition exists to benefit from this right.

It is not clear in France whether the right of publicity is transmissible *mortis causa*. However, French case law currently tends to admit that a "patrimonial" right is transmitted to the heirs.

An individual can assign their right of publicity in whole or in part and they can license their right of publicity. The licence can be exclusive or non-exclusive.

For the assignment/license of the right of publicity to be valid no specific rule applies, these contracts are submitted to the general contract law. The scope of the assignment/licence must be precisely defined (rights granted, geographical scope and duration), and a fair compensation granted.

The licensor can withdraw his consent unilaterally without justification. The licensee must be compensated for his loss.

Following the death of the licensor the contract is valid until its term and is transmitted to the heirs, unless specified otherwise in the contract.

Following the death of an assignor, contracts validly signed by the assignor before their death are transmitted to the heirs.

In the event the heirs have an independent right over the deceased individual's name, image, likeness, or other unequivocal aspects of their identity, this point is not regulated by French law and the authors do not agree on it. It is therefore not clear if the image right is transmitted to the heirs of the deceased or not (and therefore the length or such rights is not fixed either).

4.3 Enforcement

Unauthorized use of a person's name, image or likeness is reprehensible even if the use is not made commercially, as soon as the person can show that he/she has suffered a damage from that use, offering protection against alteration or denaturation of an individual's personality.

The compensation obtained depends on the commercial value of the individual's image, which can be evidenced through any relevant document (and which will be higher if this person is famous than if it is an average individual).

Freedom of speech is the most common defence to justify the use made of a third person's image (meaning that this use is informational and not purely commercial). The alleged infringer can also try to show that the person has not suffered any harm from the use made of his image or that its commercial value is extremely low, in an attempt to reduce the amount of the compensation.

Many uncertainties remain in France about the perimeter of the celebrities, the right of publicity and their transmission to the person's heirs so luxury brands should take much care when dealing with this topic.

5. PRODUCT PLACEMENT

Product placement is permitted in France.

The Audio-Visual Council (CSA) limits the product placement to cinematographic works, audio-visual fictions and musical videos, not aimed at children.

Product placement is prohibited for some products: drinks with more than 1.2 degrees of alcohol, tobacco products, medicines, firearms and ammunitions, infant formulas. It is forbidden to promote the nutritional aspects of foods or drinks containing nutrients or substances whose excessive presence in the diet is not recommended.

The content of programs involving product placement must not prejudice the editorial responsibility and independence of the media service provider. The programs must not directly encourage the purchase of goods or services, in particular by making specific promotional references to these products or services, or unjustifiably highlight the product or service.

The audience must be informed of the product placement through a logo on the screen.

Product placement made through influencers on social media is not clearly framed by French law (as this practice is quite recent). As for "classical" product placement though, brands must make sure to inform the consumers when products have been offered to influencers for their promotion or when they have been paid to wear/present them to the public.

6. PROTECTION OF CORPORATE IMAGE AND REPUTATION

A legal entity can defend itself against denigration or defamation. For instance, a legal entity is entitled to claim compensation for the damage suffered when its reputation is damaged (Conseil d'Etat, March 26, 1980, no. 02206 05701), or when its brand image has been damaged (French Court of Cassation, commercial chamber, May 15, 2012, no.11-10.278).

A fault and prejudice must be proven since the compensation of this damage is based on article 1240 of the Civil Code.

Selective distribution agreements including specific clauses aimed at protecting the corporate image/reputation of one of the parties are common in the luxury area, for example prohibition to sell the products to re-sellers whose image is below a certain defined standard.

One cannot include in an agreement a clause prohibiting minimum prices imposed by the merchant to his resellers since this is contrary to The French Commercial Code. Clauses prohibiting purchase of non-original – but otherwise legitimate – spare parts and components are not legitimate either.

Liquidated damages or stipulated fines clauses for breach by a party of any provisions protecting the reputation or corporate image of the other party are permissible, but these clauses must not imbalance the rights and obligations of the parties and the judges can intervene to modify their contractual amounts.

Controlling the secondary market and preserving the quality of service/products through trusted resellers is a hard task for luxury brands. Tools must be put in place (and those available must be used) to work together with the secondary market platforms in order to help them identify the genuine/fake products and guarantee the quality to the consumers.

AUTHOR BIOGRAPHY

Sophie Marc

Sophie Marc is a partner of the firm. She is an experienced IP attorney specialized in trademarks, designs and copyrights. She has a specific expertise in the management of worldwide portfolios of IP rights for French and foreign clients, both for prosecution and enforcement matters. Her clients operate in various areas of activities and services with a predominance in luxury, fashion and sports.

She has been a qualified French and European Trademark and Industrial Design attorney since 2005, with a Master in Private Law and a Post Graduate Degree from the University of Grenoble covering Intellectual Property, Contracts and IT Law obtained in 2000.

Sophie is a member of INTA, APRAM and CNCPI.

GERMANY

Dr. Wiebke Baars
Taylor Wessing

1. TRADEMARK

1.1. Sources of law

German trademark law is regulated in the Trademark Act of 25 October 1994 (MarkenG). This implements the Directive no. 2008/95/EC into national law, which has recently been revised by Directive (EU) 2015/2436 of 16 December 2015. In addition to the national regulation, various European provisions have an effect in Germany. EU-wide trademark protection is granted by the European Union trademark based on Regulation (EU) 2017/1001 of 14 June 2017. Furthermore, Germany participates in international treaties concerning trademark law such as:

- The Paris Convention for the Protection of Industrial Property of 20 March 1883.
- The Madrid Agreement concerning the International Registration of Marks of 14 April 1891 and the Madrid Protocol of 27 June 1989 relating to the Madrid Agreement concerning the International Registration of Marks.
- The Marrakech Agreement on Trade-related Aspects of Intellectual Property Rights of 15 April 1994 (TRIPS).

Not all law has the same priority. The legal system has a hierarchical structure. At its top is the German constitution, followed by the European treaties and, in its scope of application, EU law. The following level is German law, which is followed by individual regulatory acts. Being a civil law country, judges are bound by statutory law and not by precedent case law. However, cases by the Federal Supreme Court (BGH) are regarded to be persuasive and typically accepted as precedent. Only judgements of the Federal Constitutional Court have binding effect.

1.2. Substantive law

Under § 4 MarkenG, the following shall give rise to trademark protection:

- the entry of a sign as a trademark in the Register for specific goods and services;
- the use of an unregistered sign in trade in so far as the sign has acquired public recognition as a trademark within the affected trade circles; or
- a trademark constituting a well-known mark within the meaning of Article 6bis of the Paris Convention.

Trademark protection is either granted after registration and the scope of protection is defined by the goods and services registered, or protection is based on recognised use for certain goods and services.

However, according to § 14 III a MarkenG, a third party is also prohibited from using a sign identical with or similar to a trademark for goods or services which are not similar to those for which the trademark enjoys protection, if the trademark has a reputation in Germany and the use of the sign takes unfair advantage of, or is detrimental to, the distinctive character or the repute of the trademark.

Typically this provision extends the scope of protection of well known marks. According to German case law, a mark has a reputation according to § 14 II 3 MarkenG if it is known to a "significant part of the public" (BGH, 2 June 2017 - I ZR 75/15 No. 37 – Wunderbaum II).

GERMANY

Consequently, trademarks with a reputation can be protected against reproduction or imitation that constitutes an unjustified exploitation of the sign or is likely to cause prejudice to the owner of the mark. This protection particularly extends to luxury marks that typically have a high market recognition which will facilitate proof of their reputation in the sense of § 14 II 3 MarkenG.

1.3 Enforcement

To establish that a registered trademark is enforceable under § 14 MarkenG against acts of infringement, a trademark owner must prove that he is the owner of the mark or an exclusive licensee entitled to enforce the mark. A registered trademark is deemed to be valid as long as it has not been cancelled from the register.

An injunction against infringing trademark use can be obtained if the use refers to identical signs for identical goods and services or if there is a likelihood of confusion between the coinciding marks and their respective goods and services (§ 14 II 1 and 2 MarkenG). German law accepts that there is a interaction between the similarity of the mark, the similarity of the goods and services and the distinctiveness of the mark, which may be enhanced by reputation and market recognition. Therefore, the better known a mark is, the less similar it needs to be to establish infringement.

For proving that a mark is renowned and has enhanced distinctiveness, the trademark owner can provide written evidence about, for example, the intensity, geographical extent and duration of use of the trademark, sales figures and market share of the trademark as well as advertising spent. Owners of well known luxury brands can provide documents showing the mark's presence in the media. Evidence can be provided, for example, in the form of surveys showing the level of recognition of the mark in the market (see Court of Justice of the European Union (CJEU), 14 September 1999 - C-375/97 para 23 – *Chevy*). Even though the CJEU has stated that the degree of knowledge required in order to benefit from the protection of § 14 II 3 cannot be defined as a predetermined percentage of the public, German courts have a long tradition as accepting survey results as decisive. Degrees of recognition between 31% and 79% have been accepted. Besides that, oral testimony, affidavits and expert evidence can be admitted.

Once the reputation of the trademark has been established, the owner can enforce it against all uses "in the course of trade", which includes use as a domain name, a trade name and other distinctive signs, if used as a trademark. The German Federal Supreme Court (BGH), also decided that the use of a trademark in metatags can be an act of infringing trademark use, as long as the sign is not used descriptively. For the same reason a trademark can also be enforced against an unauthorized use in social media, provided the use takes place "in the course of trade" as a trademark.

The situation is more complex in relation to keyword advertising. Defendants have typically used identical marks as keywords to advertise goods identical to the protected ones. The BGH has, based on the CJEU's judgments on keyword advertising, established that the function of origin of a mark or trade name is regularly unaffected if it is used as a keyword if:

- The ad appears in an advertising area which is expressly designated (e.g. "Advertisement") and is clearly separated from the search results.
- The ad itself does not contain the mark and does not refer to the owner or to its goods or services in any other way.

If these conditions are met, the user who has used the mark in a search query, does not assume that the ad comes from the trademark owner or companies linked to the owner. According to the CJEU the situation may be different if the ad triggered by a keyword is so vague regarding the origin of goods or services that the internet user is unable to determine from the ad whether an economic link between the advertiser and the trademark owner exists or not (CJEU, 22 September 2011 - C-323/09, para. 45 - *Interflora*). In that case the CJEU held that the function of origin is already adversely affected and the trademark is infringed.

With respect to comparative advertising, the use of a trademark is deemed to be infringing if it is disparaging and taking unfair advantage of the reputation of the trademark or if it creates a risk of confusion. Any comparative advertising that does not meet the legal standards of objective and fair comparison and would be deemed to be an act of unfair competition also qualifies as trademark infringement (CJEU, 18 June, 2009, C-487/07 - *L'Oréal/Bellure*).

Trademark parodies do not necessarily constitute trademark infringement. The constitutionally protected freedom of art and opinion can legitimize the parody. Nevertheless, a trademark parody is inadmissible, particularly in the case of disparagement without any discernible reason and solely commercial interests of the parodist (BGH, 02 April 2015, I ZR 59/13 – *Jumping Poodle*).

Under German law claims can be made both on the grounds of trademark infringement and unfair competition. The BGH gave up its opinion that trademark law prevails over unfair competition law in its *Hard Rock Cafe* decision in 2013 (BGH, 15 August 2013, I ZR 188/11). Typically, claims for unfair competition are made before the same court in addition to trademark infringement claims, when the facts of the case, in addition to the use of the trademark, amount to separate unfair practices (for example by parasitism, misleading the consumer about the origin of a product or by passing off the product's reputation).

2. COPYRIGHT

2.1. Sources of law

Copyright law in Germany is primarily based on the Act on Copyright and Related Rights of 9 September 1965 (as revised and amended) (UrhG), which has been significantly influenced by the unification of European law. In addition to European Community legislation, other supranational regulations contained in treaties of which Germany is a contracting party also have an impact in Germany:
- The Berne Convention for the Protection of Literary and Artistic Works of 9 September 1886.
- The Geneva Universal Copyright Convention of 6 September 1952.
- The Geneva WIPO Copyright Treaty of 20 December 1996.

GERMANY

2.2 Substantive law

German law does not provide for registration of copyrights. All works resulting from a personal intellectual creation that is not conventional or customary, is copyright protected as of its creation. A non-exhaustive list can be found in § 2 UrhG, which covers, amongst others, artistic works, including works of architecture and of applied art and drafts of such works.

In order to be protectable the work's features must be original and not be exclusively determined by functional needs or follow general fashion trends. In the light of these requirements products of fashion, jewellery, furniture or accessory design may be eligible for copyright protection. The BGH held, for example, the Bauhaus Tubular Frame Chair and the Wagenfeld lamp to be eligible for copyright protection (BGH, 27 February 1961, I ZR 127/59 – *Stahlrohrstuhl*; BGH, 15 February 2007, I ZR 114/04 – *Wagenfeld Leuchte*). If the threshold of an original work is not met, other means of protection may be available such as Unfair Competition or Design Law.

When a work is eligible for copyright, the author is entitled to claim economic and moral rights in their own personal creation.

As for economic rights, the author is granted the exclusive right of reproduction and the right of distribution of original copies of the work to the public as well as the right of exhibition (§§ 15 I, 16, 17 and 18 UrhG).

The author has further rights to communicate their work to the public in non-material form, which covers the right to making the work available to the public on the internet or to broadcast or perform works amongst others (§§ 19 to 22 UrhG).

The author's moral rights cover:
- the exclusive right to determine whether and how their work shall be disclosed to the public;
- the right to reconsider or withdraw the work after it was first disclosed;
- the right to be recognised as the author of the work; and
- the right of integrity and to prohibit the distortion or derogatory treatment of the work.

These moral rights are perpetual and cannot be transferred or waived.

The author's economic rights expire at the end of a time-period of 70 years starting on the first day of the year following the death of the author.

According to § 10 UrhG the author is the creator of the work and there is a presumption in favour of the person under whose name the work has been disclosed to the public, unless otherwise proven. § 8 UrhG stipulates that where several persons have jointly created a work without it being possible to separately exploit their work, they are joint authors and the right of publication and exploitation of the work accrues jointly to them.

As in German law the copyright as such cannot be transferred, any legal entity that wishes to acquire the rights in the works created by its employees, consultants, shareholders, directors or suppliers can only contractually acquire the rights to use the works in question. Case law recognizes that the employer is granted far-reaching and exclusive rights of use by virtue of the employment contract. According to § UrhG, the employer acquires rights of use to the work created by the employee in accordance with the "transfer of purpose theory" to the extent that they are required for business purposes.

Any copyright assignment agreement with an author must comply with the following requirements:
- The contract must distinctly mention each assigned right and the scope, destination, geographical extent and time period for which the right is assigned.
- The general assignment of future works is not valid and assignment contracts need to have a clearly defined object.
- The author cannot waive his moral rights.

2.3. Enforcement

As in German law there is no copyright registration, in each case of dispute the claimant needs to demonstrate that their work meets the standards of an intellectual creation rising above the average and functional. This also applies to industrial design and may be demonstrated by oral testimony, affidavits, expert reports etc.

For establishing infringement the reproduction of the original features protected by the copyright need to be shown, substantial similarity is enough. The court will analyse the similarities – and not primarily the differences – between the infringing object and the copyrighted work.

Copyright grants a monopoly right to its owner, which can be enforced against trademarks, registered and unregistered designs, patents, domain names, trade names, pseudonyms or other distinctive signs, any use in social media or in comparative advertising, as long as they reproduce the original characteristics of the work.

The only limits to these prerogatives are the legal exceptions of §§ 44 a to 53 a UrhG. These exceptions are restrictively listed and precisely specified, there is no general doctrine of 'fair use' or 'fair dealing'. The most relevant exceptions in relation to luxury goods are:
- copies or reproductions reserved strictly for the private use of the copier;
- analyses and quotations provided that they are justified by the critical, polemic, educational, scientific or informatory nature of the work they are taken from;
- press reviews;
- publishing or broadcasting of speeches as long as they are considered as current news; and
- reproduction or performance of a work extract used as an illustration for educational purposes.

The typical defence against infringement claims is to challenge either the copyrightable character of the work (due to lack of quality of an own intellectual creation or expiry of the protection); the ownership on the copyright; or the similarities between the infringing object and the copyrighted work. The right to enforce a valid copyright might be forfeited if the copyright owner has tolerated the use for a substantial amount of time. The copyright owner cannot file any action if the claim has become time barred, which is three years for civil actions after he has learned about the infringing act.

The right holder can bring an action claiming both copyright and design infringement based on the same facts, as the purpose and preconditions of these rights are not the same: a luxurious object of industrial design may be eligible for both, copyright and design protection. Furthermore, unfair competition claims for slavish copying can be made before the court in charge of the copyright dispute in addition to the infringement claims. Following established case law regarding the protection of fashion novelties, unfair competition law, for example, grants protection against identical adoption or almost identical imitation as that the creator of a fashion novelty is deprived of the competitive advantage on the market based on his performance (BGH, 6 November 1997, I ZR 102/95).

3. DESIGN
3.1 Sources of law
German design law originates from two sources. The national source of law is the Act on the Legal Protection of Designs (DesignG) as amended on 24 February 2014, which transposes the EU Directive on the legal protection of designs (EC Directive 98/71/EC of 14 October 1998) into national law (EUDD).

In addition, the European Regulation on Community Designs ((EC) No 6/2002) of 12 December 2001 applies, as amended by Council Regulation No 1891/2006 of 18 December 2006 (EUDR).

3.2. Substantive law
In Germany designs can be registered at the German Patent and Trademark Office (GTPO) while Community designs may either be registered at the European Union Intellectual Property Office (EUIPO) or claim protection as an unregistered design under European Design Law. All designs are defined as "protecting the appearance of the whole or a part of a product resulting from the features of, in particular, the lines, contours, colours, shape, texture and/or materials of the product itself and/or its ornamentation".

Both the DesignG and the EUDD define said products as "any industrial or handicraft item, including *inter alia* parts intended to be assembled into a complex product, packaging, get-up, graphic symbols and typographic typefaces, but excluding computer programs".

A design may therefore be considered for a wide range of luxury products. Not protectable, however, are features of appearance of a product which are solely dictated by its technical function and interconnecting parts (except those that serve the purpose of allowing multiple assembly or connection of mutually interchangeable products within a modular system). Also excluded from design protection are appearances of products that are contrary to public policy or morality.

The appearance of a product can be protected by a valid design under the following requirements:
- The design must be **new**, meaning that no identical design has been made available to the public before either the date of filing of the application for registration (or the date of priority) for national or registered Community designs, or, for unregistered Community designs, the date on which the design claiming protection has first been made available to the public. The

design is not considered as being made available to the public when the disclosure was made by the designer within a 12-month time period preceding the filing for registration (or date of priority) or when the disclosure is the result of an abuse.
- The design must have **individual character**, meaning that the overall impression the design produces on the informed user differs from the overall impression that may be produced on such user by any design which has been made available to the public before.

For registered designs, the duration of the protection is 5 years renewable 4 times for 5 years (up to 25 years) whereas the protection for unregistered design is granted for 3 years after the first disclosure of the design within the European Union.

According to § 7 DesignG the right in the registered design shall belong to the designer. Where several persons have jointly created a design, the right in the registered design shall belong to them jointly. Where a design was created by an employee in the execution of his duties or following the instructions given by his employer, the right in the registered design shall belong to the employer, unless otherwise provided by contract. Designs created by consultants, agencies, shareholders, directors or suppliers need to be contractually assigned. Usual rules of contract law apply to design assignment, but for a Community design to be enforceable against third parties, the agreement must be in writing and published on the European Design register (Art. 28 EUDR).

German and European Law does not recognise a moral right in the appearance of the product; however, § 10 DesignG and Article 18 EUDR provide that the designer has the right to have their name cited before the Office and in the register.

3.3. Enforcement

A design may be enforced against all designs that do not give a different overall impression on the informed user. Registered designs are protected against unauthorized uses by third parties, in particular against the making, offering, putting on the market, importing, exporting or using of a product in which the design is incorporated or to which it is applied, or storing such a product for these purposes. For registered designs, this also applies against slavish imitation and similarities. Unregistered Community designs enjoy the protection against uses described above when they result from purposely copying the protected design.

The right holder can enforce the design against any kind of infringement, including infringement arising from use of the design in trademarks, registered designs, patents, domain names, trade names, pseudonyms or other distinctive signs or IP rights.

Exceptions to protection are granted in cases of acts done privately and for non commercial purposes or acts done for experimental purposes or citations. Furthermore a valid design can be forfeited and therefore unenforceable in the case where the design owner has tolerated the use for five years.

As defence, the alleged infringer may challenge the validity or ownership of the design right invoked (for example, citing the expiry of the protection, the existence of prior art that removes novelty or the purely functional features of the design). It can furthermore be argued that the infringing design does not produce a similar overall impression on the informed user or that the claim is time barred (three years after the claimant became aware of the infringement).

Furthermore, Article 8.2 EUDR provides the repair clause that excludes protection of the Community Design from a component part used for the purpose of the repair of a complex product. This exemption particularly effects the car industry. § 40 DesignG accepts a more limited approach by stating that such limitation only applies to the repair of a complex product with the aim to restore it to its original appearance.

The owner of the design is entitled to claim both copyright and design infringements based on the same facts. Furthermore, unfair competition claims can be made before the court hearing the design dispute in addition to the infringement claims when the surrounding facts aside from the mere use of the design amount to separate unfair practices such as slavish copying.

4. RIGHT OF PRIVACY, PUBLICITY AND PERSONAL ENDORSEMENT

4.1. Sources of law

Under German law private individuals are entitled to control the use of their name, image and other aspects of their identity. These rights are based in the general personality right, granted by Art. 2 I of the German Basic Law (GG) and § 12 (right to one's name) and § 823 I of the German Civil Code (BGB), as well as § 22 of the German Art Copyright Act (KUG), which grants the right to one's own picture which may only be published with this person's consent.

4.2. Substantive law

There are no other conditions to owning the right of publicity apart from being a human being.

The right to informational self-determination, as well as the other manifestations of the general personality right from Article 2 I in conjunction with Article 1 I GG, end with the death of a person. Simple-law provisions such as the right to one's name or data protection also end in principle with the death of a person.

In terms of fundamental law, post-mortem protection of personality derives exclusively from human dignity protected under Article 1 GG. However the claim to value and respect initially continues to exist, but fades with time.

In the event of a violation of the non-material components of the post-mortem personality right under civil law, the heirs shall be entitled to claims for defense, but not additionally to claims for damages. (BGH, 5 October 2006 - I ZR 277/03.)

However, the general post-mortem right of personality under civil law also protects the person's pecuniary interests. In the event of a violation, claims for damages may exist which can be asserted by the heirs of the deceased (BGH, 5 October 2006 - I ZR 277/03). Like the right to one's own image (§ 22 KUG), the duration of protection of the pecuniary components of the post-mortem right of personality is limited to ten years after the death of the person.

The rights and obligations provided by assignments or licensing agreements entered into by the deceased persons before their death are transmissible to their heirs.

Individuals are free to enter into exclusive or non-exclusive assignment or licensing agreements and monetize the use of their right of publicity, as a whole or in parts. There are no specific provisions under German law that govern contracts for the use of one's personality rights, so general contract law applies. It is advisable to clearly define the scope of the contract, in particular as regards its duration, geographical scope, the subject matter and uses covered or not covered. The rights to terminate the agreement also needs to be defined. Therefore, the contract remains binding until the agreed term has expired. This also applies to the heirs of the person whose personality rights are the subject of the license agreement. In addition, German law provides that continuing obligations such as license agreements can always be terminated for cause, if it cannot reasonably be expected for the licensor to adhere to the agreement, especially in cases of misconduct of the licensee.

4.3. Enforcement

The right of publicity can not only be enforced against a commercial use of an individual's name, image, likeness or other aspects of their identity. Equally, a non-commercial use (for example, for artistic reasons), can be prevented if it is not justified e.g. by freedom of art of freedom of speech. Therefore an injunction can also be obtained against a defamatory or disparaging use, even if no commercial interests are involved.

The commercial value of one's personality is relevant in order to determine the amount of damages to be incurred for an unauthorized use of an individual's name, image, likeness or other aspects of their identity. If an individual is well known and can show that they typically monetize their rights, the easier it will be to be awarded a high compensation for infringement. The BGH has awarded high damages to a well know television presenter whose image was used in so called "clickbaiting", that is, luring readers to third party advertisements on the internet (BGH, 21 January 2021 - I ZR 120/19 – Clickbaiting).

In defence, the alleged infringer may dispute the infringement of one's right of publicity on several grounds. In particular, freedom of speech, including satire and freedom of art, can legitimize the use of personal attributes, when this use is made as part of a debate of public interest, or is necessary to illustrate current events. The right to one's own picture is, for example, limited if it amounts to a portrait from the field of contemporary history (§ 23 KUG).

5. PRODUCT PLACEMENT

Product placements are permitted under German law but are subject to restrictions, mainly resulting from the State Media Treaty (MStV) and Advertising Statutes. German law defines product placement as "any form of advertising that consists of incorporating or referring to a product, service, or brand in return for remuneration or a similar consideration, so that it appears in a programme or user-generated video". Product placement requires monetary consideration. However, the free provision of goods or services can also be classified as product placement if the goods or services are of significant value. This is most relevant for expensive luxury goods. If the value of the product is higher than €100 and at the same time reaches 1 percent of the production costs of the programme or if it exceeds the amount of €10,000, the regulations for product placements are applicable. If several products are provided by the same advertising partner, they will be counted up together.

According to the MStV product placement is permitted, except in (for example), news programmes and programmes intended for political information, consumer programmes, programmes with religious content, and children's programmes. Furthermore, there are special restrictions on product placements in public service broadcasting. Here, product placements are only allowed in cinematographic works, films, series, sports programmes and light entertainment programmes.

Programmes containing product placements must meet strict requirements:
- editorial responsibility and independence concerning content and placement in the programme schedule must not be prejudiced;
- no direct encouragement of purchase, rental or lease of the placed goods or services;
- the product shall not be unduly prominently placed; and
- clear identification of product placement at the beginning and at the end of a programme, as well as at its continuation following an advertising break.

For cinematographic works only the provisions of the Unfair Competition Act (UWG) apply. The viewer must not be deceived by product placements insofar that the props used are in fact advertising.

Details of the agreed product placement in a production should be set out on a contract stating precise criteria for the form of the presentation. The parties may also agree on an obligation to return the goods. If the film producer does not comply with the agreement, damages can be claimed under civil law.

Product placement involving luxury brands is particularly relevant in the context of influencer marketing on social networks, to which the above mentioned rules also apply. Advertising by influencers must also be clearly recognisable as such and unambiguously separated from the other content of the offerings if the influencer has received consideration for his posts (BGH, 09 September 2021 – I ZR 125/20). Under Unfair Competition Law, it is also regularly necessary that the commercial purpose of the advertising (e.g. of the Instagram posts) is made clear.

6. PROTECTION OF CORPORATE IMAGE AND REPUTATION

In German law there are various possibilities to protect the image or reputation of any company (goodwill). Sources of law are primarily the Unfair Competition Act (UWG) and the German Civil Code (BGB) in combination with criminal law granting rights against the tort of defamation and slander.

Under Unfair Competition law, companies are protected against impairment of their economic interests through disparaging statements by competitors (e.g. in advertising). In addition, competitors are not allowed to harm the economic interests of other companies by claiming or spreading false facts. Furthermore, Unfair Competition law protects the good reputation of brand owners marks against unfair exploitation or impairment. The good reputation of a company and its brands is exploited, for example, if it is transferred to the products of another company through advertising (e.g. in the advertisement for a sparkling wine, persons are clearly visible wearing watches of well-known luxury manufacturers; the use of a picture of a well-known car in an advertisement for a whiskey (BGH, 09 December 1982 – I ZR 133/80)).

In addition, claims for injunctive relief can be established through general civil law provisions (§ 823 BGB), for example in the case of the exploitation of a famous trademark for political campaigns, the ridiculing of a famous trademark and other damage to reputation. The same applies to statements that affect a company's social standing as an employer or business enterprise, i.e. that challenge its reputation. In addition, § 824 BGB protects companies from untrue facts that are likely to jeopardise credit or cause other disadvantages for acquisition or advancement. This has practical significance, for example, in cases where goods of the company are disparaged on television or untrue allegations (e.g. about health hazards) are spread about them in the press.

In general, clauses that are aimed at protecting the corporate image through resale restrictions are only permissible as long as they do not constitute a restriction of competition in accordance with § 1 German Act against Restraints on Competition (GWB) or Art. 101 of the Treaty on the Functioning of the European Union (TFEU).

Prohibition to sell the products to re-sellers whose image is below a certain defined standard is only permissible if the manufacturer, re-seller and retailer are part of a selective distribution system. In such a system, the parties agree to sell the product only to authorised partners within the network who fulfil certain qualitative (and – under certain conditions – quantitative) selective criteria specified by the manufacturer. The admissibility of selective distribution systems has been confirmed in Germany for several products or groups of products, especially in the luxury product sector, such as technically sophisticated products or amongst others watches, jewellery, luxury perfumes, luxury cosmetics. Having a selective distribution for luxury goods may even justify the prohibition to sell the products on internet marketplaces, if necessary to safeguard the exclusive image of the products (CJEU, 6 December 2017 – C-230/16 - *Coty Germany GmbH/Parfümerie Akzente GmbH*).

Restrictions on the freedom to set resale prices are generally not permissible, as they constitute a restriction on competition. All clauses that aim at directly or indirectly influencing resale prices are prohibited, even if they are only applicable for specific time periods. Only in very narrow circumstances the practice of setting resale prices can be permissible, e.g. the mere recommendation of a retail price (in German: "*unverbindliche Preisempfehlung UVP*") or the setting of a maximum resale price, which does not have the effect of a price fixing.

The prohibition to buy non-original – but otherwise legitimate – spare parts and components would constitute an exclusive purchase obligation or a non-competition clause, which are only permissible if they are justified. However, if the Vertical Block Exemption Regulation (VBER) applies – i.e. the market share of the parties does not exceed 30% and the restrictive agreement does not contain any hard-core restrictions – such obligations are exempted from the prohibition of competition restricting agreements for a period of 5 years.

Stipulated fines clauses for breach of protecting the reputation or corporate image of a party are generally permissible in Germany. If stipulated fines clauses are part of general terms and conditions of a contract, they are subject to content inspections under German law. In order to avoid a declaration of unenforceability, the stipulated fines must not unreasonably disadvantage the other party. A clause is considered to be disadvantageous if the sanction (e.g. the amount of the fine) is disproportionate to the seriousness of the breach of contract.

AUTHOR BIOGRAPHY

Wiebke Baars

Wiebke Baars is a partner at Taylor Wessing. As a trademark lawyer she is specialised in advice and litigation in the fields of intellectual property law and competition law. With over 20 years of professional experience during which she has handled a multitude of well-known, primarily international client matters, Wiebke has earned herself an excellent reputation winning a number of awards in trademark and design law.

Her work focuses on German, European and international trademark applications as well as on opposition and appeal proceedings before the GPTO and the EUIPO. Another focus is the drafting and negotiation of licence agreements. Her clients – ranging from SMEs to global players - include companies in the fashion, media, toy and food industries.

INDIA

Pravin Anand, Dhruv Anand, Udita M. Patro, Kavya Mammen & Sampurnaa Sanyal
Anand and Anand

1. TRADEMARK

1.1 Sources of law

The principal sources of law relating to trademarks are the Trade Marks Act, 1999 (TMA) and the Trade Marks Rules 2017. Law relating to trademarks in India has also evolved through judicial decisions.

India has also been a signatory to the Madrid Protocol since 8 July 2013, which was designed to build efficiency and ease the process of application and registration of trademarks across various jurisdictions. India is also a member of the Agreement on Trade-Related Aspects of Intellectual Property Rights (TRIPS) since it came into effect on 1 January 1995.

In India, use is recognized as a source of trademark rights. In the case of a non-registered trademark, the remedy to the proprietor of the mark lies in the common law tort of passing off and this remedy has been recognized under the Trademarks Act, 1999 under Section 27(2). A prior user of a trademark can restrain even a registered proprietor of the same or deceptively similar mark (Section 34 TMA). Use, therefore, trumps registration. Moreover, 'use' is very broadly defined under Sections 2(2)(b), 2(2)(c) and Section 29(9) of the TMA.

1.2 Substantive law

India does define a "well-known trademark" under Section 2(zg) as a specific category. A well known trademark "in relation to any goods or services, means a mark which has become so to the substantial segment of the public which uses such goods or receives such services that the use of such mark in relation to other goods or services would be likely to be taken as indicating a connection in the course of trade or rendering of services between those goods or services and a person using the mark in relation to the first-mentioned goods or services".

Section 29(4)(c) also makes reference to a 'trademark with a reputation' in the context of dilution.

Section 11(6) lays down certain factors which the Registrar shall take into account for determining whether the mark is well-known.

Well known trademarks and reputed marks are also mentioned in Section 11(2) as a relative ground for refusal of registration of marks.

Trademarks belonging to the "luxury industry" do not enjoy a broader range of protection. The TMA does not confer special protection on any particular industry. In practice, however, infringement in the luxury space involves counterfeiting, which courts are particularly intolerable towards.

Moreover, trademarks which have been declared as well known by the Court or by the Registrar of Trademarks enjoy a special and enhanced degree of protection. Thus, well-known trademarks, including those belonging to the luxury industry, enjoy wide protection. A few notable examples of trademarks in the luxury industry which have been declared well-known are Cartier, Louis Vuitton and Revlon.

A trademark can be recognized as a well-known mark either by a declaration by a Judge in a court proceeding or by the Registrar of Trademarks pursuant to an application under Section 124 of the Trademark Rules, 2017 filed before the Registrar for declaring a said mark as "well-known".

Section 30 (3) of the TMA empowers the trademark owner to overcome a defense of lawful acquisition/exhaustion by proving that there exist legitimate reasons for the proprietor to oppose further dealings in goods whose condition of sale has been changed or impaired (material alteration which courts have also interpreted as including non-physical attributes of the product such as warranties, after sale services etc). Legitimate reasons can be many and when it comes to luxury goods, the nature of these goods are such that when they are not sold in the manner in which they are usually sold, the same will qualify as a legitimate reason.

1.3 Enforcement

In order to qualify as a well-known trademark, the following documents could be filed as evidence. Documents showing that:
- the mark is known and recognized by the relevant section of the public (such as a consumer survey);
- the duration, extent and geographical area of any use of that trademark;
- the duration, extent and geographical area of any promotion of the trademark, including advertising or publicity and presentation, at fairs or exhibition of the goods or services to which the trademark applies; or
- a list of international registrations and successful enforcement actions on behalf of the trademark in question and any order/judgement in which the Court has held the mark to be well-known.

Testimony is given in the form of affidavits and the adverse party has the right to cross examine the deponent/witness based on their testimony.

Affidavits from leading editors of fashion magazines attesting to the quality of the product sold under the trademark would bolster the case for the mark to be granted broader protection after being declared a well-known mark.

Expert evidence is particularly helpful in non-traditional trademark cases to prove distinctiveness of a mark and consumer perception.

A trademark can be enforced against a domain name, trade name and its use as a metatag. In the matter of *Kapil Wadhwa & Ors v Samsung Electronics Co. Ltd. & Anr.* 194 (2012) DLT 23, the use of a trademark as meta-tags was held to be illegal. Section 29(5) is a specific provision relating to infringement where the mark is used as part of a trading name in relation to the same goods and services for which the mark is registered. Lastly, there have been various cases, that have discussed the possibility of enhanced confusion if a mark is used as a domain name without the proprietor's consent due to the ease of diversion of customers on the Internet (*Yahoo v Akash Arora,* 78 (1999) DLT 285, *Satyam Infoway Ltd. v Sifynet Solutions Pvt. Ltd.*, (2004) 6 SCC 145).

Trademarks can be enforced against unauthorized use in social media by way of a civil suit seeking an injunction restraining such use.

For an infringement or a passing off action, what has to be shown is 'use in the course of trade' and use over social media when shown to be in the course of trade and in a trademark sense, can be stopped.

The owner of a trademark can enforce rights against its unauthorized use in comparative advertising if the advertising is not in accordance with honest practices or is detrimental to the distinctive character and repute of the mark under Section 29(8) and Section 30(1) of the TMA.

Parody is not an absolute defence to infringement and passing off. The court may take into consideration various factors to be seen cumulatively to determine whether a defendant is entitled to the defence of parody. If the use of the trademark by the other party is non-commercial, and for the purposes of criticism and fair comment, such use of the trademark would not amount to infringement. (*Tata Sons Limited v Greenpeace International* 178(2011) DLT705).

However, there have been many cases where the defendant has crossed the line and disparaged the mark in a distasteful manner either by way of a dialogue in a film (*Hamdard National Foundation & Anr. v Hussain Dalal & Ors.* 2013 (55) PTC 216 (Delhi)) or on social media (Anhueser Busch LLC v Rishav Sharma & Ors., 2020 (83) PTC 21).

A trademark owner can file a single suit claiming both trademark infringement and unfair competition against an infringing party for the same set of facts. Therefore, there is no necessity for filing separate actions.

One of the current issues that luxury brands face in expanding and protecting their trademark rights is the availability of cheap replicas and counterfeit products bearing the trademarks on e-commerce sites which leads to dilution. In such situation, it often becomes difficult to identify the seller and gauge where the seller is sourcing the counterfeits from.

2. COPYRIGHT

2.1 Sources of law

The main source of law relating to copyright in India is the Copyright Act, 1957 and the Copyright (Amendment) Rules 2021. Apart from these sources, law relating to copyright in India evolves from judicial decisions from the High Courts, the Supreme Court and decisions of the Intellectual Property Appellate Board (IPAB). The Copyright Board was earlier empowered to hear and decide certain disputes until 2017 when it was replaced by the IPAB.

India has also been a member of the Berne Convention since 28 April 1928 and thereafter the Universal Copyright Convention adopted in Geneva since 6 September 1952 and signatory to Rome Convention since 26 October 1961 (but not a member). India has also acceded to the WIPO Copyright Treaty and WIPO Performances and Phonograms Treaty (the internet treaties) which came into force in India on 25 December 2018. India is also a member of the TRIPS Agreement since it came into effect on 1 January 1995.

When a conflict arises the law with respect to copyright as codified by the statute takes precedence. There is no common law copyright and Section 16 of the Act embodies this principle. Therefore, copyright has to be in accordance with the provisions of the Act. The Courts adopt principles of international conventions only in certain circumstances, for example to fill in a lacuna or throw light upon the subject (*Entertainment Network (India) Ltd v Super Cassette Industries Ltd. & Ors,* 2008 (37) PTC 353) so long as the same is not in conflict with the municipal law of the country. Moreover, the rules are always subordinate to the Act and in case of conflict, the Act would supersede.

2.2 Substantive law

Under Section 13(1) of the Copyright Act 1957, copyright subsists in original literary, dramatic, musical and artistic works, cinematographic films and sound recordings. Literary work is further defined in Section 2(o), dramatic works is defined in Section 2 (h), musical works is defined in Section 2(p) and artistic works is defined in Section 2(c). Cinematographic film is defined in Section 2(f) and sound recording is defined under Section 2(xx). The list of copyrightable works are therefore specifically enumerated and defined.

Objects of industrial, fashion or accessory design are copyrightable, subject to Section 15(1) and (2) of the Copyright Act, 1957. Under Section 15(1), the copyright will not subsist in a design which has been registered under the Designs Act, 2000. Under Section 15(2), copyright in any design which was not registered under the Designs Act, shall cease as soon as any article to which the design has been applied has been reproduced more than 50 times by an industrial process by the owner of the copyright.

The following rights are covered by copyright as outlined in Section 14 of the Copyright Act, 1957:
- The right of reproduction.
- The right to issue copies of the work.
- The right to perform/communicate it to the public.
- The right to make a cinematograph film or sound recording.
- The right to make any adaptation.
- The right to make translations.
- To sell or give on commercial rental (for computer programs and cinematographic films) a copy of the computer program.
- To store the work in any medium by electronic or other means.

Moral rights are covered under Section 57 of the Copyright Act, 1957 and includes the right to claim authorship of the work and a right against destruction, mutilation or modification of the work. These rights are categorized as 'special rights' and are independent of the author's copyright.

A legal entity can acquire rights in the works created by its employees under a contract. This is necessary since, in the first instance, the author of a work is considered the first owner of copyright therein.

Section 17 of the Act is a deeming provision which recognizes an employer as the first owner of copyright in the case of a contract of service for certain works. This however, can also be subject to an agreement that can overcome this deeming provision.

As regards freelance artists, suppliers and consultants, they would generally retain copyright being under a 'contract for service'.

The requirements of a valid copyright assignment are outlined in Section 19 of the Copyright Act, 1957 and are as follows:
- that it is in writing and signed by the assignor;
- that it identifies the work and specifies the rights assigned, duration and territorial extent of the assignment;
- that it specifies the amount of royalty and consideration payable to the author; and
- that the assignment of a work shall not be contrary to the terms and conditions

of the rights already assigned to a copyright society of which the author is a member.

There is limited jurisprudence on whether an author can transfer or waive their moral rights in India. However, it has been observed in *Sartaj Singh Pannu v. Gurbani Media Pvt Ltd & AnR.*, 220 (2015) DLT 527, that as long as the waiver is voluntary, it cannot be opposed to public policy. However, strong evidence of such voluntariness must be present.

The inherent nature of the right itself indicates that it may not be assignable and is inalienable. The right can however be exercisable by the legal heirs of the author under Section 57(2) of the Act.

The term of copyright is dependent upon the nature of the work. For literary, artistic, dramatic and musical works, copyright shall subsist during the lifetime of the author and for 60 years following the death of the author as outlined in Section 22 of the Copyright Act, 1957. For cinematographic films, recordings and government works, copyright shall subsist until 60 years from the beginning of the calendar year following the year of its publication.

2.3 Enforcement

Copyright registration is not required to enforce a copyright.

However, certificate of registration of copyright is often useful in that it serves as *prima facie* evidence of ownership in a court of law.

Industrial designs are protected in India under the Designs Act, 2000. Copyright in any design which is capable of being registered under the Designs Act, 2000 and which has not been so registered, shall cease as soon as the article to which such design has been applied has been reproduced more than 50 times by an industrial process under Section 15(2) of the Copyright Act, 1957. Moreover, Section 52(1)(w) states that the making of a three-dimensional object from a two-dimensional artistic work, such as a technical drawing, for the purposes of industrial application of any purely functional part of a useful device will not amount to infringement.

The test of copyright infringement has been succinctly laid down in *R.G. Anand v. Deluxe Films* (1978) 4 SCC 118, wherein the Supreme Court held that one of the surest tests to establish copyright infringement is to determine whether or not the reader, spectator, or viewer after having seen or read both works would be of the unmistakable opinion that the alleged infringing work is a copy of the first.

Actual copying is not necessary and the courts can presume copying based on a showing of substantial similarity between the two works. This is however subject to the defence of independent creation.

The owner of a copyright can enforce their copyright against the proprietor of a trademark if any part of the trademark amounts to a reproduction of an original artistic work of the copyright holder in which copyright subsists. In fact, under Section 11(3)(b) of the TMA, a trademark shall not be registered if its use in India is liable to be prevented by virtue of the law of copyright.

As regards other categories:
- Copyright can be enforced against a registered design.
- Copyright can be enforced against a registered patent especially drawings in a specification.

- Copyright cannot be enforced against a domain name or trading name or a pseudonym since courts have recognized that these categories do not merit copyright protection due to lack of originality which is a pre-requisite for copyright protection. *A priori*, copyright cannot be enforceable against these works.

Copyright can be enforced against its unauthorized use in social media if the substantial portion of the work has been reproduced and such use of the work does not amount to fair use or is not covered by the activities exempt from infringement under Section 52 of the Copyright Act, 1957.

Copyright can be enforced against unauthorized use in comparative advertising if a substantial portion of the protected elements of the original work have been used, subject to fair use.

Generally, parodies come under the defence of fair use under Section 52(1)(a)(ii). Courts have also held that sometimes a parody becomes a completely new work with a transformative use, and therefore would not infringe the copyright of the owner of the work.

An exhaustive list of exceptions to copyright infringement (fair dealing) is outlined in Section 52 of the Copyright Act, 1957. In addition to these, the Courts have also developed some tests to determine if a particular activity qualifies as fair dealing. These are:

- amount and substantiality of dealing or reproduction (*RG Anand v. Delux Films & Ors.*, AIR 1978 SC 1613);
- extent justified by the purpose of the reproduction (*The Chancellor Masters & Scholars of the University of Oxford v Rameshwari Photocopy Services*, Judgment dated September 16, 2016 in CS (OS) 2439 of 2012, The High Court of Delhi); and
- intention to derive profits from unfair competition (*Kartar Singh Giani v Ladha Singh*, AIR 1934 Lah 777).

Some of the grounds under which a copyright in a work can be challenged are as follows:
- the work is not original;
- the work covers an idea more than an expression; and
- the term of copyright has expired or the copyright owner had formally renounced it.

The Limitation Act, 1963 prescribes a period of 3 years (Article 88) for filing a copyright infringement suit from the date of infringement. However, various judgements have held that each violation of copyright and trademarks gives rise to a recurring cause of action. Therefore, delay, if not inordinate or amounting to laches or acquiescence is not problematic.

Current issues that luxury brands face in expanding and protecting their rights in copyright include:
- Large scale counterfeiting activities by entities which copy the protected elements of an original artistic work.
- Section 15(2) of the Copyright Act which has the effect of extinguishing copyright in a work if the same is registrable as a design and has been applied on an article which has been multiplied more than 50 times.
- Infringement of copyright has many exceptions which whittles down the exclusive nature of the right.

3. DESIGN

3.1 Sources of law

In India, the Designs Act, 2000 along with the Design Rules, 2001 lay down the statutory framework of design law. The judicial decisions also have a significant impact on the development of design law.

India is a member of the TRIPS Agreement which requires its members to provide protection for design. India is also a signatory of the Paris Convention and follows the Locarno classification of goods for industrial designs.

The Designs Act, 2000 is the primary source of law supplemented by the Design Rules, 2001 and judicial decisions.

3.2 Substantive law

According to Section 4 of the Designs Act, 2000, a product is eligible for registration, if:

- it is new or original (it was held in the case of *Bharat Glass Tubes Ltd. v. Gopal Glass Works Ltd., 2008* (37) PTC 1 (SC) that "new or original" means that the design which has been registered has not been published anywhere or it has been made known to the public);
- it has not been disclosed by prior publication or use or in any other way;
- it is sufficiently distinguishable from known designs or their combination; and
- it contains no scandalous or obscene matter and is not contrary to public order or morality.

However, an unregistered design is not protected under the Indian Design law.

In order to obtain a valid registration, the following conditions must be satisfied:

- The design should be new or original. The novelty may reside in the application of a known shape or pattern to new subject matter.
- The design should relate to features of shape, configuration, pattern or ornamentation applied or applicable to an article.
- The design should be applied or applicable to any article by any industrial process.
- The features of the design in the finished article should appeal to and are judged solely by the eye.
- Any mode or principle of construction or operation or anything which is in substance a mere mechanical device, would not be a registrable design.
- The design should not include any trademark or property mark or artistic works as defined under the Copyright Act, 1957.

Unregistered design rights are not protected under the Designs Act.

Unlike under the Copyright Act, there is no automatic assignment in case of Design and therefore, a design created by its employees, directors, suppliers, shareholders, consultants can be acquired by a legal entity by virtue of assignment clauses in contracts. Moreover, transmission can take place through mortgage, license or operation of law.

In order to be valid and enforceable, the assignment agreement has to be in writing and should contain all details regarding the rights being transferred and the obligation being imposed. The assignment has to be duly signed by both the parties involved.

While drafting a design assignment agreement, it is necessary to ensure that the agreement includes provisions pertaining to terms of assignment which specifies the rights and obligations of the parties, the time period for the assignment and specifies the procedure of renewal, a representation and warranties clause and a confidentiality clause in order to prevent any disclosure of information. Moreover, the geographical area to which the agreement pertains to must be provided. Since the assignment is a contract, it must satisfy the requirements of Section 10 of the Contract Act, 1872.

The Designs Act does not specifically contain any concept of moral rights, which is provided under Section 57 of the Copyright Act, 1957. Under the Designs Act, two possibilities may exist:

- When an underlying work of art is created which is subsequently applied to an article which leads to a design right. In such a case, moral rights may co-exist with the design right. In India, moral rights are inalienable rights and they cannot therefore be waived/transferred. (*Amar Nath Sehgal v Union of India*, 2005 (30) PTC 253 Del).
- When the design is inseparable from the article, in which case, moral rights may not be created, since moral rights fall outside the scope and purview of the Designs Act.

In India, a copyright in a design is for a period of 10 years from the date of registration and can be extended to a maximum of 15 years (Section 11 of Designs Act, 2000).

Unregistered design has no statutory protection in India since a design can only be in accordance with the provisions of the Designs Act which requires registration. However, this does not preclude a party from asserting other causes of action like copyright (subject to Section 15 (2) of the Copyright Act) and passing off.

3.3 Enforcement

Under Section 22(1) of the Designs Act, 2000, a fraudulent or obvious imitation of the design thereof, in respect of a similar article, for the purpose of sale or importation of such article, without the written consent of the registered proprietor, amounts to piracy of a registered design.

In *Vega Auto Accessories (P) Ltd. v. S.K. Jain Bros. Helmet (I) Pvt*, the Hon'ble Court opined that while comparing two designs, "their sameness of the features does not necessarily mean that the two designs must be identical in all points and should differ on none - they have to be substantially the same". Therefore, actual copying is not necessary so long as there is substantial similarity.

It would appear that a design cannot be enforced against a trademark. Moreover, if the subject matter of the design has already been used as a trademark, the novelty in the design will be destroyed which would defeat any design action.

There have been various decisions including a judgement by a three-judge bench of the Delhi High Court holding that a suit for infringement of a design is not maintainable against another registered proprietor of a similar or identical design (*Micolube India Ltd v Rakesh Kumar*, 199 (2013) DLT 740).

A design cannot be enforced against a patent. Design law is concerned with the appearance of the article to be judged solely by the eye whereas patent law strictly deals with functionality. In fact, Section 2(d) of the Designs Act excludes from the definition of 'design', which is in substance a mere mechanical device and any mode or principle of construction.

A design cannot be enforced against a domain name. The scope of protection of a domain name is akin to a word trademark which is entirely different in scope from what design protection confers.

A design cannot be enforced against a trade name. Trade name is a concept under trademarks. The name under which an entity conducts or carries out trade is known as the 'trade name'.

Other IP rights such as Geographical Indications, circuit designs, plant variety protection, traditional knowledge and trade secrets do not intersect with design law.

A design may be enforced against its unauthorized use in social media if it is published or exposed or caused to be published/exposed for sale by any person for the purposes of obtaining commercial benefit (Section 22 (1) (c), Designs Act).

Comparative advertising can never result in design infringement since there is no misappropriation of the registered design or any obvious or fraudulent imitation made which is actionable under the Designs Act. Other causes of action are available to restrain an impermissible comparative advertisement.

There is very limited jurisprudence on whether a design can be enforced against its unauthorized use in parody and it would depend on a case-to-case basis.

All grounds for cancellation of Registration of a design available under Section 19 of the Designs Act, 2000 are available as a defence in an action for infringement (Section 22 (3), Designs Act).

There is no provision for a repair clause or any other comparable limitations in India.

Acquiescence on the part of the owner may be a ground for Courts not to grant an injunction against the infringer. Acquiescence is not mere delay but involves a positive act on the part of the proprietor.

In certain cases, suppression of material facts has also resulted in injunctive relief being denied to the design proprietor.

After three years from the last act of infringement, a claim for design infringement becomes time barred. However, every act of infringement will give rise to a fresh cause of action from which limitation will start again.

As to whether a design holder can take action claiming both design infringement and copyright infringement and/or unfair competition for the same set of facts - if the design is registered under the Designs Act, the Design would lose its copyright protection under the Copyright Act. If it is a design registrable under the Designs Act but has not so been registered, "the Design would continue to enjoy copyright protection under the Act so long as the threshold limit of its application on an article by an industrial process for more than 50 times is reached". But once that limit is crossed, it would lose its copyright protection under the Copyright Act.

Design infringement and copyright infringement actions are distinct causes of action which can be combined in one suit.

As regards whether passing off can be claimed in a suit for design infringement, the overwhelming position is that an action for passing off will be maintainable so long as there is a clear demarcation between features of a product over which design rights are claimed and aspects and embellishments for which passing off may be asserted.

Current issues that luxury brands face in expanding and protecting their design rights are:

- Proprietors are often faced with electing between trademark protection or design protection for certain articles involving shape of a product. If the product is used as a trademark, it may not qualify as a valid design since the use would destroy its novelty. At the same time, a design right is a strict monopoly right granted for 15 years and has fewer exceptions compared to those in trademark law. Moreover, substantial evidence of use is required to show secondary meaning in respect of unconventional trademarks like shape since these are often considered inherently non-distinctive.
- Section 15 (2) results in extinguishing copyright if design protection is not sought at the inception (before 50 articles are made). This leaves creators/proprietors remediless since it is often difficult for them to envision how commercially successful a design may turn out to be. By not applying for design registration, they lose both copyright and design protection.
- One of the most pressing issues faced by luxury brands in India is counterfeiting and the copying of designs to produce replicas, primarily in the apparel and auto industries.

4. RIGHT OF PRIVACY, PUBLICITY AND PERSONAL ENDORSEMENT

4.1 Sources of law

The law in India protects publicity and privacy rights of individuals. In cases such as *Titan Industries v. Ramkumar Jewellers,* 2012 (50) PTC 486 (Del) and *D.M. Entertainment Pvt. Ltd v. Baby Gift House* MANU/DE/2043/2010, Courts have protected the publicity rights of celebrities against commercial exploitation. The right is attributable to public figures by virtue of them having acquired a status and a personality which grants commercial value to individual persona. Privacy rights of individuals are protected irrespective of whether they are celebrities or popular figures since privacy is recognized as a fundamental right as a facet of right to life and personal liberty guaranteed under Article 21 of the Constitution of India, 1950.

There is no express provision in any present statute that protects right of publicity. The said right is protected under common law.

4.2 Substantive law

To own a right of publicity, aside from being a living human, the individual must have attained fame and popularity among the public at large and must be a recognizable figure.

There is no specific law relating to the protection of an individual's right to publicity after their death.

Publicity rights being property rights have monetary value attached to it. The individual may assign their name or other indicia for commercial gain.

The individual may grant permission to another person to use their name or other indicia for commercial gain through a license (exclusive or non-exclusive).

There is no specific statutory provision governing the requirements for an agreement for the assignment/license of the right of publicity. The requirements would be the same as any assignment or license agreement which are both agreements governed under the Indian Contract Act, 1872.

Breach of any of the material terms of the contract would entitle the licensor to withdraw consent by terminating the agreement. In the context of right to publicity, this may include using the persona/image for an illegal purpose or for a purpose which was not agreed upon.

As a property right, the right of publicity is inheritable and will legally bind the successors. As the parties to the contract change, a new agreement is signed.

Following the death of an assignor the legal representatives inherit the rights.

In the event the heirs have an independent right over the deceased individual's name, image, likeness, or other unequivocal aspects of their identity there is very limited jurisprudence in this regard in India. It appears that the contract would be controlling.

If the right of publicity is transmissible mortis causa, it will not expire until such time as there is a significant commercial value attached to the publicity rights.

4.3 Enforcement

The right of publicity can only be enforced against a commercial use of that individual's name, image, likeness, or other unequivocal aspects of their identity.

It is necessary to prove that that individual's name, image, likeness, or other unequivocal aspects of one's identity have a commercial value to obtain an injunction or other remedies for the unauthorized use.

The major challenges faced by celebrities are false endorsements and unauthorised use of persona which would lead to lowering of their image in the eyes of the public at large.

5. PRODUCT PLACEMENT

Product placement is permitted in India. There are 2 scenarios which can be envisaged:
- if product placement happens pursuant to a legitimate contract between the proprietor of the brand and the producer of the audio-visual film; or
- if products bearing a trademark or copyright are shown in an audio-visual work without the proprietor's consent

The facts of each case would have to be seen to determine whether it is actionable. There have been cases where products shown in a bad light have been blurred since the visual or aural depiction/rendition of a mark amounts to infringement without the proprietor's consent. As regards copyright, if the artistic work is merely incidental or by way of background to the principal matters portrayed in the film, the same may not be actionable (Section 52(1)(u) of the Copyright Act).

There are restrictions placed on advertising certain products as per the Code of Advertising Practice, also known as the ASCI code.

Some of the products and services banned from advertising are:
- Tobacco Products.
- Alcoholic beverages.
- Human Organs.
- Infant milk food.
- Prize chits and money circulation schemes.
- Prenatal determination of sex.
- Physicians.
- Legal Services.

In the event the other party fails to perform the agreement the brand owner can file a suit for specific performance of a contract. Moreover, injunctive relief can also be sought seeking removal/blurring of the infringing content from the audio visual work in addition to claiming damages.

Challenges faced by luxury brands include the following:
- There are instances when certain well-known brands have been shown in a disparaging manner in films/advertisements (for example, the G4S case, where a premier security guard service was shown in bad light, *ICICI Bank Ltd. v Ashok Thakeria & Ors.,* 2014 (58) PTC 258 (Delhi)).
- Even if not shown in a disparaging manner, certain brands, due to their exclusivity, may not like to be associated with certain works of art.
- To be actionable, the use must be tarnishing or likely to cause confusion as to the source of the goods/services. This may prove to be difficult since a film is considered an artistic work and does not easily fit as a competitor to the brand.
- Each case would therefore depend upon its own unique facts.

6. PROTECTION OF CORPORATE IMAGE AND REPUTATION

The laws regarding right of publicity and/or privacy do not extend to legal entities/corporations, these rights are only applicable to natural persons.

Specific clauses can be incorporated into agreements for the protection of corporate image as long as they are not in violation of any statutory laws.

Such clauses may be included through contract so long as they are in compliance with existing laws (for instance price ceiling legislations). Liquidated damages are generally permitted and may be included through contract for protection against breach. To avoid unenforceability, parties must be able show actual loss suffered. Any prohibition which is anti-competitive may invite action under the Competition Act, 2002. Some IP statutes such as the Patents Act, 1970 (Section 140) and the Designs Act, 2000 (Section 42) also have provisions prohibiting such restrictive clauses.

Some of the challenges faced by luxury brands in the secondary market are as follows:
- In the absence of contract and due to the operation of doctrine of exhaustion, a brand owner may have limited control on the downstream distribution of his products which may raise various concerns such as diluting the exclusivity of the brand.
- The price of the original product may be affected by resellers offering the product to consumers.

- Under Section 30(2)(d) TMA, if a mark is used by a person in respect of goods forming part of, or as an accessory to, other goods for which the trademark has been used, there will be no infringement where the use of the mark is reasonably necessary to indicate that the goods are so adapted.

AUTHOR BIOGRAPHIES

Pravin Anand

Pravin Anand is the Managing Partner and Head of Litigation at Anand and Anand. Awarded the INTA 2021 President's Award, AIPPI Award of Merit and recognised as the "Most Innovative Lawyer" for the Asia Pacific Region by Financial Times, Pravin has experience of appearing in more than 2500 cases in over 42 years of his practice as an IP lawyer. Some landmarks in his career include Patent lawsuits that transformed pharmaceutical and bio-technology enforcement regime in India including *Merck v. Glenmark*; *Roche v. Cipla*; the Monsanto case; and a large number of other suits on behalf of Pfizer, BMS, AstraZeneca, etc. Also to his credit are: India's first Anti-anti-suit injunction (*InterDigital v Xiaomi*); Software Patent law suit conferring protection (Ferid Allani case); development of damages culture recognising compensatory, exemplary and aggravated damages (*Philips v. AmazeStore*); India's first post-trial SEP judgment (*Philips v. Bhagirathi*); development of unique remedies like the "Tree Planting Order" (Merck case); and order benefitting adolescent girls (Hermes case).

Dhruv Anand

Dhruv is a Partner at Anand and Anand. His work covers a wide array of cases from luxury brands, FMCG to pharma and life sciences including copyright enforcement. He has been involved in significant copyright cases such as the DU photocopy case, enforcing the moral rights of a famous sculptor, represented copyright societies and more. He has lately been involved in a dispute concerning the rights of singers to receive royalties. Dhruv has been instrumental in enforcing and upholding the patent rights of many pharmaceutical companies such as Bayer, Merck, Pharmacyclics and Eisai in cases involving complex patent law principles.

Udita M Patro

A Managing Associate at Anand and Anand, Udita is involved extensively in IP litigation and dispute resolution involving all forms of IP including Trademarks, Copyright, Patents, Designs, domain names, and anti-counterfeiting work including brand enforcement for luxury brands, contractual and advisory work. She has been involved in big-ticket litigation matters for leading Pharmaceutical companies, including Merck v Glenmark, which was the first patent infringement lawsuit in India wherein a permanent injunction was granted in favour of the patentee after trial.

Sampurnaa Sanyal

Sampurnaa is a Litigation Associate at Anand and Anand where she is engaged extensively in IP litigation and dispute resolution with respect to trademarks, patents and copyright. She is also involved in research and client advisory work.

ITALY

Fabrizio Jacobacci
Studio Legale Jacobacci & Associati

1. TRADEMARK

1.1 Sources of law

In Italy, trademark rights are governed by national and European Union law as well as international conventions.

The main source of law relating to trademarks in Italy is the Code of Industrial Property (CIP) (Law Decree No. 30 of 10 February 2005), which repealed and reorganized all prior legislation on industrial property, including the old Trademark Law. The CIP also contains a number of rules relating to the litigation of intellectual property rights that complement those of the Code of Civil Procedure.

In addition, Italy is party to a number of international treaties and, as a Member State of the European Union, Italian trademark law is also affected by Community legislation, in particular, by EC Directive no. 2004/48 on the Enforcement of IP rights and Directive no. 2436/2015 to approximate the laws of the Member States (the "Trademark Directive"). In addition, Regulation no. 2017/1001 on the Community trademark and Regulation no. 1151/2012 on quality schemes for agricultural products and foodstuffs which replaced the previous Regulation (EC) No 510/2006 on Geographical Indications.

Court decisions are not sources of law in Italy, since they are not binding for future cases between different parties. However, they may have a persuasive effect on future decisions, especially if rendered by higher courts. According to well-established principles and to the Italian Constitution, EU and international law prevails over national legislation.

Under Italian law, trademark protection can be obtained either by way of registration or by way of use. However, "use on a not merely local scale" is necessary to obtain protection in a form that is almost identical to that of a registered trademark.

The construction of the requirement of "use on a not merely local scale" has resulted in inconsistent decisions that identified the threshold to exceed the mere local use differently in terms of geographical extension. The recent trend however seems to be that any use that covers at least one main region of Italy is sufficient.

1.2 Substantive law

The general rule is that the scope of protection granted to trademarks is limited to the goods and services identical or similar to those for which the trademark is used or registered.

However, pursuant to Articles 12.1(e) and 20.1(c), of the CIP, a registered trademark having a reputation in Italy (i.e. a trademark that has acquired a reputation for at least some of the goods and services for which it has been registered), is also protected in relation to goods and services dissimilar from those for which it has been registered provided that:
- the two marks are similar;
- the use of the later mark can be detrimental to the repute or distinctiveness of the earlier mark or it enables the user to draw an unfair advantage from them; and
- the use is without due cause.

The interpretation of these provisions, as well as of the corresponding article in the Trademark Directive, has caused much debate and has produced a substantial number of judgements.

According to the decisions of the CJEU and of Italian courts, a trademark has a reputation if it is "known by a significant part of the relevant public for the products or services it covers" (see CJEU, *General Motors*, 14 September 1999, C-375/97). Therefore, reputation must satisfy a quantitative requirement, namely degree of knowledge of the earlier mark among the relevant public and how large a segment of the relevant public knows the mark. The qualitative aspects of the reputation may become relevant at a later stage, when the trademark proprietor must prove that the reputation attached to his mark has suffered detriment or that unfair advantage has been taken of it.

Italian law protects trademarks having a well-known status – that differs from that of trademark having a reputation – in accordance with Article 6bis of the Paris Union Convention. A well-known trademark is an unregistered mark (or at least unregistered in the country where protection under Article 6bis is sought) that is well-known by the public in Italy even though the mark in question is not used in the country and it has therefore acquired the well-known status for reasons other than its use.

According to Article 12.1(a) and (f), a well-known trademark may be invoked to prevent the registration of a later identical or similar mark for identical or similar goods and services, and if the mark is question in addition to being well-known it has also a reputation, also for dissimilar goods and services. This is an exception to the requirement that only registered trademarks can be protected for dissimilar goods and services.

Courts occasionally use the adjective 'famous' to designate a trademark as having a particularly high reputation, but the acknowledgement of this status is of no significant consequence in term of protection.

In short, there are no particular rules governing the trademarks of the luxury industry, nor protecting the "aura" of luxury surrounding them in a way that differs from that of a trademark having a reputation belonging to another industry. However, the proof that a trademark not only has a reputation, but also has an "aura" of luxury, may be helpful in establishing the additional conditions that must be satisfied by the proprietor to stop third parties from using a similar mark, namely, the detriment to the repute or distinctiveness of the mark or the unfair advantage.

1.3 Enforcement

There is no recognized test to prove that a trademark has a reputation. This is assessed based on a number of concurring factors and the trademark proprietor should submit as much evidence as possible to prove that the trademark is well known by a substantial portion of the relevant public.

In particular, the following is usually very helpful, if not necessary, to prove a reputation:
• sales details during the 5 years preceding the litigation;
• details of advertising expenditures during the 5 years preceding the litigation;
• market share data searched and created by independent and reliable agencies;

- copies of advertisements (videos, magazine ads, on-line, radio broadcast, etc.);
- market surveys produced by independent well-established agencies; and
- documents and material relating to promotional / sponsored events, such as sport /cultural events.

The purpose of the above is to provide a full picture of the intensity, geographical extent, duration of use of the trademark, the scale of the investments made by the undertaking in promoting the trademark, the market share and so on (see CJEU, *General Motors*).

To the extent this is possible, facts should be proved by documentary evidence that must be as objective as possible. For example, a mere spreadsheet recapitulating sales is not relevant evidence, while the same spreadsheet accompanied by a declaration made by an external auditor that he/she has verified the accuracy of the spreadsheet is persuasive evidence. Oral testimony is better used to confirm the origin and content of documentary evidence, thus, in case of doubt, the external auditor can be heard as a witness.

Affidavits – i.e., sworn declarations - have no greater evidentiary value than a simple declaration. Statements under oath can be usefully rendered only during testimony in court and not by way of affidavit.

Courts are willing to consider expert evidence even though they do not give it a substantial evidentiary weight to prove the reputation of a trademark.

Market surveys are often used to support a number of claims, from acquired distinctiveness of a trademark, to the actual existence of confusion between two signs or, more often, to prove the share of public who know the trademark and associate it with a specific undertaking.

When resulting from an activity of one of the parties, survey evidence is given some value by the courts as long as the questionnaire appears to have been drafted in order to avoid leading questions and the survey has been carried out by a respectable, recognized entity. Appreciation may be higher if the party applies to the court to order a survey evidence and this survey is carried out by an expert appointed by the court. In general, however, Italian courts very rarely resort to survey evidence carried out by experts in trademark disputes.

In case one of the parties produces the survey, the same shall provisionally bear its costs, whereas the court will normally charge these costs to the losing party at the end of the proceeding. Although market survey may have some impact in determining the outcome of the case, the courts do not regard them as the most relevant means of evidence. Further, there is no established threshold of recognition beyond which a trademark is considered to have a reputation, so establishing that a certain percentage of the public knows a certain mark is not overwhelming evidence of reputation (CJEU, *General Motors*).

Once the proprietor has proven the reputation of the trademark together with the detriment or unfair advantage, he can stop any use of an identical or similar mark made in the course of trade, i.e., intended for commercial reason.

Metatags pose a different range of problems. Since the beginning, the traditional approach of Italian courts is that the use of a third party's mark as a metatag does not amount to trademark infringement, but unfair competition (Tribunal of Rome, 18 January 2001, Tribunal of Milan, 8 February 2002 and Tribunal of Naples, 28 January 2001).

More recent decisions have ruled that the use of trademarks as key words (metatags have become technically obsolete) may amount to trademark infringement if the use is likely to confuse the public because of the manner in which it is made (Tribunal of Milan, 26 February 2009 and Tribunal of Palermo, 7 June 2013).

The use of a trademark in comparative advertising that may be detrimental to the reputation of the mark, takes unfair advantage of it, or creates a risk of confusion, amounts to trademark infringement. The Tribunal of Milan ruled that presenting the compared product as identical except for the mark to the product of reference is an attempt to attract consumers thanks to the reputation of the competitor's mark and not by an objective comparison between the respective products characteristics (Tribunal of Milan, 27 June 2013).

The use of a trademark in parodies for the purpose of criticism, controversy or mere humour is a legitimate exercise of freedom of speech, as long as the use is not for commercial use. On the contrary, if the parody is not the end, but a mere means to convey a commercial message, then the use may amount to trademark infringement. The circumstance that the original mark has been distorted for the purpose of parody may exclude confusion and therefore infringement. However, in the case of a trademark having a reputation, the same is not only protected if there is a likelihood of confusion, but also if the use may be detrimental to the mark and may enable the user to draw an unfair advantage.

In our society, luxury goods function as status symbols, they define class, social distinction, and even personal beliefs and values. Luxury companies utilize their trademarks as symbols to signal status and market their products or services. It is not a surprise, therefore, that trademarks have become their most valuable assets and no efforts are spared to constantly expand their scope of protection, often by testing the law in an attempt to stretch it to its furthest limits. In this respect, protection of shape marks and of colours continue to be the battleground on which the luxury industry focuses its efforts.

In relation to shape marks, the evolution has not been the most favourable. In the *Hauck v Stokke* case (C-205/13), the Court held that even if a shape is not indispensable to the function of the goods, the same is not protectable if it results from its nature. This has raised the threshold for obtaining and preserving trademark protection. On the opposite front, in the *KitKat* case (Case C-215/14), the CJEU stated that only the manner in which the goods at issue function is decisive, not the manner of manufacture; this seems to be, however, a modest victory for brand owners as the distinction is likely to have only a marginal practical impact.

At national level, Italian courts do not show any inclination to invalidate shape marks easily, but at the same time, they construe their scope of protection by excluding that infringement may occur when the similarity is limited to those elements that result from the nature of the allegedly infringing goods. In line with this approach, the Court of Appeal of Torino upheld the validity of the registration for the iconic shape of the Vespa scooter and its infringement by one of the three scooters accused of infringement (Judgement April 16, 2019). Tribunal of Rome dismissed a claim for infringement based on the Omega shape trademark of Ferragamo (Judgement July 8, 2020) observing that the similarity between the shape mark and the accused products was found only in relation to elements that are inherent to the nature of such products.

2. COPYRIGHT

2.1 Sources of law

The main Italian law regulating copyright is Italian Copyright Law (ICL) (Law No. 633 of 22 April 1941) on the protection of copyright and of other rights related to its exercise, as supplemented and amended by a number of subsequent laws.

A few residual provisions concerning copyright are also contained in the Italian Civil Code (Articles 2575-2583).

In addition to the national legislation, a number of directives enacted in the copyright field and implemented in Italy also governs Italian copyright law. Finally, Italy is party to a number of international treaties regarding copyright law, generally aimed at setting common rules and a minimum level of protection in member states.

Court decisions are not sources of law in Italy, since they are not binding for future cases between different parties. However, they may have a persuasive effect on future decisions, especially if rendered by higher courts. According to well-established principles and to the Italian Constitution, EU and international law prevails over national legislation.

2.2 Substantive law

According to Articles 1 and 2 of the ICL, copyright protects creative works belonging to literature, music, fine arts, architecture, theatre and cinematography, irrespective of their form of expression, as well as computer programs and databases. Finally, it also protects objects of industrial design, provided they have an artistic value.

The protection of objects of industrial design has been hotly debated in Italian courts over the past thirty years. The highly subjective character of the artistic value requirement – let alone its compliance with EU law as we shall see below in the Enforcement section - has caused commentators and courts to issue the most diverse opinions. Recently, case law seems to have found a criterion to establish that if an object of industrial design is copyrightable, namely, by ascertaining if the same has been recognized as a work of (applied) art in the relevant circles. Therefore, objects that have become part of permanent collection in museums or that have enjoyed the attention of art critics and, more generally, have been able to sail through and transcend the time in which they were created, are usually recognized as having an artistic value (Tribunal of Milan, 13 September 2012). This approach, however, fails to take into account that the work is protected by copyright as of its creation and not when the public or museum curators perceive it as a noteworthy object of design. Courts have recognized this limitation and have stressed that the inclusion of the object in dispute in museum collections or in temporary exhibition is a mere confirmation of its original artistic value (Tribunal of Milan, 9 January 2014) and it is not a requirement for establishing copyright protection. This approach is hardly compatible with the necessity to protect fashion industry products. Even successful products are quickly replaced and products of the fashion industry are often recognized as "iconic", i.e., capable of transcending the time in which they were created years if not decades after their launch. Therefore, exclusive reliance on copyright instead of other forms of protection such as design – either registered or not – is not a sound approach.

ITALY

Italian copyright law covers both economic and moral rights.

Economic rights are the rights to make any type of use of the work such as, without limitation, the right of publication; reproduction; transcription; public performance; broadcasting; making available or otherwise communicating to the public; distribution; elaboration; translation; rental and loan. These rights may be assigned or licensed in whole or in part, or waived and they have a limited duration of 70 years from the death of the author.

Moral rights consists in the author's right to:
- be recognized as the author, the so called 'right of paternity';
- oppose any distortion, mutilation or other modifications of the work which could damage its honour or reputation, the so called 'right of integrity'; and
- withdraw the work from the market in case the work no longer represents the author's views, the so-called 'right of repentance'.

All these rights are perpetual and may not be waived or assigned. The relatives of the author may, after their death, exercise the right of paternity and the right of integrity. These rights, however, are not acquired by the relatives' *mortis causa*, but are a right of personality belonging to them in their unique capacity as relatives that may well not coincide with that of heirs.

Finally, the ICL also provides for specific and limited economic rights – ie related rights – concerning specific kinds of works and granted to certain categories of beneficiaries, such as phonogram producers; producers of cinematographic or audiovisual works; radio or TV broadcasting companies; performers; authors of 'simple photographs' (that is, photos that are not creative enough to be considered works of art); and makers of non-creative databases.

Individuals create artworks, either alone or in a group. The general rule prescribes that the author of the artwork is also the owner of all economic rights, but the rules suffer from an important exception. The copyright in works of employees created in the performance of the employment contract belong to the employers. On the contrary, works created by consultants or suppliers belong to them, unless the agreement stipulates otherwise or they have been created under the direction and for use by the principal, in which case the principal acquires the right to use the work for which it paid the agreed consideration. However, such right does not include the right to license third parties or to make copies of the work for use by third parties.

The position of directors of a company may pose a delicate problem if the work has been created in the performance of the director's duty using the company's resources. In that case, it seems that the copyright should belong to the company. This approach cannot be applied to shareholders who have no duties *vis-à-vis* the company.

The contract by which copyright is assigned in whole or in part or is licensed must be proved in writing (Article 110 ICL) and not by way of testimony. Pure oral agreements are, therefore, valid, but unenforceable in the event their existence is denied. As a consequence it is a sound precaution to specifically regulate the assignment of copyright in writing. Such assignment must be drafted bearing in mind that the law, in order to protect the author, provides that the contract by which an author agrees to assign the copyright in all his future works or in all categories of work is null and void if the author obligation are not limited to a specific period of time.

2.3 Enforcement

The creation of the work is the only necessary requisite for copyright. While authors can register a variety of works with the SIAE (the Italian main collecting society), the registration is not necessary for the right to come into existence. The use of the copyright notice has no legal value and failing to affix it has no consequence.

In the absence of a registration system that provides a presumption of ownership, copyright enforcement requires producing evidence that the work has been created by the party that is seeking enforcement or proof of acquisition from the original author. Evidence other than that of assignment can be given by any means, including testimony. A general rule regularly applied by Italian court, however, is that if a party has been making a public use of the copyright in a certain work for a long time without being challenged, it is presumed that that party is the owner of the copyright, until the opponent produces evidence to the contrary.

To succeed in an infringement action is not necessary to prove actual copying or the intention to copy. It is sufficient to prove that essential elements of the original work have been reproduced, in whole or in part, in the copy. Case law often held that infringement occurs when the original work can be 'read' in the subsequent version.

While the law does not expressly mention the intention to copy as a requirement for establishing infringement, the knowledge deriving from access to the original work will be relevant for the assessment of damages, as no damages can be awarded where infringement was not wilful or negligent.

Copyright can be enforced against any subsequent right, including trademarks, designs, patents and other IP rights that may fall within the scope of protection granted by copyright law to the artwork. Since names – including names of fictional characters are rarely protected under copyright law; the commercial use of the name of fictional characters is unlikely to infringe an earlier copyright.

Unlike trademarks, which are protected against uses in the course of trade, copyright is also protected when the alleged infringer is not making a commercial use of it, except in very narrow, specific cases.

Under Italian law, there are no general defences or exceptions based on fair use or fair dealing. The defendant may only rely on the specific exceptions provided by ICL

The use of a copyrighted work for the purpose of parody has been the subject of frequent disputes in Italy. Art. 5.2(k) of Directive 2001/29 provides that Member States may provide for exceptions to the right of reproduction in the case of "use for the purpose of caricature, parody or pastiche". As a rule, a parody of a copyrighted work does not infringe the original work if it satisfies the essential characteristics for a parody. Namely, "first, to evoke an existing work, while being noticeably different from it, and secondly, to constitute an expression of humour or mockery" (CJEU, *Vandersteen*, 3 September 2014, C-201/13, Tribunal of Venice, 7 November 2015).

Although there is no statute of limitation to bring an action for copyright infringement, the claim for damages must be commenced no later than 5 years from the last act of infringement.

Also, importantly, action for copyright infringement can be cumulated with other types of actions, such as design infringement and unfair competition. All these actions can be brought before the same court and decided together.

Given the complex issues arising from the use of trademarks to protect the shape of product, copyright could offer an attractive alternative. The term of protection is not perpetual as in trademarks, but is far longer than that accorded by a design registration. However, not all shapes are eligible for copyright protection. As illustrated in the previous paragraphs, shapes of products are protected only if they have an artistic value and the difficulty in establishing, with sufficient certainty, the presence of such an element has often led luxury brands to rely on copyright when no other intellectual property rights was available.

Thus said, the CJEU (*Cofemel*, Case C683/17) dictates that the national legislation may not impose separate and specific requirements for the protection of object of industrial design. In paragraph [29], the court makes clear that the "concept of 'work' […] constitutes […] an autonomous concept of EU law which must be interpreted and applied uniformly, requiring two cumulative conditions to be satisfied. First, that concept entails that there exist an original subject matter, in the sense of being the author's own intellectual creation. Second, classification as a work is reserved to the elements that are the expression of such creation".

The court then moves on to clarify that the concept of a 'work' entails the existence of a subject matter that is identifiable with sufficient precision and objectivity and such precision and objectivity is not attained where an identification is essentially based on the sensations, which are intrinsically subjective, of an individual who perceives the subject matter at issue. Therefore, a condition such as "artistic value" may fail to meet the requirement of precision and objectivity required by the CJEU. The CJEU reiterated the same principle in the *Brompton* case (C-833/18). Although the issue at stake was whether copyright protection applies to a product whose shape is, at least in part, necessary to obtain a technical result, the CJEU seized the opportunity to repeat that to qualify as a "work" the item must be original, i.e. the author's own intellectual creation and be an expression of that creation. "The subject matter reflects the personality of its author, as an expression of his free and creative choices" (*Brompton*, paragraphs [22] and [23]). These conditions are both necessary and sufficient, so that the addition of the "artistic value" requirement appears to violate EU law.

3. DESIGN
3.1 Sources of law
The provisions contained in the CIP implemented in accordance with Directive No. 1998/71 govern Italian designs. Community designs are governed by Council Regulation (EC) No. 2002/6 of 12 December 2001 (hereafter 'ECR'). In addition, Italy is party to the Paris Convention for the Protection of Industrial Property of 20 March 1883, as revised and amended.

Court decisions are not sources of law in Italy, since they are not binding for future cases between different parties. However, they may have a persuasive effect on future decisions, especially if rendered by higher courts. According to well-established principles and to the Italian Constitution, EU and international law prevails over national legislation.

3.2 Substantive law

Italian design rights can be only obtained by way of registration with the Italian Patent and Trademark Office (UIBM), while Community designs may either be registered at the Office for Harmonization in the Internal Market (OHIM) or unregistered, the latter being subject to a different set of rules.

The object of protection of design rights is the appearance of the whole or a part of a product resulting from the features of, in particular, the lines, contours, colours, shape, texture and/or materials of the product itself and/or its ornamentation.

Italian and Community law defines the term 'product' as "any industrial or handicraft item, including *inter alia* parts intended to be assembled into a complex product, packaging, get-up, graphic symbols and typographic typefaces, but excluding computer programs".

Therefore, design rights protect a very wide variety of features except for those features that, in the case of components, are not visible during normal use and those that are solely dictated by their function.

Appearances of products that are contrary to public policy or morality are not eligible for protection.

In order to benefit from design protection, the design must satisfy two separate requirements:

- The design must be new. No identical design has been made available to the public before either the date of filing of the application for registration (or the date of priority, if applicable) for national or registered Community designs, or, for unregistered Community designs, the date on which the design for which protection is claimed has first been made available to the public. The nature of the product to which the prior design relates is not relevant (*Group Nivelles* - Joined Cases C-361/15 P and C-405/15 P).
  The disclosure made by the designer, a successor or a third party based on the knowledge of the design obtained from the designer in the 12-month period preceding the filing of the design application or the disclosure made as the result of an abuse do not deprive the design of novelty.
  Similarly irrelevant is the disclosure that could not reasonably have become known in the normal course of business to the circles specialised in the sector concerned, operating within the Community.
- The design must also have individual character, meaning that the overall impression that the design produces on the informed user differs from the overall impression that may be produced on such user by any design that has been made available to the public. Differently from the assessment of novelty, the identification of the product to which an earlier design applies, or in which the latter is incorporated, is relevant for the assessment of individual character. It is through the identification of the product concerned that it will be possible to determine whether the informed user of the product to which the later design applies, or in which the later design is incorporated, is aware of the

earlier design. Only if that latter condition is fulfilled, the earlier design may prevent the later design from being recognised as having individual character.

The maximum duration of the protection for registered designs is 25 years whereas the protection for unregistered design is granted for 3 years after the first disclosure of the design within the European Union.

The owner of the design is the registrant or the person under whose name the unregistered design was disclosed.

It is however important to remember that registered/unregistered design are potentially eligible for copyright protection, in which case, since the rules governing ownership are not the same, the owner of the copyright, which almost unavoidably pre-dates the design, can seek a declaration of invalidity of the design. This situation can be avoided by securing the assignment of the copyrights from the author (independent designer, design agency, etc.) by way of a written agreement.

The assignment of design rights does not need to satisfy specific formalities. However, the rule to apply in order to resolve conflicts among concurring assignees is that the first to record the assignment prevails on all other assignees, including that who bought the right first. Recordation of the assignment is not necessary for its validity, but highly recommended.

Designers enjoy very narrow moral rights in relation to their creations. They are only entitled to be recognised as the authors of the design in the register.

3.3 Enforcement

The scope of protection of design rights encompasses all identical designs as well as those that do not produce a different overall impression on the informed user. Unregistered Community designs enjoy the same scope of protection, but only in respect of designs that have been made with the intention to copy the protected design. A number of factors, including prior knowledge of the design, degree of similarity, etc., are taken in account in order to establish if the similarity is the result of copying or of coincidence.

Registered and unregistered designs are protected against any unauthorized uses by third parties, such as the making, offering, putting on the market, importing, exporting or using a product in which the design is incorporated or to which it is applied, or storing such product for these purposes.

The design proprietor is entitled to enforce its rights against any kind of infringement, including infringement arising from use of the design in trademarks, registered designs, patents, domain names, trade names, pseudonyms or other distinctive signs or IP rights, even though a lot of these instances appear to be merely theoretical.

Like copyright, some limited uses do not fall within the scope of protection:
- private use with no commercial purpose;
- experimental use; or
- use for illustrative purposes such as teaching.

The most common defence to a claim for infringement is to challenge the validity or ownership of the design right and/or to argue that the litigious design does not produce a similar overall impression on the informed user, or that the design invoked is actually closer to the prior art than to the alleged infringing product. In relation to an action for damages, the usual 5-year statute of limitation would also apply.

Finally, Article 8.2 ECR for Community design and Article 241 of the CIP for Italian designs provides that a component used for the purpose of the repair of a complex product is excluded from the scope of protection of design.

Actions for design infringement can be cumulated with both copyright infringement and unfair competition claims before the same court.

4. RIGHT OF PRIVACY, PUBLICITY AND PERSONAL ENDORSEMENT

4.1 Sources of law

Private individuals are entitled to control the use of their name, image and other aspects of their identity in accordance with Articles 6 - 10 of the Italian Civil Code and Articles 96 – 98 ICL, whether for commercial use or for any other purpose that is not consented by the law. In addition, the relatives of said person have a more limited right to prevent the use of the person's name and image. More specifically, they may prevent the use of the name for family reasons that deserve protection and the use of the image that may be detrimental to the respectability and reputation of that person or of their relatives. Said relatives' rights survive the passing of the person whose name or image is used.

4.2 Substantive law

Any individual is entitled to the right to the name, likeness and personal identity. These rights, that include the right of publicity, i.e., the right to make a commercial use of one's name, are identified – together with certain other rights - as rights of personality and they cease with the passing of the individual. Relatives may have some residual separate right that, however, belongs to them as relatives and not as successors.

Traditionally, personality rights could not be assigned or licensed. However, the commercial use of one's name or image – the right of publicity – has become a frequent object of commercial transactions and it is well accepted that the same can be licensed, on an exclusive or non-exclusive basis, although not assigned.

There are no specific formalities required for the validity of a license concerning the right of publicity. However, the possibility of an oral license makes no commercial sense, although there have been instances where the agreement has been considered to have been concluded by implied consent of by a positive conduct (later regretted). The law on the protection of personal data is, however, changing this approach since the consent must be always express.

Although they may appear reasonably simple agreements, drafting of licenses (when the use of a celebrity name or image is used for a relatively long period of time) requires a number of precautions. First, the obligations that are imposed on the licensor in terms of their behaviour in relation to the licensee's products and business and in general must be clearly identified. The goodwill attached to a specific celebrity may well turn into a liability should the celebrity behave in a way that is damaging to the licensee and its business and this should be a cause for termination of the license upon notice given by the licensee.

Similar precautions should be taken by the licensor in the event the licensee is involved in practices that are contrary to the licensor's beliefs or ethical principles or, more generally, are incompatible with the way the licensor is perceived by the public. In all these cases, the licensor should be entitled to withdraw their consent to the use of the name and image.

Under Italian law, the passing of the licensor extinguishes the right of publicity. In theory, the licensee could continue using the name and image of the licensor without their consent and without paying their successors any consideration. Therefore, a contract usually provides that after the passing of the licensor the licensee cannot continue using the (now exhausted) right of publicity unless they obtain the relatives consent. A far preferable approach, however, is to register the name and image of the licensor as trademarks that, differently from the right of publicity, can be transferred *mortis causa*.

After the death of the licensor, the relatives could theoretically object to the use of the name or image of the deceased person. However, it seems difficult to argue that such use is detrimental to the respectability of the deceased since they had previously consented to it.

4.3 Enforcement

As an exception to the other personality rights, Italian courts have recognised since the early 1980's that the exclusive licensee also has standing to sue for a violation of the right of publicity.

The right of publicity can be enforced against any unauthorised use, whether for commercial purpose or not and the typical remedy is the injunction. However, the commercial value of the image or name have an impact on the assessment of damages.

The commercial value can be proved by any means. The most obvious is to produce copy of the license agreement showing that other parties were willing to pay a consideration for the use of that individual right of publicity. The fame or celebrity of the individual will generally create the presumption that the right of publicity of that person has a commercial value.

The main defence used to seek the dismissal of a claim for violation of the right of publicity is to argue that the image:
- was taken at a public event; and that
- the use was not made for commercial purpose, but for the prevailing purpose of information.

The case law has made clear that the information purpose must be prevailing purpose of the use and not a mere excuse to make a commercial use of the person in question.

Luxury brands often use celebrities – including their own well-known designers – to endorse and promote their brand or (as they frequently state) as ambassador for the brand. Some even incorporate a celebrity's name or likeness on their goods. The main risk of hiring a celebrity to promote or endorse a product is the unexpected or disgraceful behaviour of those individuals, or unforeseen events such as death. Stakeholders will view any adverse behaviour at an event or by a celebrity as a reflection of that company's culture, values or operational ineptitude. The damage is essentially reputational and Luxury brands should take the necessary precautions in their contract by stipulating that any actual or alleged criminal act or distasteful conduct from the celebrity will trigger the termination of the contract.

5. PRODUCT PLACEMENT

Product placement is governed by Directive no. 2010/13 of the European Parliament and Council as amended by Directive no. 2018/1808 of the European Parliament and of the Council. In Italy, the law regulates product placement with two separate legislative instruments, namely Ministerial Decree 30 July 2004 concerning product placement in movies and Legislative Decree N. 2010/44 for TV programmes.

Product placement in films is permitted if the placement is obvious, sincere and correct and coherent with the context of the story. Also, it is necessary that all product placement be listed in the credits at the end of the film.

Product placement is permitted in TV programmes if the presence of promotions within the programme is announced at the beginning of the programme and after each advertisement interruption as well as being listed in the end credits.

Finally, all products that are subject to an advertising ban, such as tobacco products cannot be objects of product placement. In addition, Article 10 of Legislative Decree N. 44/2010 - in line with Directive no. 2010/13 - imposes limits on the placement of alcoholic beverages and also prohibits the product placement of medicines in accordance with Directive no. 2007/65.

There are no specific remedies in the event a products placement contract is breached, other than the general remedies applicable to contract, namely damages and specific performance. The difficulty in enforcing an order for specific performance means that the brand owner is left with the only realistic option of seeking compensation for the damages suffered and the termination of the agreement.

Luxury brands are not immune from the most common risk involved by product placing, namely the irritation of viewers when confronted with a prominent product placement or a sequence that seems designed to sell, rather than entertain. This could interrupt the viewing experience, reflecting badly on the offending brands and the more so in the case of a luxury brand.

Although drafting an appropriate product placement contract is key for a successful product placement, in addition, educating the producer on the values of the brand to ensure that the exposure of the brand is in line with its perceived image. Luxury brands must be specifically careful in detailing all conditions of the product placement, as for the feature itself, the agreement should include the duration of the feature, whether or not there will be close-ups, and any other details regarding the appearance of the products. Importantly, brand owners should decide whether the producer could feature products from competitors in the same work. Investing financial resources to appear alongside competitors is not desirable.

6. PROTECTION OF CORPORATE IMAGE AND REPUTATION

Legal entities are also entitled to the protection of their image and reputation that may be damaged by third parties with an emphasis on the economic damages that may be suffered (legal entities are not capable of suffering psychological or biological damages). Having said that, the rules that apply to individuals cannot be applied to legal persons.

The name of a legal entity is a distinctive sign of the entity and as such is protected against the risk of confusion. In addition, if the company has acquired a reputation, any use in the trade of its name that may be detrimental to it can be prohibited.

The contractual protection of the image and reputation of a company is possible, but the provisions aimed at protecting it should be checked for potential violation of competition rules.

In particular, the Block Exemption (Commission Regulation (EU) No 330/2010 of 20 April 2010) with respect to vertical agreements allows selective distribution systems provided that the specific requirements in the Block Exemption are met and that the market share does not exceed 30 per cent.

On this basis, a restriction on the sale of products to certain re-sellers (that are not part of the selective distribution system) may be acceptable under the Block Exemption, and if these requirements are met, such prohibition on such sales may be allowed.

On the contrary, a restriction preventing selling below a certain price or outside of specific time periods in an agreement would be considered a "hardcore restriction" that can never be exempted under either the Block Exemption regulation or under Italian competition law.

Liquidated damages are generally permissible under Italian law. However, the amount of liquidated damages must be proportionate to the breach, otherwise the court has the right to reduce the amount provided in the contractual clause. The breach of the clauses protecting the corporate image or reputation would generally be considered a legitimate ground for application of liquidated damages.

AUTHOR BIOGRAPHY

Fabrizio Jacobacci

Fabrizio specializes in litigation and arbitration, most notably in the area of competition law and intellectual property, with particular emphasis on Life Sciences, including the regulatory aspects related to medical devices and pharma products. He has acquired an international reputation for his handling of various complex patent and trademark disputes.

Fabrizio is a frequent speaker at international conferences on intellectual property matters, including for the Intellectual Property Section of the New York State Bar Association, the International Trademark Association, the International Bar Association and Marques. He is a lecturer at the WIPO post-graduate specialisation course on intellectual property, jointly organized by WIPO and Turin University, and a member of the editorial board of the "European Trademark Reports" published by Sweet & Maxwell.

JAPAN

Koichi Nakatani
Momo-o, Matsuo & Namba

JAPAN

1. TRADEMARK

1.1 Sources of law

The Trademark Act and the Unfair Competition Prevention Act (UCPA) are the principal sources of law. Supreme Court precedents substantially function as sources of law.

If using unregistered well-known trademarks or famous trademarks, then such well-known or famous unregistered trademarks can obtain protection under the UCPA.

Well-known or famous unregistered trademarks can be protected by Prior Use if the commencement of the use is prior to registered trademarks.

1.2 Substantive law

The Trademark Act provides for the categories of unregistrable trademarks (upon examination or subject to cancellation) to protect well-known or famous trademarks.

The UCPA protects "indications of goods or business (names, trade names, trademarks, mark, containers or packaging for goods which are connected with a person's operations, or any other indication of a person's goods or business [...])," which are "well-known among consumers" or which are "famous". "Famous" indicates a higher degree of fame than "well-known" does.

Use of signs identical or similar to an indication of goods or business that is "well-known" among customers is deemed unfair competition if the likelihood to cause confusion exists, whereas "famous" indications of goods or business are protected even where there is no likelihood to cause confusion.

Both the Trademark Act and the UCPA distinguish between famous trademarks and well-known trademarks.

Under the Trademark Act, Article 4-1-10 is considered to protect both well-known trademarks and famous trademarks. Article 4-1-15 and 4-1-19 are interpreted to protect only famous and extremely well-known trademarks.

Under the UCPA, the difference lies in whether it is necessary to demonstrate the requirement to cause confusion (for well-known marks) or not (famous marks) in order to be deemed as unfair competition.

The "aura of luxury" should not play a role either. In practice, courts will apply the same general principles to luxury brands and do not recognize any broader protection.

1.3 Enforcement

According to the Examination Guidelines for Trademarks published by the Japan Patent Office (JPO), the fact that a trademark is well-known or famous needs to be proved by evidence such as:
- printed matter (newspaper, magazines, catalogues);
- invoices, receipts;
- photographs showing the trademark;
- certificate by an advertisement agency;
- trade association or consumers certificate;
- public organization certificate;
- articles in general newspapers, trade journals and the internet; and

- outcome reports of the questionnaire intended for consumers regarding awareness of the trademark.

The JPO and courts would take into account various factors:
- a trademark actually in use and goods or services for which it is used;
- the start date, duration, or the area where it is used;
- the volume of production and scale of business (number of stores, business area, an amount of sales;
- appearance in general newspapers, trade journals, magazines and the internet; and
- the outcome of the questionnaire regarding consumers' awareness of the trademark.

Usually, oral testimony is not used for trademark protection cases.

Affidavit is not common for trademark protection of luxury brands, but it is sometimes used to show sales, strategy and advertisement for the brand in Japan with other documents.

In order to show the likelihood of confusion, the reputation and the degree of awareness or fame of the brand, a Questionnaire Survey conducted by experts is sometimes used.

The owner of a trademark can seek an injunction of a domain name.

A trademark cannot be enforced against a trade name if the use of the trade name is in a general manner and the owner of the trade name does not have the purpose of unfair competition.

If other distinctive signs are categorized as commercial use, especially for advertisement of the products, brands or services, then it may become infringement.

There have been Court decisions (for example, 10 October 2019 IP High Court) that recognize that using a third party trademark in description metatag may cause infringement. However, another IP High Court decision did not recognize that keyword metatag caused infringement.

Whether a trademark can be enforced against its unauthorized use in comparative advertising depends on whether the use in a social media or comparative advertising is deemed as trademark use. One of the points is whether such use in social network services contributes to advertising of the products or services.

There is no provision for general fair use in parody. The *Frank Muller* Case in the IP High Court (12 April 2016) held that parody use of a Frank Muller watch did not constitute trademark infringement. In another case, *KUmA/PUMA* in the IP High Court (27 June 2013), found trademark infringement in a parody case for PUMA logo. The Court does not provide the conditions or tests for infringement in parody.

A trademark owner can take action claiming both trademark infringement and unfair competition for the same set of facts. It is possible to bring parallel proceedings.

One of the issues for luxury brands is the import of pirate products for personal use. This is a loophole used by importers of pirate products. In order to resolve this issue, the Trademark Act was amended in May 2021. New article 2-7 defines that "Import" in the amended act clearly prohibits any action to bring infringement products from a foreign country into Japan by people who reside outside of Japan, by themselves or via any third party for any reason. As a result of this, personal use import of pirate products would be prohibited.

2. COPYRIGHT

2.1 Sources of law

The substantive law is the Copyright Act. Japan has executed many treaties with respect to copyright protection, including the Berne Convention; Universal Copyright Convention; Rome Convention; Geneva Phonograms Convention; WIPO Copyright Treaty; WIPO Performances and Phonograms Treaty; and WTO/TRIPS Agreement.

Supreme Court precedents substantially function as sources of law.

The provision of the treaty will prevail. However, there are no conflicts at present.

2.2 Substantive law

Copyrightable work should be as a "production in which thoughts or sentiments are expressed in a creative way and which falls within the literary, scientific, artistic or musical domain." Article 10 provides open list, including scripts and other literary works; musical works; choreographic works and pantomimes; paintings, sculptures and other artistic works; architectural works; maps, diagrammatical works of a scientific nature; cinematographic works; photographic works; and computer programs.

Objects of industrial, fashion or accessory design can be copyrightable, however, only a very limited number of industrial products can satisfy the requirements for copyright protection.

The Court grants to an industrial product only if it is deemed comparable to fine arts or it has qualities of fine arts with following factors: whether or not the work has a high level of aesthetic expression or artistic qualities; whether or not it is produced only in pursuit of aesthetic expression, without substantial restrictions thereon for practical purposes; and whether or not it can serve as an object of art, or a complete artistic work, apart from its practicality.

Article 21 to 28 of the Copyright Act sets forth the following type of rights: reproduction; performance; screen presentation; public transmission; recitation; exhibition (limited to artistic work or unpublished photographic work); distribution (limited to cinematographic work); transfer (work other than cinematographic work); rental (work other than cinematographic work); translation and adaptation; and exploitation of a derivative work (original author).

As for moral rights (Art.18 to 20), the author has the right to offer and make available to the public any work which has not yet been made public; the right to determine whether or not to indicate its name as the author of the work; and the right to maintain the integrity of its work and its title. These rights are personal and exclusive to the author and cannot be transferred (Art. 59).

"Neighboring rights" are protected. This term refers to the rights of performers, broadcasters, and other individuals who do not author works, but play an important role in communicating them to the public.

Rights of producers of phonograms (Articles 96 to 97-3), Broadcasting organizations (Articles 98 to 100) and Wire-broadcasting organizations (Articles 100-2 to 100-5) are also protected.

Article 15(1) of the Copyright Act specifically provides that authorship of an employee "in the course of his duties" is attributed to the employer "unless otherwise stipulated in a contract, work regulation, or the like in force at the time of the making of the work".

Contract provision to assign the rights are required for copyrightable work carried out by consultants or suppliers.

Where a shareholder or director is also an employee, the work for hire presumption will apply. Otherwise, express contract provisions shall provide for copyright assignment.

No formalities are necessary to assign copyright. However, to assert a copyright assignment against a third party, copyright registration in the Agency for Cultural Affairs (or SOFTIC for computer programs) is required. The registration has to be substantiated by submitting relevant documents providing evidence that the parties have agreed to the assignment.

Moral rights are non-transferable and cannot be waived.

In principle the term of protection is until the end of the 70-year period following the death of the author (Article 51). There are some exceptions. First, the term of protection for anonymous or pseudonymous works and works under the name of a juridical person or other corporate body is until the end of the 70-year period following the making public of such works (Articles 52, 53). With respect to cinematographic works, the copyright continues to subsist until the end of the 70-year period following the making public of such works, and if the work has not been made public within the 70-year period following its creation, until the end of the 70-year period following the work's creation (Article 54).

The Berne Convention adopts the principle of reciprocity with respect to the term of protection. Therefore, if the term of protection in the country of origin is shorter than above, the shorter term of protection applies (Article 58).

2.3 Enforcement

Neither copyright registration, copyright deposit nor copyright notice is required to enforce a copyright.

Copyright registration may be obtained at the Agency for Cultural Affairs (or SOFTIC for programming works). The merit of registration lies in the point that a person whose true name is registered will be presumed to be the author of the work (Article 75-3) and to assert a copyright assignment against a third party.

The Supreme Court has held that "copying of a work is the reproduction of a work based on the existing work, and from which the details and forms of the existing work can be perceived". If it can be acknowledged as having been based on the existing work and is of substantial similarity from which the details and forms of the original work can be perceived, it will establish an infringement of copyright.

It may be possible for copyright to be enforced against a trademark, registered design/design patent, patent, domain name, trade name, pseudonym or other IP rights. In order to protect by copyright, such distinctive signs must be a "production in which thoughts or sentiments are expressed in a creative way" and "which falls within the literary, scientific, artistic or musical domain" and oftentimes, extremely short phrases are considered to not meet the requirement.

The use of copyright in social network services or comparative advertising may constitute copyright infringement, if such use falls under infringement.

The Copyright Act does not provide general fair use provisions or parody exceptions. Any unauthorized use will be decided on a case-by-case basis and considered copyright infringement if it meets the criteria.

Articles 30 to 47-8 of the Copyright Act limit copyright and neighboring rights in the cases indicated thereunder, for the purpose of harmonizing the economic benefits of the author and the benefits of the society which uses the information. The list is limited. In that sense, cases in which the exercise of copyrights are acknowledged, although they may be far from "fair", are individually listed in detail, and rights are limited in only such cases. The limited list includes (but are not limited to): reproduction for private use; use for evaluation by a certain prospect licensee; use for experimental purposes; quotations; reproduction in school education; performances not for profit-making; reproduction for judicial proceedings; reproduction of artistic works in copyright assignment or license; reproduction by the owner of the reproduction of a computer program (install, backup, etc.); ephemeral reproduction for maintenance or repairs; and record of software works for execution of a program by duplication or transmission of a computer program.

With respect to neighboring rights, these are essentially limited in the same instances as above.

The right to demand compensation for damages for copyright infringement lapses by prescription if not exercised: within 3 years from the time when the right holder became aware of such damages and of the identity of the person who caused it; or within 20 years from the act of infringement.

For luxury brands, copyright protection is frequently used to protect its internet homepage, photography of the brands and catch copy of advertisements. In addition to them, although not so common, some artistic logos might be protected. If luxury brands retain an external designer to create their logo, the luxury brand should ask that designer to assign copyright and to commit not to exercise their moral rights.

3. DESIGN
3.1 Sources of law
The Design Act, the UCPA and the Copyright Act are the principal sources of law. Supreme Court precedents substantially function as sources of law.

Treaties take precedence over domestic laws, however, there are no hierarchical differences at moment.

3.2 Substantive law
The Design Act exclusively protects registered designs defined as "the shape, patterns or colors, or any combination of them, of an article which creates

an aesthetic impression through the eye" as long as it does not fall under the category of unregistrable designs.

The UCPA provides protection for unregistered design by prohibiting acts of unfair competition for 3 years after the date the goods were first sold in Japan, regardless of notoriety of the configuration. Well-known design or Famous design is also protected by the UCPA.

A design is protectable under the Copyright Act if the design is deemed as a copyrightable work.

To obtain a design right a design owner is required to show the design:
- creates an aesthetic impression through the eye;
- has industrial application;
- has novelty and is not easily created;
- is not identical with or similar to a part of a design which application has been filed prior to the date of filling of the said application;
- does not fall under the category of unregistrable design;
- complies with the requirement, one application per design; and
- there is no prior application.

A legal entity shall have a non-exclusive license on design rights obtained for designs made by an employee, which, by the nature of the said design, fall within the scope of its business and created by an act categorized as a present or past duty of the said employee. Besides this non-exclusive license, a legal entity is required to execute an assignment agreement to acquire the rights in the designs created by its employee, consultant, shareholder, director or supplier.

Unless a design falls under the category of non-exclusive license for "work for hire", any provision in any agreement, employment regulation or any other stipulation provided in advance that the right to obtain a design right or that the design rights for any design made by an employee shall vest in the employer, or that an exclusive license for the said design shall be granted to the employer, shall be null and void.

Besides the above, there is no specific requirement in the laws for a design assignment agreement to be valid.

An employee is entitled to receive reasonable remuneration where he assigns the design right or grants an exclusive license to the employer in accordance with an agreement, employment regulation or any other stipulation. The value of the remuneration shall not be considered unreasonable in light of circumstances where a negotiation between the employer and the employee took place in order to set among others, standards for the determination of the said remuneration and their disclosure, the opinions of the employee, regarding the calculation of the amount of the remuneration received and any other relevant circumstances.

Unless a design is protected under the Copyright Act, the designer shall not obtain moral rights.

Registered design protection lasts 20 years (15 years for the application filed before 31 March 2007) without the possibility of renewal.

Under the UCPA, unregistered design protection lasts 3 years from the date the goods were first sold in Japan unless the design of the goods is well-known or famous.

Copyright protection lasts for 70 years following the death of the author.

3.3 Enforcement

Actual copying is not always necessary to establish design infringement.

Under the Design Act, a design owner can exercise its exclusive right to manufacture or sell an article that is identical or similar to the registered design. Whether a registered design is identical with or similar to another design shall be determined based upon the aesthetic impression created by the designs through the eye of their consumers. There is no actual copying requirement.

Under the UCPA, it is prohibited to assign, lease, display for the purpose of assignment or leasing, trade in goods that imitate the configuration of another person's goods within 3 years from the date the goods were first sold in Japan (see Section 3.2 Design: Substantive law). In addition, if a design is considered as an indication of goods or services and is well-known or famous among consumers, an identical or similar design will constitute infringement. There is no actual copying requirement.

A design is enforceable against a trademark, a registered design/design patent, patent, domain name, trade name or other IP rights if these are infringing the design according to the Design Act, the UCPA or the Copyright Act.

However, the Design Act provides that one cannot enforce its registered design where that registered design or a design similar to that registered design, is similar or conflicts with another person's prior right with a previous filing date (i.e., registered design, patented invention or registered utility model, trademark right, or copyright).

In general, it must be noted that rarely do trademarks, patents, domain names and trade names fulfil criteria for designs (see definition at 3.2), and thus would not be held identical or similar to the allegedly infringed design under the Design Act.

A design can be enforced against its unauthorized use in social media, comparative advertising or parody, if such use falls under one of the categories of infringement under the Design Act, the UCPA or the Copyright Act.

There is no "repair clause" in Japan. The defenses that are available to an alleged infringer under the Design Act are general ones, for example: design right invalidity defense; prior use; prior application; or restriction on the effect of the design right restored by retrial.

A design owner cannot enforce their design right if it is deemed as abuse of right under the Civil Code.

For the protection under the UCPA, see Section 3.2 Design: Substantive law.

The right to demand compensation for damages lapses after 3 years from the time when the right holder became aware of such damages and of the identity of the person who caused it; or within 20 years from the act of infringement.

It is possible for a design holder to take action claiming both design infringement and copyright infringement and/or unfair competition for the same set of facts and bring parallel copyright proceedings and/or unfair competition proceedings.

Before the recent amendment of the Act, only one design was acceptable for one prosecution. However, with changes to modern industry, one design may be used for several products. Therefore, the amendment allows a design right owner to file several design prosecutions for one design.

4. RIGHT OF PRIVACY, PUBLICITY AND PERSONAL ENDORSEMENT

4.1 Sources of law

Case law in Japan does recognize the right of an individual to control the commercial use of his or her name, image, likeness, or other unequivocal aspects of one's identity.

There is no statutory source relating to the right of publicity - it is recognized through judicial precedents which refer to the Constitution, the Civil Code, the Copyright Act, or a combination of the three.

4.2 Substantive law

To own a right of publicity, persons must be of distinction or a celebrity, such as actors, performers, singers or sportspersons. Protection is granted to both Japanese and foreign individuals. It is not necessary for individuals to make commercial use of their identity. The Supreme Court (13 February 2004) held that only natural persons can enjoy a right of publicity and damages for its infringement.

Case law does not provide for protection of the right of publicity to extend after the individual's death, although post-mortem rights have been under discussion.

Although there are no judicial precedents officially recognizing post-mortem rights, in practice successors of the deceased individual often require prior approval and payment of royalties to use that individual's name or image, and have indeed obtained and been paid by publishers or TV companies.

The Supreme Court recognized publicity rights ("*Pink Lady*" Judgment, 2 February 2012) as originating from personal rights which are in principle not transferrable. However, the IP High Court partially admitted transferability of publicity rights regarding a baseball team and its players (Heisei 18(ne) No.10072).

An individual's right of publicity can be licensed for advertisement, distribution of merchandising products, derived goods or productions (films, animations, CD's, etc.). There is no restriction on whether it must be exclusive.

There are no requirements for validity.

Given the particular nature of publicity rights, a licensor can withdraw the consent to its use whenever the licensor's image, goodwill or name is objectionable, namely defamatory, obscene or unlawful and/or their reputation damaged. In order to avoid this issue, a clause requiring prior written approval for usage should be included and the possibility to withdraw in case of breach.

Following the death of the licensor, since post-mortem rights do not currently exist in Japan, in principle the contract becomes unenforceable.

The agreement may expressly provide whether the agreement binds successors.

There is no set length of protection or post-mortem rights so the rights are likely to lapse after the death of the assignor.

In the event heirs have an independent right over a deceased individual's name, image, likeness, or other unequivocal aspects of their identity, a licensing agreement should expressly provide for how to deal with this situation. If there is no express prior clause, the licensee or assignee may be faced without any rights.

4.3 Enforcement

Since publicity rights aim to protect financial value, the right of publicity is infringed where use is made without the right holder approval, in cases where the image is used for promoting a product to attract audience or customers.

It is not strictly necessary to prove that an individual's name, image, likeness, or other unequivocal aspects of one's identity have a commercial value to obtain an injunction or other remedies for the unauthorized use. However, as an example, the Yokohama District Court (Hensei 1 (wa) No.581) ruled that a poet did not have any right of publicity as poets do not control their name like a celebrity who uses his or her name in order to attract an audience.

The issue of whether the use of a prominent person's name or likeness is actionable should be determined by weighing the interest in exclusively controlling one's name or likeness against the guarantee of freedom of expression and the burden that prominent members of society may reasonably be expected to bear.

Use in news report or literary works is guaranteed by freedom of expression. The alleged infringer must demonstrate lack of intent to free ride on the individual's promotional value.

Limited use of photos and names is allowed with reasonable purpose and extent.

As an example of the current issues that celebrities and others face when exercising their right of publicity when working with luxury brands, the IP High Court found that publicity of Jill Stuart and using their photography without authorization constituted publicity infringement. The infringer was a long term experienced local distributor. This distributor finally obtained trademarks for Jill Stuart by assignment from Jill Stuart brand. However, Jill Stuart terminated the distribution agreement after the trademark assignment. IP High Court found publicity infringement, and recognised that Jill Stuart damages were around JPY1,000,000 (10K USD).

5. PRODUCT PLACEMENT

There are no legislative provisions on product placement in Japan. The use of "subliminal techniques" in broadcasting is generally prohibited in Japan, although there is no specific regulation regarding surreptitious advertising or product placement.

There are several self-regulation industry bodies which restrict advertising of certain products due to their nature and in order to protect minors. For example, the tobacco industry and alcohol industry have self-regulation.

In the event another party fails to perform the agreement, assuming there is an express agreement regulating the product placement, the damaged party may sue the non-compliant party for breach of contract and IP rights infringement in order to obtain an injunction order and/or damage remedies.

Since there is no restriction on product placement and no criticism against product placement, luxury brands provide a product/brand to Japanese TV or movies at a certain level. As of the present time, there is no specific concern in this respect.

6. PROTECTION OF CORPORATE IMAGE AND REPUTATION

Publicity and Privacy rights are protected under interpretation of Article 13 of the Constitutional law for the right to "life, liberty, and the pursuit of happiness" and for the right for people to be "respected as individuals."

There is no case that recognizes the right of publicity for corporations or legal entities.

It is generally possible to include specific clauses in agreements aimed at protecting the corporate image/reputation of one of the parties, under freedom of contract principles. One might include prohibition to sell the products to re-sellers whose image is below a certain defined standard and this clause is common in a selective distribution contract and can be included in a "right of publicity" agreement provided it does not contravene provisions of the Antimonopoly Act.

Prohibition to sell below a certain price, or to do so outside of specific time periods, and prohibition to buy non original – but otherwise legitimate – spare parts and components are both possible, provided it does not constitute an infringement of the Antimonopoly Act.

Article 420-1 of the Civil Code provides that the parties may agree on the amount of the liquidated damages with respect to the failure to perform the obligation. However, if the claiming party has partially contributed to the loss suffered, the principle of contributory negligence will work to reduce the amount of recoverable damages.

For luxury brands concerned about the secondary market, this is protected by First Sale Doctrine, which is not specified in legislation but protected by case law. Repair and reconditioning services are also allowed, however, redesign for sales is not allowed.

AUTHOR BIOGRAPHY

Koichi Nakatani
Koichi Nakatani is a partner of Momo-o Matsuo & Namba, representing many fashion brands in Japan. He has 25 years of international legal experience in IP law. He obtained a L.L.B from Keio University in 1992 and a L.L.M. for Intellectual Property Law and Policy from the University of Washington in 2007.

NETHERLANDS

Tjeerd Overdijk, Herwin Roerdink
& Nadine Reijnders-Wiersma
Vondst Advocaten

NETHERLANDS

1. TRADEMARK

1.1 Sources of law

The Netherlands is a member of the Benelux union, along with Belgium and Luxembourg. Registered Benelux trademarks are protected by the Benelux Convention on Intellectual Property Rights. Additionally, the trade name of a company is protected in the Dutch Trade Name Act. Furthermore, a company can register a community trademark for the entire EU territory, under the EU Trademark Regulation. The Netherlands is member of the Paris Convention on Protection of Industrial Property, the Agreement on Trade-Related Aspects of Intellectual Property Rights (TRIPS), as well as the Madrid Agreement and Madrid Protocol.

In the Benelux, use as a source of trademark rights is not recognized. Nevertheless, the non-use of a trademark for an uninterrupted period of five years can lead to lapse of the right. Furthermore, the registration of a trademark that is already in use can lead to filing in bad faith, which renders the right null and void.

1.2 Substantive law

Benelux law and practice contain a distinction regarding well-known trademarks to a certain degree, in the sense that the owner of well-known and registered trademarks can take action against the use of another trademark, on the grounds that their trademark is famous/well-known, and the opponent either takes unfair advantage of the use or the use is detrimental to the distinctive character or repute of the trademark.

In general, trademarks belonging to the luxury industry do not enjoy a broader range of protection. There is one exception, however: a trademark owner may not oppose the resale of products that have been put on the market in the EU by them or with their consent. However, in its landmark *Dior*-judgment the ECJ ruled that trademarks with an 'aura of luxury' can be excluded from this exhaustion rule in cases in which the reseller causes serious damage to the reputation of the trademark.

1.3 Enforcement

The court is not required to use witness statements, affidavit or expert evidence to establish that a trademark is entitled to broader protection. In examining whether the sign has a reputation, the national court must take into account all the relevant circumstances of the case, If, for the purpose of this test, the court deems it necessary to call witnesses and use expert evidence, the court is free to do so.

A trademark can be enforced against a domain name, provided that the use of the trademark takes an undue advantage or is detrimental to the distinctive character or reputation of the trademark.

A trademark can be enforced against a trade name when the general requirements for trademarks infringement are fulfilled without a valid reason. When the trade name is older than the trademark, there is such valid reason, and the trademark cannot be enforced.

A trademark can be enforced against other distinctive signs when the general requirements of trademark infringement are fulfilled.

A trademark can be enforced against its use in a metatag if the use of the trademark takes an unfair advantage or is detrimental to the distinctive character or reputation of the trademark.

A trademark can be enforced against its unauthorized use in social media if there is infringement, which includes the existence of a risk of confusion. Enforcement may only be initiated against the user posting the content, not against the social media network itself.

In general, comparative advertising is allowable under Dutch and Benelux law under certain conditions, namely that it may not cause confusion to the public without a due cause and may not take unfair advantage of the reputation of a trade. Also, that the advertisement may not cause confusion and goods or services may not be presented as counterfeit.

Trademark law in the Benelux has no parody exception.

The slavish imitation of a design can lead to unfair competition and is an unlawful act if the "imitated" product has its own place in the market, the imitation causes confusion among the public, and the imitation was avoidable, without impairing the soundness and usefulness of the product. It is possible to bring parallel proceedings.

Current issues for luxury brands. The registrability and scope of protection of trademarks is a constant theme for vigilance.

On one hand, it is harder to obtain trademark rights as the Trademark Office, the Bureau of Intellectual Property, is becoming more and more choosy and critical when it comes to distinctiveness in order to prevent generic words or names being monopolized by individual brand owners. Nowadays, it is often much more difficult to create a distinctive mark by adding a few figurative elements to a non-descriptive word or term.

On the other hand, the realm of trademarks seems to become bigger as the defence that a sign is purely used as a decorative element is less easily accepted, which is good news for the owners of trademarks for luxury goods.

However, the owners of brands for luxury goods may have to accept that their trademarks are being mocked or derided by opinion makers and artists and in many such cases the freedom of information and press have become important elements in deciding such disputes, for example in the Dom Perignon case decided by the CJEU. This is clearly a development that limits the scope of protection for brand owners.

Another area of concern is the enforcement options for infringements that occur on online platforms, online auctions and social media, in particular the options under strict privacy rules and the limited liability of the providers of online market places, which makes it more difficult to obtain the necessary information on the identity of trademark infringers.

2. COPYRIGHT

2.1 Sources of law

The principal source of law in the Netherlands is the Dutch Copyright Act. Relevant international treaties are the Berne Convention, Universal Copyright Convention and the TRIPS Agreement.

When conflict arises, international treaties take precedence in the Netherlands.

2.2 Substantive law

Dutch law provides for an open list of copyrightable works, listing works in the field of literature, science and art. This includes applied arts.

Objects of industrial, fashion or accessory design are copyrightable if they fulfil certain requirements, for example a work must be amenable to human perception, have its own original character and bear the personal stamp of the creator.

The right to exploit is covered by copyright, that is, to publish and copy the work. Additionally, the author of the work has moral rights, including the right to attribution and the right to oppose alterations of the work. Lastly, makers of graphic works or fine arts have a resale right.

A legal entity may obtain the shareholder's copyright in its work when works are made public as originating from it, without naming any natural person (the shareholder/employee/contractor) as the creator. However, there must be a connection between the work of the shareholder and the legal entity in order to establish that the work of the legal entity originated in the public domain.

A director can be described as an employee. Only a person who is a director-major shareholder, or occupies a similar position, is not considered an employee.

Suppliers will need a specific copyright assignment agreement to transfer the copyright.

For a copyright assignment agreement to be valid it must be in writing and signed by both parties. Since 2015, the Copyright Act also contains provisions on agreements with authors. The author has the right to receive a fair remuneration. Furthermore, terms that are unreasonably onerous for the creator are open to be nullified.

An author can only partly transfer or waive their moral rights; the right to attribution can be waived. The right of the maker to oppose alteration of the work can only be waived insofar as it concerns changes in the work or in the designation of the work.

Copyright protection in the Netherlands expires 70 years after the makers death or, when no maker is known, 70 years after the first publication of the work.

2.3 Enforcement

There are no registration formalities necessary to obtain or enforce a copyright.

Objects of industrial designs are considered 'works' in the Netherlands and therefore capable of protection by copyright if they meet certain requirements, such as a work must be amenable to human perception, have its own original character and bear the personal stamp of the creator.

Actual copying is not a necessary requirement to establish infringement (but would constitute infringement *per se*). Editing or copying in altered form may also constitute infringement provided that the overall impression is the same as that of the original work.

The owner of a copyright may claim infringement of their copyright in case a trademark encompasses a copy of the work, for example in cases of figurative trademarks. Obviously this is only relevant in case the copyright holder and the trademark holder are not the same person/entity.

The owner of an older copyright can invoke the invalidity of a design and/ or may claim that a design constitutes a copy of their work and should therefore be deemed to infringe the copyright. The holder of a registered design is also presumed to be the copyright holder. This presumption does not hold up against the actual creator of the work, if he can prove that he is the owner of the copyright.

Copyright cannot be enforced against patent.

A copyright may be enforced against its use in a domain name, trade name or pseudonym, when the name is a copyrighted work, although it might be hard to prove that a single word or short combination of words is original enough to be copyright.

The unauthorized use of a copyrighted work on social media may be considered a publication within the meaning of the Copyright Act.

In terms of comparative advertising if the advertisement discloses a copyrighted work without the consent of the copyright owner, the copyright can be enforced.

Use in parody is an exception under Dutch copyright law, if the use of the work is in accordance with what is reasonably permissible according to the rules of social discourse. When assessing a reliance on the parody exception, a fair balance must be struck between the interests of the copyright holder, on the one hand, and the freedom of expression on the other hand. To this end, all circumstances of the case must be taken into account.

In terms of defences available to alleged infringers Dutch copyright law does not contain a fair use-doctrine. Limitations to copyright are listed exhaustively. Moreover, the Dutch courts are used to apply the three-step test of Article 5 para 5 of the Infosoc Directive which says that the application of a limitation should not conflict with a normal exploitation of the work and does not unreasonably prejudice the legitimate interests of the author.

Under some circumstances enforcement actions can be held to be abusive and like any right holder a copyright owner should stay away from abusing his right. There is a general statute of limitation for tort actions of 5 years after the occurrence of the infringement or 5 years after the right holder has become aware of the infringement and the wrongdoer.

Current issues for luxury brands. In the area of copyright we see a trend that the Dutch courts are moving towards higher thresholds for affording copyright protection to designs of products. This development is also relevant for manufacturers and designers of luxury goods, as they might see a lessening of the number of designs which will be afforded protection on the basis of copyright.

Furthermore, the manufacturers of luxury goods may have to accept products being derided by opinion makers and artists and, in many such cases, the freedom of information and press have become important elements in deciding disputes, e.g. in the *Dom Perignon* case decided by the CJEU. This is clearly a development that limits the scope of protection for copyright owners.

Another area of concern is the enforcement options for infringements that occur on online platforms, online auctions and social media, more in particular the options under strict privacy rules and the limited liability of the providers of online market places, which makes it more difficult to obtain the necessary information on the identity of infringers.

More in general, there is a trend to afford lower cost awards to IP right holders, which makes it more costly to pursue infringements of the copyright for their products. This comment is also valid for trademarks and designs.

3. DESIGN

3.1 Sources of law

Principal sources of law and regulation related to designs are the BCIP at Benelux-level and the Community Design Regulation at EU-level. Furthermore the TRIPS Agreement and the Paris Convention are relevant sources of law, as well as the Hague-Agreement and the Locarno-Agreement.

The Paris Convention and the TRIPS Agreement have priority in the event of conflicting laws.

3.2 Substantive law

Under Dutch and Benelux law, only registered designs are protected. Products protectable by way of registered design are the appearance of objects or parts of products, derived in particular from the lines, outline, colors, shape, texture or materials of the product or its ornaments. Excluded from protection are connectors, interfaces and external features of a product that are determined solely by their technical function.

To obtain a valid registered or, where applicable, unregistered design right, the design needs to be new (novel) and have its own character.

The employer is considered the designer if an employee creates a model or drawing in his function.

If a design or drawing is designed to order, the person who placed the order is considered the designer. This is only the case if the design is ordered to be used in trade or industry, which means the client is considered the designer only if he continues to market the object made according to the design.

A design assignment agreement must be written and cover the entire Benelux-area to be valid. Registration is not required, although a transfer of design rights has no third party effect if it is not registered.

When drafting a design assignment agreement with employees, consultants, shareholders, directors and suppliers it is important to obtain as much information as possible about the existence, validity and title of the rights.

The designer can only partly transfer or waive their moral rights - the right to attribution can be waived.

The registration and the protection lasts for five years after the application date, and can be extended with consecutive terms of five years, with a maximum of 25 years.

An unregistered design protection (at EU-level) lasts for 3 years.

3.3 Enforcement

Holders of unregistered designs can only act against deliberate imitation of their design. Holders of registered designs can oppose the use of a product in which the design is incorporated or to which the design is applied and which has the same appearance as the registered design, or which does not produce upon the informed user a different overall impression.

A design can be enforced against a newer design. A design cannot be enforced against a patent, domain name or tradename since these rights do not cover what is covered by design protection.

A design can be enforced against its unauthorized use in social media if the requirements for finding infringement have been met. The publication or offering of a design through social media can constitute an infringement in the same way as in the analog world or other media platforms.

Designs may be used by a person other than the right holder for the purpose of illustration, provided this is compatible with fair trade practices. Use in comparative advertising can, under certain circumstances, constitute an unfair trade practice.

There is no legal parody exception in Benelux design law, but the enforcement of a design against use in parody may possibly infringe free speech.

The exclusive right to a design does not include the right to oppose acts done privately and for non-commercial purposes. A design right cannot be enforced against its use in repair parts or further marketing of products that have been put into circulation in the EU or EEA by them or with their consent.

Under certain circumstances enforcement actions can be held to be abusive and, like any right holder, a design right owner should stay away from abusing their right. There is a general statute of limitation for tort actions of 5 years after the occurrence of the infringement, or 5 years after the right holder has become aware of the infringement and the wrongdoer.

A design holder in the Netherlands may combine design infringement and copyright infringement and/or unfair competition for the same set of facts in the same action. It is therefore not necessary to bring parallel and/or separate copyright infringement and/or unfair competition proceedings as they may be combined in a single proceeding before a Dutch court.

Current issues for luxury brands. Luxury goods are typically the kind of products which are eligible for multiple forms of protection: trademark, design rights and copyrights. Each of these protection systems has its own advantages and drawbacks, so it is always a challenge to make the right choices when it comes to obtaining protection.

Design rights seem to have become less popular as it is more difficult to assess in advance the value of design rights in addition to copyrights and trademarks.

Also, a particular area of concern is how to define the interested circle or the relevant public or part thereof that can sometimes be decisive for the outcome of a design right infringement case. There are some decided cases from Dutch courts which call for a quite specific approach on this subject, which may be interesting for owners of design rights for luxury goods. The reason: the more specific the target group that is viewed for the purpose of determining the part of the relevant public and the general impression conferred on it by a certain design, the bigger the scope of protection for the design in question will become.

Another development that may be viewed with interest and which offers a brighter perspective for owners of design rights is the protection accorded to parts of products, such as the shape of a specific part of the hood of the car, which increases the possibilities for manufacturers of luxury goods against the supply of non-original parts. Such was the ruling in the recent *Ferrari* case decided by the ECJ.

Furthermore, in the same way as for trademarks, an area of concern for owners of design rights is the enforcement options for infringements that occur on online platforms, online auctions and social media, in particular the options under strict privacy rules and the limited liability of the providers of online market places, which makes it more difficult to obtain the necessary information on the identity of trademark infringers.

NETHERLANDS

4. RIGHT OF PRIVACY, PUBLICITY AND PERSONAL ENDORSEMENT

4.1 Sources of law

The law in the Netherlands does not recognize the right of an individual to control the commercial use of their name, image, likeness, or other unequivocal aspects of one's identity. However, a person who has been portrayed has a so-called portrait right, right to privacy and personality rights.

4.2 Substantive law

No additional conditions exist to "own" a portrait right. The individual has to satisfy they have a reasonable interest to invoke their portrait right.

In considering whether the right of publicity survives the death of the individual, Dutch copyright law distinguishes two different situations:

- If the picture was commissioned the portrait may not be exploited without prior consent of the surviving relatives within ten years. After that period, the portrait may be exploited without such consent.
- If the picture was not commissioned the surviving relatives also have the right to invoke the portrait right if they have a reasonable interest to do so but are always bound to consent, regardless of whether ten years have passed.

An individual cannot assign their right of publicity in whole or in part. They can consent to the exploitation (i.e. publication) of their portrait, and the portrait may not be exploited without such consent if the portrait was commissioned. If the portrait was not commissioned, it may be published, unless the legitimate interest of the portrayed or their surviving relatives opposes such publication.

A(n) (exclusive) license/assignment to promote or exploit the intellectual property and portrait right of a person can be granted, either on an exclusive basis or on a non-exclusive basis.

For an agreement to be valid the licensee needs to grant a representative power of attorney, ideally by notary deed or draw up a license agreement.

Like any agreement, a license or consent may be terminated by revoking or withdrawing it.

In the event of the death of the licensor the agreement may continue (but depending on its terms) and it will be up to the heirs to decide for how long the right of publicity can continue to be exploited.

In the event of the death of the assignor the agreement will continue, unless it includes a clause under which the death triggers an option to terminate the agreement.

The law states the surviving relatives (as mentioned above) can invoke the portrait rights individually.

After the death of the person portrayed, only their spouse, registered partner, parents and children can oppose the use.

4.3 Enforcement

To derive protection from their portrait right, the person portrayed must have a reasonable interest. This may be a commercial interest, but it can also be a non-commercial interest such as the protection of privacy of the person concerned, or their next of kin. Other circumstances that may be taken into account are that there is a danger of mockery, when there is nudity involved, or an undesirable associative or disqualifying context.

The alleged infringer can defend themselves by arguing that consent was given by the person portrayed, or by arguing that the person portrayed has no reasonable interest or "provoked" the disclosure himself.

5. PRODUCT PLACEMENT

Product placement is not allowed in the media offerings of public media organisations.

Product placement is permitted for commercial media companies, which may include those providing commercial media services on demand if they meet the criteria set out in the Policy rule on classification of commercial media services on demand.

Product placement in commercial media offerings is restricted in several ways. Firstly, the advertisement must be recognizable as such. Secondly, the usage of subliminal techniques is prohibited and thirdly, surreptitious advertising is banned.

For content published after 19 December 2009, additional conditions must be taken into account. Product placement is not allowed in news and current affairs programs, programs intended to inform consumers objectively and impartially about products or services, programs of a religious or spiritual nature, and programs intended for children under twelve years of age. The placement of products within a program may only occur if the editorial statutes of the institution include safeguards for the editorial independence. Furthermore, product placement is not permitted for medicinal products, medical treatments, nor for alcoholic beverages between 06:00 AM and 9:00 PM.

In the event a party fails to perform an agreement, the brand owner may terminate the agreement or file a claim for the agreement to be dissolved. He may also claim compensation for damages as a result of the breach of contract.

Unique concerns faced by luxury brands. The recent implementation of the Audiovisual Media Services Directive in the Dutch Media Act may lead to difficulties for luxury brands. All economical services where the main purpose is to provide videos that have a mass media character, provide a catalogue through which the videos are ordered, and with editorial responsibility are to be regarded as commercial media services. As a consequence, channels on video platform services are more quickly subject to the product placement regime of the Dutch Media Act.

6. PROTECTION OF CORPORATE IMAGE AND REPUTATION

Laws regarding right of publicity and/or privacy do not extend to legal entities/corporations.

It is possible to include specific clauses in agreements aimed at protecting the corporate image/reputation of one of the parties and this is often done in (selective) distribution agreements or sponsorship agreements. Such agreements may not violate EU competition law. The CJEU has formulated the criteria that a selective distribution system must meet.

The prohibition to sell below a certain price is not allowed, since it is considered a hardcore restriction of the competition. A prohibition to sell outside of a specific time period is not a hardcore restriction and may be allowed if it does not have anti-competitive effects.

The prohibition to buy non original – but otherwise legitimate – spare parts and components is not considered a hardcore restriction, so it may be allowed if it does not have anti-competitive effects.

Stipulated fine clauses may be included in all sorts of agreements, including distribution agreements. Under Dutch law such clauses are not interpreted purely linguistically, but in light of the parties' intentions.

AUTHOR BIOGRAPHIES

Tjeerd Overdijk

Tjeerd Overdijk studied Law at the Leiden University and has been a lawyer since 1984. He has been an all-rounder in the field of intellectual property for more than 25 years, with a special interest in matters balancing on the edge of intellectual property and information technology, such as the enforcement of rights on software, trademark and copyrights on the Internet, database rights, software and business method patents and trademark and domain name disputes. He is a WIPO panelist for domain name disputes in .nl. Tjeerd is also one of the very few specialists in plant variety rights. He is a co-author of the loose-leaf intellectual property textbook 'Intellectueel Eigendom' (chapter on copyright) and of a monograph on Intellectual Property & ICT (chapter on patent law).

Herwin Roerdink

Herwin specializes in intellectual property, (online) marketing and data protection. He advises and litigates on the protection, exploitation and enforcement of trademark rights, copyrights, design rights and trade name rights. He also has a strong focus on anti-counterfeiting, data protection, (online) marketing, licensing, franchise and distribution. He has represented several clients in enforcement proceedings by the Authority for Consumers & Markets (ACM) and the Dutch Data Protection Authority (AP) as well as representing clients in various sectors, including FMCG, fashion/luxury goods, internet, media/entertainment, automotive and charity. He frequently lectures and publishes on intellectual property, marketing and data protection law. Herwin is co-author of Sweet & Maxwell's book 'Data protection & Privacy', the book '50 questions on privacy', the chapter 'The trustee and intellectual property' in the Insolvency Practicebook and the Copyright chapter in the loose-leaf textbook Intellectual Property.

Nadine Reijnders - Wiersma

Nadine studied Civil Law and Information Law at the University of Amsterdam. During her studies, she was author of the biweekly Kluwer IP Patent Case Review newsletter. Nadine started her career as an attorney-at-law at and Amsterdam based IP boutique, where she worked mainly in the (pharmaceutical) patent litigation practice. As per September 2014, Nadine joined Vondst. She advises and litigates in the broad intellectual property practice, i.e. trademarks, designs, copyrights and patents.

SOUTH KOREA

Won Joong Kim & Dae Hyun Seo
Kim & Chang

1. TRADEMARK

1.1 Sources of law

Trademarks may be protected under the Korean Trademark Act (TMA), while well-known marks can be protected under the Unfair Competition Prevention and Trade Secret Protection Act (UCPA). International conventions to which Korea is a signatory, such as the Agreement Establishing the World Intellectual Property Organization, the Paris Convention for the Protection of Industrial Property, the Madrid Protocol on the International Registration of Marks and the Agreement on Trade-Related Aspects of Intellectual Property Rights (TRIPS), have the same legal effect as domestic laws.

While protection is provided to non-registered marks that are famous in Korea, "use" *per se* will not be recognized as a source of a trademark right in Korea.

1.2 Substantive law

The law makes a distinction between "well-known" and "famous" marks. A well-known mark is considered as a mark that is recognized by a majority of customers in the relevant industry, while a famous mark is recognized by a majority of customers within and beyond the industry.

Trademarks belonging to the "luxury industry" do not enjoy a broader range of protection.

1.3 Enforcement

The fame of the mark must be established in order to prove that a trademark is entitled to broader protection in Korea. The courts generally review sales and advertising figures, sales volume and duration, global registration status, and any other evidence showing that the mark was exposed to local traders and consumers as an indication of source.

The well-known status of a mark may be substantiated by the above evidence or in an affidavit duly executed by a person who has access and knowledge of such information. Oral testimony and expert evidence are also acceptable forms of evidence.

For <.co.kr> or <.kr> level domain names, trademark owners may file an administrative proceeding with the Internet Dispute Resolution Committee (IDRC) or file a civil action based on the UCPA and/or the Internet Address Resources Act (IARA) in order to transfer or de-register an unauthorized domain name that contains their trademark. An IDRC action is similar to a Uniform Domain Name Dispute Resolution Policy (UDRP) proceeding, and petitioners may rely on claims under the IARA that are similar to those under the UDRP, except that trademark infringement claims can be also raised under the IARA. The anti-cybersquatting provision of the UCPA can also be applied as long as the trademark is well-known to Korean consumers.

A registered trademark can be enforced against a trade name, but TMA Article 51 limits the extension of such trademark right if the trade name indicates the trademark in a common manner.

A trademark can be enforced against other distinctive and source-identifying signs.

A trademark cannot be enforced its use as a metatag.

If the trademark is used as a source identifier in social media in relation to similar/identical goods/services, then the owner may have a claim for infringement. Also, if the trademark is used to cause dilution or mislead the public as to an affiliation between the trademark owner and account holder, then there may be claims available under the UCPA.

With unauthorized use in comparative advertising the key is to establish whether the trademark was used as a source identifier in the advertisement. Most comparative advertisements do not use a third party's trademark as a source identifier, and thus it is generally difficult to assert infringement under these circumstances. The trademark owner may explore other regulatory claims as well as Article 2(1)(vi) of the UCPA, the Fair Labeling and Advertising Act and other advertising related regulations if any of the statements in the advertisement are false.

It is possible for a trademark to be enforced against its unauthorized use in a parody if the parody mark is used as a source identifier. The owner may also assert likelihood of confusion over the source of the goods and/or dilution under the UCPA. Further, the owner may seek redress under the "catch-all" provision of the UCPA, which prohibits acts of infringing another person's achievements through considerable effort and investment, in contravention of fair trade practice or competition order.

A trademark owner can claim both trademark infringement and unfair competition in the same civil and/or criminal proceedings. It is also possible to bring parallel and/or separate proceedings.

The issues that luxury brands face in expanding and protecting their trademark rights in South Korea include:
- Finding the proper protection of trademark rights to respond to the development of information technology, such as applying for new types of goods and services, and dealing with new types of infringement in virtual environments (for example, metaverse, NFTs, and so on).
- Luxury brands are also finding ways to collaborate with online platforms given that most infringement activities have moved online.

2. COPYRIGHT

2.1 Sources of law

The Korean Copyright Act (CA) is the relevant local law regarding copyrights, while Korea is also a member country of the Universal Copyright Convention, the Geneva Phonogram Convention, the TRIPS Agreement, the Berne Convention for the Protection of Literary and Artistic Works, the WIPO Copyright Treaty and the International Convention for the Protection of Performers, Producers of Phonograms and Broadcasting Organizations and the WIPO Performances and Phonograms Treaty.

In principle, the CA and treaties have equal effect and there is no order of priority. However, if there is a conflict between these sources, the more recent or special laws are applied depending on the circumstances or parties involved.

2.2 Substantive law

The CA non-exhaustively lists examples of categories of protected works according to the forms they take, but even if a type of work is not included in this list, it may still be protected under the Act. The list reads as follows:
- novels, poems, theses, lectures, recitations, plays, and other literary works;
- musical works;
- theatrical works, including dramas, dances, pantomimes, etc.;
- paintings, calligraphic works, sculptures, crafts, works of applied art, and other artistic works;
- architectural works, including architecture, architectural models, and design drawings;
- photographic works including photographs and other works prepared by similar methods;
- cinematographic works;
- maps, charts, design drawings, sketches, models, and other diagrammatic works; and
- computer program works.

Objects of industrial design may be copyrightable as applied art. The industrial design or applied art must possess the fundamental elements of a copyrightable work, which is "creativity" and "expression of human emotion or idea," in addition to having artistic value that is physically or conceptually separable from the function of the industrial article.

The rights of reproduction, public performance, broadcasting, transmission, exhibition, distribution, renting and making derivative works are covered by copyright. According to the CA, the copyright holder also has moral rights, which include the rights of public disclosure, preservation of integrity or identity of the work, and attribution of authorship.

The CA deems an employing legal entity, organization, or other person to be the "author" and own copyright in a work, if all of the following conditions are satisfied:
- the work is created by an employee within the scope of employment, subject to the employer's supervision;
- the work is published in the name of the employer (except computer program); and
- there is no separate or particular contract or employment regulation providing that the status of the author, or ownership of the copyright in, the work-for-hire should belong to the employee.

If the above three conditions are met, then the legal entity is the copyright holder of the work.

Consultants are not considered as an "employee" as identified in the above provision, and thus the legal entity would have to receive an assignment of the copyright to the work through a separate agreement.

Shareholders are not considered an "employee" as identified in the above provision.

If the director was subject to the employing legal entity's supervision, then it is possible for the director's work to be considered a work made for hire.

Suppliers are not considered an "employee" as identified in the above provision.

As long as the parties agree to an assignment of the copyright, a copyright assignment agreement does not have to satisfy any particular formalities to be valid. However, in the event that the copyright holder has executed duplicate assignment agreements, it is possible that protection would be granted only for the assignment that has been recorded with the Korean Copyright Commission.

It is not possible for an author to transfer or waive their moral rights.

Copyright protection lasts for the life of the author plus a term of 70 years after death. Works made for hire have a protection term of 70 years after the work is made public, but if the works have not been made public or published within 50 years of its creation, the protection term is then for 70 years after its creation.

2.3 Enforcement

The CA provides that a protected work may be registered with the Ministry of Culture, Sports, and Tourism, which delegates its authority for registration to the Copyright Council. Although a copyright deposit or notice is not required, a person who desires to register the copyright in a work must submit an application to the Copyright Council with specified information.

Industrial designs are capable of protection by copyright under certain conditions, and any type or form of evidence may be produced to establish the foregoing (see Section 2.2 Copyright: Substantive law).

Copyright infringement is assessed by proving that the infringer created its work based on a third party's copyright work, and that there is substantial similarity between the compared works. Actual copying is not necessary, and substantial similarity is sufficient to establish infringement.

Despite a valid trademark registration, if the trademark conflicts with a copyright of a third party that existed prior to the trademark application filing date, then the trademark registrant is not allowed to use their own registered mark without the copyright owner's authorization (Article 53 of the Trademark Act).

Despite a valid design registration, if the design conflicts with a copyright of a third party that existed prior to the design application filing date, then the design registrant is not allowed to use their own registered design without the copyright owner's authorization (Article 95 of the Design Protection Act).

There is no specific provision with regard to the enforceability of a copyright against a patent, domain name, trade name, pseudonym, or other IP right. However, in principle, the copyright holder's consent is necessary if the foregoing IP rights conflict with a copyright.

A copyright may be enforced against its unauthorized use in social media or comparative advertising, as long as the conditions identified above are met and there are no other exceptions applicable, such as fair use.

There is no settled law or precedent with regards to the use of a third party's copyright in parody. However, a lower court decision has acknowledged copyright infringement against a party's production of an album and music video that was a parody of a famous song.

The CA provides exceptions to copyright infringement. For instance, an alleged infringer may have an available defence against infringement if use of the copyright work was for any of the following uses: private, educational, library and other archival reproduction, non-profit performance and broadcasting, current news reports, reproduction for judicial proceedings, temporary sound or visual recording by a broadcaster, exhibition or reproduction of fine art, temporary reproduction on a computer, reproduction for the handicapped, and free use of public works.

The fair use defence is also included in the CA, and expressly permits the use of copyrighted works for the purposes of reporting, criticism, education and research, etc. to the extent that such use does not conflict with the ordinary use of the works, and does not unreasonably prejudice the legitimate interests of right holders.

There is no time limit for seeking injunctive relief in an infringement action. However, a claim for damages must be brought within three years from when the copyright owner became aware of the infringement, or ten years from the date of infringement.

Parallel importation of genuine goods are permitted under Korean law, and luxury brands are not able to stop parallel importers from using their trademarks within such permissible scope, but they have been able to stop parallel importers from using their copyright works (for example, an advertisement issued by the luxury brand owner) based on copyright infringement.

3. DESIGN

3.1 Sources of law

Product designs that are registered with the Korean Intellectual Property Office (KIPO) are protected in Korea under the Design Protection Act (DA). Unregistered designs can be protected under the UCPA and/or CA in certain circumstances. Further, Korea is a signatory to the Agreement Establishing the World Intellectual Property Organization and the Paris Convention for the Protection of Industrial Property, and thus they have the same legal effect as domestic laws.

In principle, the DA and treaties have equal effect. However, if there is a conflict between these sources, the more recent or special laws are applied depending on the circumstances or parties involved.

3.2 Substantive law

The subject matter protected by the DA is industrial designs. The DA defines "design" as "the shape, pattern, color, image, or a combination of these in an article (including part of an article) which produces an aesthetic impression in the sense of sight". A typeface can also be protected under the DA, as well as moving designs and image designs regardless of whether they are displayed on a screen or not. As for an image design that is not displayed on a screen, such image design should be used for the operation of a device or exhibits a function.

Unregistered designs cannot be protected by the DA, but under the UCPA, any act of assigning, renting, displaying, importing or exporting a product which imitates the appearance of another party's product (e.g., the shape, pattern, color, or combination of such attributes) within three years after the creation of a design is deemed to be unlawful.

In order to obtain a grant of a valid design registration, a design must possess novelty and creativity. More specifically, prior to the filing of the design application, such design must not be:
- identical or similar to one which has been publicly known or used in Korea or in a foreign country; or
- identical or similar to one which has been described in a publication circulated in Korea or in a foreign country.

Further, a design may not be registered where a person with ordinary skill in the particular field of design could have easily created the design from a widely known design in Korea, or from a design publicly known or used in Korea, or in a foreign country.

As for unregistered design rights, the "dead copy" provision (that is, a product which imitates the appearance of another party's product (e.g., the shape, pattern, color, or combination of such attributes) is not applicable where:
- the imitation product is manufactured more than three years after the date of manufacture of the original product; or
- the product shape is commonly used for the subject goods.

The basic principle underlying the Korean laws on in-service inventions is that intellectual property rights (including patents, utility models and designs) inherently belong to the employee who created the invention. That is, an employee has an inherent right to obtain a registration for their design.

There are two ways for an employer to have vested title to in-service inventions. One is to enter into a pre-invention assignment agreement with the employee, thereby the employee agrees to assign any and all future in-service inventions to the employer. The other is to adopt an employment rule (e.g. an invention compensation policy) expressly providing for employee-inventors' assignment of any and all future in-service inventions to the employer. When an employer succeeds in gaining the rights to the in-service invention in accordance with a contract or employment rule, the employee is entitled to "reasonable compensation" from the employer – even if the employer ultimately decides not to pursue a design registration and, instead, decides to keep the invention as a trade secret.

Consultants are not considered an "employee" as identified in the above provision, and thus the legal entity would have to receive an assignment of the design through a separate agreement. However, depending on the facts, the consultant's work may be considered an in-service invention if he/she was actually working for the legal entity as an employee.

If a director was subject to the employing legal entity's supervision, then it is possible for the director's work to be considered an in-service invention.

Shareholders and suppliers are not considered to be "employees", and thus the legal entity would have to receive an assignment of the design through a separate agreement.

As long as the parties agree to an assignment of the design, a design assignment agreement does not have to satisfy particular formalities to be valid. However, for the design assignment itself to be valid, the assignment must be recorded with KIPO.

The Korean Invention Promotion Act (KIPA) sets forth a set of rules governing two aspects:

- the procedural requirements for an employer to acquire ownership in and title to an in-service invention; and
- factors in determining reasonable compensation that the employee is entitled to when the employer acquires the in-service invention.

KIPO also has published guidelines in connection with in-service inventions. Therefore, KIPA rules and KIPO guidelines should be taken into consideration when drafting a design assignment agreement.

There are no moral rights in relation to designs.

Once registered, a design is protected for twenty years from the application filing date.

As discussed above, the "dead copy" provision is not applicable if the imitation product is manufactured more than three years after the date of manufacture of the original product.

3.3 Enforcement

It is an infringement of the rights to a registered design to use an identical or similar design without authorization from the owner of the registered design. Substantial similarity is sufficient to establish infringement.

As for protection of unregistered designs under the "dead copy" provision, the compared designs must be nearly identical.

According to Article 95 of the DA, a registered design or a design similar to the registered design may be enforced against another's trademark, design, patent, copyright, or utility model if an application for the foregoing was filed earlier than the filing date of the registration of the design concerned. In cases of conflict between the design right and other person's patent right, utility model right, trademark right, copyright, the owner of the registered design in question shall not commercialize the design without permission from the owner of the relevant design right, patent right, utility model right, trademark right or copyright, or without complying with Article 123 (trial for granting a non-exclusive license in connection with relevant design right, patent right, utility model right or trademark right).

There must be an infringement of the registered design right for a design to be enforced against its unauthorized use in social media, comparative advertising or parody.

There is no "repair clause" in Korea nor are there any comparable limitations. Invalidity of the design is the most common defence raised by alleged infringers.

An otherwise valid registered design can be deemed unenforceable if there are validity issues. There is no time limit for seeking injunctive relief in an infringement action. However, a claim for damages must be brought within three years from when the design registrant became aware of the infringement, or ten years from the date of infringement.

A design holder may file one action claiming design and copyright infringement, as well as unfair competition, for the same set of facts. It is possible to bring parallel and/or separate proceedings.

Current issues that luxury brands face in expanding and protecting their design rights include:
- Finding the proper protection of design rights to respond to the development of IT technology, such as applying for new types of designs and articles, and

dealing with new types of infringement in virtual environments (for example, metaverse, NFTs, and so on).
- Luxury brands are also finding ways to collaborate with online platforms given that most infringement activities have moved online.

4. RIGHT OF PRIVACY, PUBLICITY AND PERSONAL ENDORSEMENT

4.1 Sources of law

There is no law in South Korea recognizing the right of an individual to control the commercial use of his or her name, image, likeness, or other unequivocal aspect of their identity. Furthermore, the lower court decisions are also split on this issue of one's right to publicity, and there is no Supreme Court precedent in this regard.

For those lower courts that have recognized the right to publicity, they have relied on constitutional laws, such as personal rights, the right to pursue one's happiness, or the right to own property.

4.2 Substantive law

The lower court decisions that recognize the right of publicity have at minimum, required commercial value in such right. As such, there have been instances where the court has recognized the infringement of publicity rights even for non-public figures as long as there is commercial value in their name or likeness.

There is no statute or Supreme Court decision regarding the right of publicity and whether such right survives the death of the individual. Moreover, the lower courts that have addressed this issue are inconsistent as well.

Although not a Supreme Court decision, a lower court has held that it is possible to assign one's right of publicity.

It is possible for an individual to license their right of publicity. Such license can either be exclusive or non-exclusive, and it is common practice for celebrities that enter into contracts authorizing third parties to use their name, likeness, or other aspect of their identity.

There are no set requirements for an agreement involving the assignment/license of the right of publicity to be valid.

As there is no statute with regard to the right of publicity, there are no unique conditions and the parties are free to enter into an agreement according to their desired terms.

The lower courts are split on the issue of how to treat a license agreement following the death of a licensor or assignor. While one court ruled that the right of publicity extinguishes upon the right holder's death, another court has recognized that such right can be passed on to one's heirs.

There is no law or precedent in South Korea regarding the assignee's or licensee's position in relation to heirs that have an independent right over the deceased individual's publicity right.

Similarly, there is no Supreme Court decision on the right of publicity being transmissible *mortis causa*. A lower court decision has recognized that the right of publicity term corresponds to the copyright term, while others have not.

4.3 Enforcement

Although not a Supreme Court decision, some lower courts have enforced the right of publicity against infringing commercial use. Further, it would be possible to assert one's constitutional rights against a third party's unauthorized use of one's name or likeness despite lacking a commercial aspect.

The right to publicity is not recognized by law or precedents, but for those cases that have addressed this issue, the commercial value of one's name, image, or likeness was generally presumed for purposes of obtaining a remedy against its unauthorized use.

Rather than traditional modeling contracts that involve the celebrity's consent to use the celebrity in an advertisement for a certain period of time, new types of contracts are increasing where the celebrities themselves directly create the video or advertisement content relating to the luxury brand and publicize on their own online channel, social media, etc. This is one of the current issues facing luxury brands when working with celebrities.

5. PRODUCT PLACEMENT

Product placement is permitted if certain requirements are met under the Broadcast Act.

The Enforcement Decree of the Broadcast Act specifies various limitations with regards to product placement (e.g., the type of broadcast and product, and method). For instance, product placement is only permitted on programs related to entertainment and culture, and it is prohibited to refer to the product or recommend purchase/use. Also, the logo or brand shown on the product cannot exceed a quarter of the screen.

In the event the other party fails to perform the agreement the brand owner should give them an opportunity for corrective measures, then, if they have not been taken, the owner can terminate the agreement and also petition for damages incurred due to such failure to perform.

There has been a recent controversy in Korea involving advertisements by famous local YouTubers that failed to disclose the fact that they were compensated for offering a review of a particular product online. As a result, the Fair Trade Commission amended their review guidelines regarding labelling and advertising so that an advertisement would be considered unfair if a product is advertised without disclosing an economic relationship between the advertiser and product owner.

6. PROTECTION OF CORPORATE IMAGE AND REPUTATION

There is no law regarding right of publicity and/or privacy for legal entities/corporations. However, it may be considered an unlawful tort for a party to harm the reputation or credibility of a legal entity, and such party may be subject to damages.

It is generally possible to include specific clauses in agreements aimed at protecting the corporate image/reputation.

It is possible for a party to include a clause regarding re-sellers, but such condition may be perceived as an unfair trade practice prohibited by the

Monopoly Regulations and Fair Trade Law (MRFTL). When determining if there is a risk for impeding fair business practices under the MRFTL, the Korea Fair Trade Commission will review the totality of the circumstances, including the party's intent, purpose, and the effect of the party's actions, in addition to the nature of the product in question, transaction terms, and whether the party is in a dominant position within the relevant market, as well as the contents and degree of harm on the transacting party.

The MRFTL prohibits the maintenance of resale price, but will allow a business to implement actions to prevent its products from being sold higher than a certain price as long as there are business justifications.

Prohibition against buying non-original, but legitimate, spare parts and components are generally permissible, but depending on the circumstances, such prohibition may be considered a violation of the MRFTL for possibly hindering fair trade.

It is permissible to include a liquidated damages clause for protecting the reputation or corporate image of the other party in an agreement, and such provision is considered valid by a court. However, the court may ultimately order a decrease in the payment amount if it determines that the liquidated damages pursuant to the agreement is excessive compared to the market position of the parties, the proportion between actual damages compared to the liquidated damages amount, and expected amount of actual losses.

One of the unique concerns of luxury brands in the secondary market is that they are encountering a new type of trademark infringement issue involving third parties that recondition (reform or customization) old luxury handbags into new bags for sale.

AUTHOR BIOGRAPHIES

Won Joong Kim (Patent Attorney)
Ms. Kim is a trademark attorney in the firm's Trademark/Design Practice Group. Her practice focuses on trademark / design prosecution and domain matters. Ms. Kim also assists in litigation, enforcement, and dispute resolution cases involving intellectual property issues.

Dae Hyun Seo (Attorney)
Dae Hyun Seo is an attorney at Kim & Chang with a diverse range of experience in intellectual property practice, including trademark, patent, copyright, transactions/licensing, trade secret and unfair competition. Mr. Seo represents multinational corporations as well as major Korean companies and has also advised various domestic and international clients on all aspects of intellectual property law, including patents, trademarks, copyrights, trade secrets and unfair competition. Furthermore, he regularly advises IT companies, including game companies, on a wide range of legal issues relating to IP disputes and industry-specific issues such as licensing and governmental regulations.

SPAIN

Rubén Canales, Eleonora Carrillo, Carolina Montero,
Fernando Ortega & Ignacio Temiño
Jacobacci Abril Abogados

1. TRADEMARK

1.1 Sources of law

The primary sources are national and European Union law, as well as international treaties ratified by Spain. Specifically, the national statues are the Spanish Trademark Act 17/2001, of December 2001 and the Royal Decree No. 687/2002, of 12 July 2002, approving the regulation for implementing the Spanish Trademark Act.

The European Regulations applicable to Spain as a Member State of the European Union are the European Union Trademark Regulation 2017/1001, the European Union Trademark Delegated Regulation 2018/625 and the European Union Trademark Implementing Regulation 2018/626. In addition, the European Union law includes the relevant prior Directive approximating the laws of the Member States relating to trademarks 2015/2436.

The main international treaties applicable in Spain are:
- The Madrid Agreement Concerning the International Registration of Marks of 14 April 1891 as amended on 28 September 1979.
- The Protocol Relating to the Madrid Agreement Concerning the International Registration of Marks of 27 June 1989, as amended on 12 November 2007.
- The Common Regulations under the Madrid Agreement Concerning the International Registration of Marks and the Protocol Relating Thereto, as in force on 1 February 2019).
- The Trademark Law Treaty (TLT), of 27 October 1994.
- The Singapore Treaty on the Law of Trademarks, of 27 March 2006.
- The Nice Agreement Concerning the International Classification of Goods and Services for the Purposes of the Registration of Marks, of 15 June 1957, as amended by the Stockholm (1677) and Geneve (1977) Acts and as amended on 28 September 1979.
- The Madrid Agreement for the Repression of False or Deceptive Indications of Source on Goods, of 14 April 1891.

Last but not least, case law and doctrine are clarifying sources. Indeed, the case law of the Spanish Supreme Court, the Spanish Constitutional Court and the Court of Justice of the European Union complement the foregoing sources when interpreting the applicable law provisions and regulations, and the doctrine of law experts can also be used for such interpretation purposes by the Spanish Courts.

The Trademark Act provides the owner of an unregistered mark with the same rights granted to the owner or a registration only in the event that the unregistered mark is well-known in Spain within the meaning of Article 6bis of the Paris Convention. On the other hand, the level of protection of a well-known unregistered mark is lower than, and should not be confused with, the one regarding a (registered) trademark enjoying reputation.

An unregistered well-known trademark within the meaning of Article 6bis of the Paris Convention can be the basis of an opposition against the registration of a later trademark application, while an unregistered trademark having only a standard or low degree of distinctiveness cannot. However, in the case of a well-known unregistered trademark, the protection is limited to goods / services identical or similar to those for which the well-known character is acknowledged, as opposed to a reputed (registered) trademark which is also protected against goods or services different from those covered by the registration. Furthermore, proving that the unregistered mark was well known in Spain by the filing or priority date of the later application is a crucial condition to prevail in the opposition.

Therefore, an unregistered mark which is merely used but does not enjoy a well-known character in Spain is not considered an enforceable right, nor it is protected by the Spanish law. Any possible defence of such a mark would need to be sought in the Spanish Unfair Competition Act 3/1991 of 10 January 1991.

1.2 Substantive law

Until the reform entered into force in 2019, Spanish law distinguished between three kinds of registered trademarks:
- trademarks not enjoying any notoriety;
- well-known trademarks; and
- trademarks with a reputation.

The difference between the two latter categories was that well-known trademarks were those considered well-known by the relevant sector of the goods and services covered by the registration, while trademarks with a reputation were those which the public in general is considered acquainted with (irrespective of the market sector involved).

Starting from the reform, the Spanish Trademark Act was adjusted to be in line with the European Union law and now distinguishes only between two kinds of trademarks regarding their distinctiveness: trademark not enjoying a reputation and reputed trademarks.

Registered trademarks not enjoying reputation do not benefit from the special protection acknowledged to reputed trademarks, namely, they are protected only against later marks for goods or services identical or similar to those for which they are registered.

Registered trademarks which enjoy reputation do have an enhanced protection in Spain. They enjoy a broader scope of protection and can successfully be enforced against later third party marks, which cover or are used in connection with goods and/or services similar or different from those covered by the earlier registration, provided that the use of the later mark, without due cause, may take an unfair advantage from the reputation of the earlier trademark (free-riding) or cause a detriment to it (dilution, blurring or tarnishment). Likelihood of confusion is not a requirement to apply the enhanced protection attributed to reputed/famous registered trademarks.

Prior to the reform, the Trademark Act expressly provided that the more reputed a trademark is, the more different the products and services of a trademark application can be and yet allow the owner to successfully oppose the application. Despite this having been removed from the current provision, it will certainly keep being applied as a logic rule in the assessment of oppositions based on reputed trademarks.

Trademarks belonging to the "luxury industry" do not enjoy *per se* a broader range of protection, apart from that provided by law for standard trademarks, whether well-known or reputed. However, very often the "aura of luxury" surrounding these trademarks plays a positive role when it comes to successfully enforcing them, actually granting them a *de facto* broader and stronger protection.

The positive and persuasive effect of this almost psychological effect is often seen both among trademark examiners and Judges' decisions leading to a successful outcome for the luxury industry trademark owner.

1.3 Enforcement

In order to achieve an enhanced broader protection for reputed or famous trademarks, it must be proved that they are generally known by the relevant sector of consumers to which those products or services are destined, or that they are familiar to all the public in general (of any market sector), respectively. Sufficient proof of either of these two categories may include many kinds of evidence: oral testimony, affidavits, expert evidence, surveys amongst consumers, documentary evidence such as advertisements, sales data and market share, geographical scope and duration of use, marketing activities, advertising data investments, promotional material, advertising of any kind, references on Google or other search engines and in social media, certificates issued by chambers of commerce or well-known, famous and/or reputed trademarks associations, as well as independent published rankings of trademarks, among others. Case law precedents are also useful but not binding (neither for the SPTO or the Courts).

There is not a specific test or threshold that must be reached to establish that a trademark is entitled to broader protection because it is reputed or famous. In Spain, a trademark can be enforced against a domain name, a trade name and any other distinctive sign, as well as against company names. Enforcing a trademark against its use as a metatag and/or keyword is possible too but the use should be analyzed on a case by case basis, considering that Internet users are not so easily misled. A trademark can be enforced against its unauthorized use in social media where such use is for commercial purposes, according to the general standards of trademark infringement rules; when the use is for non-commercial purposes the enforcement might succeed only if it is denigrating or detrimental to the trademark or its owner. Comparative advertising is permitted in Spain (Unfair Competition Act, Law 3/1991, of 10 January, and the General Publicity Act, Law 34/1988, of 11 November) provided that the trademark is used in the market for the products or services of the competitor which are compared with the advertiser. The comparison must be made in an objective manner between one or several essential characteristics of the products or services, which are relevant, verifiable, and representative, including price.

It must be stressed that Spanish courts do not accept the simultaneous enforcement of the same facts under the Trademark Law and the Unfair Competition Law - the latter is usually restricted to unregistered trademarks and/or very specific acts outside the scope of the trademark protection.

2. COPYRIGHT

2.1 Sources of law

The principal sources of law and regulation relating to copyright are national and European Union law, and international treaties ratified by Spain. The relevant national statutes is the Spanish Intellectual Property Act, Royal Legislative Decree 1/1996, of 12 April 1996, currently in force after several amendments.

The main international treaties applicable in Spain are:
- Berne Convention for the Protection of Literary and Artistic Works of 9 September 1886.
- Geneva Universal Copyright Convention of 6 September 1952.
- Rome Convention for the Protection of Performers, Producers of Phonograms and Broadcasting Organizations of 26 October 1961.
- Agreement on Trade-Related Aspects of Intellectual Property Rights (TRIPS) of 15 April 1994.
- WIPO Copyright Treaty (WCT) and WIPO Performances and Phonograms Treaty (WPPT) of 20 December 1996.
- Beijing Treaty on Audiovisual Performances of 24 June 2012.

The case law of the Spanish Supreme Court and the Court of Justice of the European Union complement the above when interpreting the applicable laws and regulations.

The order of priority when a conflict arises is as follows:
- European Union Law and international treaties ratified by Spain;
- Spanish Constitution;
- the Spanish law provisions and regulations;
- custom;
- general principles of the law;
- case law; and
- doctrine.

2.2 Substantive law

Original literary, artistic or scientific works, expressed by any means or on any medium, are subject to copyright protection under Spanish law. The Spanish law provides an open list of examples of copyrightable works that includes books, speeches, conferences, music (with or without lyrics), dramatic plays and musicals, choreographies, theatrical plays, motion pictures and any audio-visual works, sculptures and paintings, drawings, cartoons, comics, projects, plans, architectural and engineering designs, graphics, maps and designs in connection with topography, geography and, in general, science, photographs and software.

Copyright is independent, compatible and cumulative with the industrial property rights that may exist on a work. Therefore, it is possible that objects of industrial, fashion or accessory design are capable of being protected by copyright provided that they are original artistic creations expressed by any means or on any medium. This means that the same requirements as the listed works are required to be protected by Copyright.

The rights covered by copyright consist of both moral and economical rights, which jointly grant full disposition and exclusive right to the exploitation of the work to the author, with no limitations except those established by the Law.

The moral rights are unwaivable and inalienable, and grant the author the right to:
- decide whether their work is to be disclosed and in what way;
- determine whether such divulgation is to be made with their name, under a pseudonym or sign or anonymously;
- claim of their authorship of the work;
- demand respect to the integrity of the work and object to any distortion, modification, alteration or attack on it that might be prejudicial to their legitimate interests or detract from their reputation;
- modify the work respecting the rights acquired by third parties and the requirements of protection of goods of cultural interest;
- withdraw the work from commerce by changing their intellectual or moral convictions; and
- access the unique or rare copy of the work when it is under someone else's possession, in order to exercise the right of disclosure or any other right that corresponds to them.

A legal entity acquires the economic rights in the works created by its employees only if this is expressly agreed in writing.

The copyright assignment agreement must be freely expressed in writing with clear transfer of the rights. The transfer of exploitation rights will be limited to those expressly indicated in the agreement, as well as its duration and territory. The assignment of rights will be considered as non-exclusive unless the exclusivity is expressly agreed.

The main precautions to consider when drafting a license of copyright are that the global assignment of economic rights on future works is forbidden by law, commitments not to create any future work will be null and void and assignment of economic rights will not cover any divulgation methods inexistent or not yet discovered at the time of the assignment, even if this is expressly agreed. Lack of mention of the duration of the assignment will limit it to five years, and lack of mention of the geographical scope will limit the assignment to the country in which the assignment was made.

Copyright protection lasts during all the author's life plus seventy years after his death.

This seventy years period is calculated from the first day of the year after the year in which the author deceases. Copyright of authors who died before 7 December 1987 has a longer protection, namely eighty years from the death of the author. However, there are two moral or personal rights that are perpetual, namely, the right of acknowledgment of their authorship and the respect to the integrity of the work.

2.3 Enforcement

In Spain, it is possible to obtain a copyright registration. However, this copyright registration is not required to create or enforce copyright, obtain damages for its infringement or any other relief. A copyright deposit is not required either; nevertheless, both the registration or deposit and a copyright notice are highly advisable for enforcement purposes.

The consequences for failure to apply for and successfully complete a copyright deposit or registration are that the plaintiff will have to prove the copyright (namely its content, authorship and date of creation and/or divulgation) through other means of evidence different from the registration or deposit.

Objects of industrial designs are as capable of protection by copyright as any other work. In order to prove that an object of industrial design is capable of protection by copyright the most advisable evidence is an expert opinion, although any other kinds of evidence may complement it.

Copyright infringement is assessed when sufficient substantial similarity exists between the two works. No actual copying is necessary to establish infringement. Proof of copying can, however, increase the economic compensation the infringer is condemned to pay the copyright owner. Furthermore, copying may also amount to or involve criminal responsibility.

Copyright can be enforced against a trademark, a design, a patent, a domain name, a trade name, a pseudonym and any other intellectual property right.

Any use of a copyrighted work requires the authorization of the author or the copyright holder. Thus, copyright can be enforced against its unauthorized use in social media, according to the general standards of copyright infringement rules.

Furthermore, use of copyright in comparative advertising with other copyright, due to the nature of copyright, would be almost impossible when respecting the rules on comparative advertising, which must always focus on objective proven facts, not subjective opinions or impressions.

In general, copyright is difficult to enforce against its unauthorized use in parody because the Spanish Intellectual Property Act expressly admits such parody, provided it does not create a risk of confusion with the original work or damage to the work or its author. This is hardly ever a black or white case. On the contrary, there is a great deal of uncertainty about the enforceability, because of the subjective component of the analysis of the parody. Therefore, enforcement of copyright against parody is in general far more difficult than enforcement of a trademark against it.

Fair use, fair dealing or similar doctrines do not exist in Spain, and only the defences mentioned above can play a successful role in the defence of an alleged infringer and are usually interpreted within rather narrow limits by Spanish Courts, so all use made must be for those mentioned purposes and be reasonable, not abusive, proportional with the result sought and, obviously, indicating the source: both the work and its author.

There are no grounds on which valid copyright can be deemed unenforceable, owing to any misconduct of the copyright holder. Only an express waive by the author to the exploitation rights so that the work becomes of free use can cause a partial unenforceability.

The time limit for bringing an infringement action is five years from the moment in which it could be taken. Usually, the moment in which it could be taken is considered to be when the copyright owner learnt about the infringement. However, a later time may also be admitted provided that for serious reasons beyond the copyright owner's control, the action could not have been taken despite the knowledge of its existence. Furthermore, an economic compensation can only be sought for the period of five years before the filing of the infringement action.

The current problems faced by luxury brands to extend and protect their copyrights are mainly found in the unauthorized uses of their works through the Internet or digital media, because despite the progress made for the protection of works in these media, today there are still difficulties for their proper protection. Fortunately, the regulations are being modified to avoid these unauthorized uses (or at least make it more difficult).

3. DESIGNS

3.1. Sources of law

In Spain the principal sources of law and regulation relating to design are Spanish Law 20/2003 on Legal protection of Industrial Designs, Spanish Regulation 1937/2004 and the Hague Agreement of November 6th 1925. International designs are constituted by two Acts currently in force: the Geneva Act of 2 July 1999, and the Hague Act of November 28 1960. The Spanish Supreme Court's decisions and the ECJ develop the Spanish sources of law regarding designs.

The priority of the sources of law are as follows:
- Law (International treaties, EU provisions and Spanish laws);
- Custom; and lastly
- General principles of law.

3.2. Substantive law

A design can protect the appearance of the whole or a part of a product resulting from the features of, in particular, the lines, contours, colours, shape, texture and/or materials of the product itself and/or its ornamentation (that is, pieces destined to be assembled into a complex product, packaging, get-up, graphic symbols, typographic typefaces).

Novelty and individual character, as far as it is defined in Spanish law (according to EU regulation), are necessary to enjoy the rights on both registered and unregistered designs.

The right to the Community design shall vest in the designer or his successor in title. Rights to designs developed by employees belong to the employer if it has been developed in the execution of employee's duties or following the instructions given by his employer (unless otherwise agreed by the parties).

Although there is no moral right, Spanish design law establishes the right of the author of the design to have their name included in the application. Whether the designer can waive their this right is something not included in the law nor clarified by the Courts

Regarding the possibility of assigning the rights on the design to third parties, the Spanish law states that it must be in writing to be valid and may only be opposed against third parties once the assign has been registered before the Spanish Patent and Trademark Office.

Protection of a Spanish registered design can last up to a maximum of twenty-five years from the application date (by paying official fees). Unregistered design protection lasts three years from the date on which the design was first made available to the public within the Community.

3.3. Enforcement

The holder of the design can ask for prohibiting the making, offering, putting on the market, importing, exporting or using a product which incorporates the design. In case of registered designs, products whose characteristics differ only in irrelevant elements will be considered identical to the design. Unregistered designs provide the right to prevent the acts referred before only if the contested use results from copying the design.

A design can be enforced against a trademark, another registered or unregistered design, a patent, a trade name, and other IP rights. Commercial use of a design in social media can also be enforced against according to the general standards of design infringement rules.

Although it is very uncommon, comparative advertising of designs would be possible if it meets the requirements stated in the Unfair Competition Law 3/1991.

Use in parody is an unauthorized use of the design, but in general terms would be admitted since parody does not meet commercial purposes. However, if the holder can evidence damages to the reputation of the design derived from the parody, payment of damages could be requested.

The defence available to an alleged infringer is essentially lack of similarity, apart obviously, from challenging the validity or ownership of the design. No other grounds exist apart from limitations of rights.

According to the law, the time limit for bringing an infringement action is five years from the moment in which it could be taken. Nevertheless, the case law states that there is no statute of limitation in case of continues infringement.

In general terms, acting against the same set of facts on the basis of design law, copyright and/or unfair competition is rejected by the Spanish courts.

4. RIGHT OF PRIVACY, PUBLICITY AND PERSONAL ENDORSEMENT

4.1. Sources of law

Spanish law recognizes the right of an individual to control the commercial use of their name, image, likeness, or other unequivocal aspects of one's identity.

The principal sources of law and regulation relating to the right of publicity are national and European Union law, and international treaties ratified by Spain, namely the Spanish Constitution, the Spanish Publicity Act, Law 34/1988, of 11 November, the Unfair Competition Act, Law 3/1991, of 10 January, and the Organic Law 1/1982 of 5 May, for the civil protection of the right to honor, personal and family privacy and self-image.

The case law of the Spanish Supreme Court and the Court of Justice of the European Union complement the above when interpreting the applicable laws and regulations if such interpretation is needed.

4.2. Substantive law

The right of publicity is inherent to any individual. An individual cannot pass their right of publicity in whole or in part. However, an individual can license their right of publicity, either on an exclusive or non-exclusive basis.

Although it survives the death of the individual, and is transmissible *mortis causa*, the heirs of the deceased individual own those rights in a limited manner, being entitled only to enforce them in specific situations (i.e. uses and actions damaging the reputation).

The requirements necessary for an agreement for the license of the right of publicity to be valid in Spain are those of any other agreement under Spanish law, namely, free will expressing clearly and unequivocally the licensed rights.

The main precautions to consider when drafting a license of the right of publicity are determining precisely the scope of the license (both geographically and the kind of use), duration and causes of termination, within which, importantly, setting up the exact terms in the event of any dishonorable conduct damaging the public image of the individual. Thus, at the very least, a termination right for this cause should be established, together with compensation for the damages the licensee may suffer as a consequence of that detriment to the licensor's public image, if they affected the licensee.

The licensor can withdraw the consent to its use at any moment, but if the withdrawal is not grounded on any authorized situation ruled in the license agreement, the licensor may be forced to pay damages to the licensee if there is not justified reason. The withdrawal will not affect the past uses and actions as it has no retroactive effect.

4.3 Enforcement

Standing to sue for a violation of the right of publicity corresponds to the individual or their successors. If the damage to the image of a deceased individual is serious and there are no successors, the public prosecutor may do so as well. An exclusive or even a non-exclusive licensee may be entitled to sue depending on if the license agreement stated so and in what terms and conditions. However, this is a very personal right, so even if it was agreed between licensee and licensor, a Judge may require the individual to join the proceeding as co-plaintiff.

The right of publicity can be enforced against commercial use of the individuals name, image, likeness, or other unequivocal aspects of their identity, such as their voice. It would be more difficult to enforce it against any other aspects of their personality, but the actual chances of success of the enforcement would depend on such aspect/s being analyzed on a case-by-case basis, and whether or not the public recognizes the identity of the individual.

It is not necessary to prove that that individual's name, image, likeness, or other unequivocal aspects of one's identity have a commercial value to obtain an injunction or other remedies for the unauthorized use.

Even though it is true that a commercial value is not necessary to achieve those goals, when such value can be assessed and it is significant, this may allow the individual to obtain a higher economic compensation for losses and damages, besides increasing the chances of an injunction being granted. In order to prove such commercial value, all kind of evidence may be produced and should be admitted by Spanish Courts, including oral testimony, affidavits, expert reports, or documentary evidence, among others.

The defenses available to the alleged infringer are basically freedom of speech, freedom of information and expression, fair use, especially of a public figure image for informative purposes, and parody, with variable chances of success depending on the specific circumstances of the case and the kind of use made.

5. PRODUCT PLACEMENT

The Spanish regulation configures product placement as a "right" of the audiovisual communication service providers as a manifestation of the broader "right to make commercial communications".

Product placement is regulated in Spain by Law 7/2010 of 31 March, General Law on Audiovisual Communication and the Royal Decree 1624/2011 approving the Implementing regulation of the law.

Product placement is allowed in motion pictures, short films, documentaries, television series, sports programs and entertainment programs, in exchange of a payment. Where no payment is agreed, only the free supply of certain products or services, such as material help to the production or awards, the products or services must have a significant value. When the program is produced by the service supplier the public must be informed of the existence of the product placement at the beginning and at the end of the program, and after advertising breaks too.

In other types of programs, product placement is only permitted in exchange of free provision of the products or services, as well as economic help for the production or awards of the program.

A new Preliminary draft of the General Law on Audiovisual Communication is being discussed that in its current version would generally allow product placement in all programming except news and programs with current news content, consumer protection programs, religious programs and children's programs.

Product placement must meet the following requirements:
- Not to condition the responsibility or editorial independence of the medium.
- Not to directly incite the purchase or rental of the products, giving undue prominence to them in the program.
- To indicate the existence of product placement-at the beginning, end and after each advertising break- when the program is produced by the service supplier

When the appearance of a product in a program does not comply with these requirements, it will be considered as a covert advertising of the brand or product, which is forbidden by our legislation.

The brand owner can try to stop the communication by means of an injunction, but it would be very difficult to obtain it unless there are extraordinary circumstances and sufficient time for a Court to grant such injunction timely. In most cases, damages would be the only feasible remedy available.

6. PROTECTION OF CORPORATE IMAGE AND REPUTATION

The laws regarding right of publicity and privacy extend in general to legal entities and corporations (public ones excluded) which enjoy these rights of publicity and privacy with a similar scope and restrictions as individuals. However, it is important not to confuse corporate image, reputation and honor. Although these concepts are close, they are not similar. While corporate image and reputation of legal entities and corporations can only be protected via Intellectual Property and Unfair Competition Laws, honour is a "fundamental right" that also applies to them and as such is protected by our Constitution and especially by the Organic Law 1/1982 and Civil Code. However, cases involving the violation of a corporation's honour are mostly residual in Spain and the plaintiffs tend to mix the concept of commercial tarnish (usual in Unfair Competition and Trademark Laws) with affection of honor (in this regard, we can mention Supreme Court case 7th November 2019 ECLI: ES:TS:2019:3529 where the defendant addressed a false domain name including the plaintiff's trademark to a well-known porn site).

It is generally possible to include specific clauses in agreements aimed at protecting the corporate image / reputation of one of the parties, especially if it has an "aura of luxury" (being the last trend to exclude online marketplaces). The practice is frequent in selective distribution but must comply with ancillary European Regulations on competition (vertical agreements) since the protection of prestige is not always compatible with restrictions of sales and other limitations. In this regard, the resellers must be chosen on the basis of objective criteria of a qualitative nature that are laid down uniformly for all potential resellers and applied in a non-discriminatory fashion and that the criteria laid down do not go beyond what is necessary (C-230/16 *Coty Germany Gmbh v Parfümerie Akzente GmbH*).

It is possible in Spain to include fines clauses for breach by a party of provisions protecting the reputation or corporate image. Besides the already known competition restrictions, the clauses must not be abusive. Moreover, it must be clear in the agreement that the protection of the reputation is one of the main aspects of the negotiation and regarding damages, it is always advisable to exclude the fine from the final compensation. Finally, attention must always be put onto fair uses of the trademark, especially in repair shops, as the ECJ has confirmed in numerous times since C-63/97 *Bmw v. Deenik*.

AUTHOR BIOGRAPHIES

Rubén Canales
Law degree in 2007 at the University of Salamanca. Copyright Law Degree by the University Carlos III of Madrid. Member of the Madrid Bar and ENATIC (Digital Lawyers Association). Rubén joined the Entertainment Department & Telecommunications, Media and Technology area and collaborates with the IP litigation department

Eleonora Carrillo
Spanish trademark attorney and professional representative before the EUIPO. She joined Jacobacci & Partners in 2006 and heads the LATAM Desk of the Jacobacci group, aimed at strengthening relationships between the firm and the Latin American jurisdictions. She has extensive experience in all trademark and design matters in Spain and the EU. She is the author of numerous publications on trademarks and gives presentations in conferences. She also regularly lectures at Spanish post-graduate law schools on specific IP topics.

Carolina Montero
Law degree in 1997 at the Complutense University of Madrid. Master degree in Community Law by the Alcala de Henares University Member of the Bar Association of Madrid. Detailed experience advising in European and Spanish Trademark prosecution. She handles foreign client portfolios providing analysis and counsel on all IP matters and related issues and also on advertising and marketing.

Fernando Ortega
Degree in law by Complutense University of Madrid (2003), attorney at Law admitted in Madrid Bar since 2003 and Master degree in Intellectual Property by the University Pontificia Comillas of Madrid (ICADE) in 2004. With deep experience and a thorough knowledge in IP issues, including both civil and criminal litigation, as well as advising clients in negotiations and drafting different types of agreements. He collaborates with publications in specialized press.

Ignacio Temiño
PhD in Law and degree in Law by the University of Valladolid (1995), Attorney at Law admitted in Madrid Bar since 1997 and Spanish Patent and Trademark Agent as well since 2003. Ignacio has been Adjunct professor of Civil and Trade Law at the University as of 2001. His practice is extensive in Intellectual Property Law, especially in prosecution and litigation matters in Patent and Trademark Law, and also in Copyright (contractual and litigation) where he has valuable knowledge and practice.

TAIWAN

Crystal J. Chen & Nick J.C. Lan
Tsai, Lee & Chen

1. TRADEMARK

1.1 Sources of law

Taiwan is a jurisdiction governed by the statutory law. The Trademark Act is the dominant source of law relating to trademarks from obtaining through to maintenance of rights, as well as violation of the trademark right.

Due to the unique political situation, Taiwan is not a signatory of most international conventions or treaties, including the Paris Convention for the Protection of Industrial Property and the Berne Convention. But, by means of joining the World Trade Organization (WTO) in 2002, Taiwan is obligated to observe the TRIPS Agreement for the protection and enforcement of intellectual property rights. Court decisions, though highly valued, do not have binding effects on subsequent cases with different facts.

The Trademark Act adopts the principle of first-to-file. A mark need not actually be in use before it is eligible for registration. A person who wishes to obtain the trademark right must apply for registration for protection. Mere use of a mark without registration will not establish a trademark right, although the Fair Trade Act protects a non-registered sign, symbol or name if it is proven to be well-known enough to identify the source of goods or services.

1.2 Substantive law

Although there is no classification based on the degree of distinctiveness of a well-known trademark in the Trademark Act, the case law tends to grant a different scope of protection based on different degrees of distinctiveness of a well-known trademark.

Any unauthorized use of a trademark which is identical or similar to a well-known trademark will be deemed as trademark infringement if such use may cause confusion or dilution of distinctiveness or reputation of said well-known trademark (Articles 70.2 of the Trademark Act). When two trademarks are identical or similar, likelihood of confusion usually occurs when both parties' designated goods and services are also identical or similar. However, when both parties' goods or services are very different, there may not be any likelihood of confusion among the relevant consumers. Under such circumstances, the court tends to request the trademark owner to prove that the trademark has become well-known to general consumers. In view of the high degree of fame, even goods and services of the accused trademark are not similar to those of the well-known trademark, likelihood of dilution on the distinctiveness or reputation of the well-known trademark may occur (IP Court Judgment No. 107-*Ming-Shang-Sue*-43).

Except for the protection on the well-known trademark above, there is no specific rule for luxury brands. Notwithstanding the foregoing, the "aura of luxury" surrounding them might, to some extent, facilitate the establishment of their well-known status.

1.3 Enforcement

A trademark may be entitled to a broader protection when there is sufficient evidence to support the degree of fame for a trademark. There is no formality requirement on the exhibits represented in the court. Oral testimony, affidavit and expert evidence are all admissible exhibits. The court will decide whether to adopt the exhibits by discretion.

As a specific protection for well-known trademarks, a well-known trademark can be enforced against any unauthorized use of said trademark as the name of a company, a business, or a group, a domain name or any other name that identifies a business entity if there is likelihood of confusion by relevant consumers, or likelihood of dilution on the distinctiveness or reputation of the well-known trademark (Articles 70.2 of the Trademark Act).

Any trademark that has not reached a well-known status may also be enforced against unauthorized use on a domain name or distinctive signs as long as said unauthorized use is considered as "use of a trademark…in the course of trade where such trademark is capable of being recognized by relevant consumers as a trademark" (Article 5 of the Trademark Act).

To enforce a non-well-known trademark against an unauthorized use as a metatag or a trade name may involve the Fair Trade Act and the Company Act since such use might not be perceived as use of a trademark.

A trademark can be enforced against any unauthorized use in social media when:
• such use is considered as a use of trademark; and
• there is likelihood of causing confusion to relevant consumers.

A trademark can be enforced against its unauthorized use in comparative advertising when the unauthorized use does not constitute a nominative fair use "in accordance with honest practices in industrial or commercial matters" (Article 36 of the Trademark Act).

A trademark can be enforced against its unauthorized use in parody if such use is considered as a use of trademark and there exists likelihood of confusion (IP Court Judgment No. 108-*Ming-Shang-Shang*-5).

Article 22.2 of the Fair Trade Act stipulating infringement of a well-known symbol of goods expressively excludes its application on any registered trademark. A trademark right owner cannot claim both trademark infringement and unfair competition for the same set of facts concerning use of a trademark.

Current issues the luxury brands face are that more and more copycats plagiarize the appearance or shape of the luxury products. However, it is difficult for luxury brands to obtain three-dimensional trademarks for their products, since the degree of distinctiveness required for three-dimensional trademarks is much higher than general trademarks. If registration of a three-dimensional trademark cannot be obtained, the luxury brands can only pursue remedies under the Fair Trade Act and the Copyright Act.

2. COPYRIGHT

2.1 Sources of law

In Taiwan, the Copyright Act is the exclusive source of law relating to copyrights. Court decisions, although highly valued, do not have binding effects on subsequent cases with different facts.

2.2 Substantive law

The Copyright Act provides protection for any creation in the field of literary, scientific, artistic, or other intellectual domain. Article 5 of the Copyright Act provides an open list of copyrightable works, which includes oral and literary works, musical works, dramatic and so on.

Objects of industrial, fashion or accessory design are not treated separately and they are copyrightable if they can satisfy the general requirements for copyright protection, namely, the creation must be:
- an expression of an ideal but not an ideal itself;
- original and creative;
- the work of mind; and
- in the field of literary, scientific, artistic, or other intellectual domain.

Copyright covers the moral rights and economic rights subsisting in a completed work. Economic rights include the author's exclusive right to reproduce, distribute and display the work and so on. An author can enjoy the following moral rights under the Copyright Act:
- right of attribution: the author has the right to be identified as the author of the work;
- right of disclosure: the author has the right to disclose the work to the public and decide the conditions of said disclosure; and
- right of integrity: the author has the right to prohibit others from distorting, mutilating, modifying, or otherwise changing the content, form, or name of the work, thereby damaging the author's reputation.

A legal entity can be the initial author of a work-made-for-hire created by its employees in the absence of agreement to the contrary. A legal entity can be the initial owner of the work made by its consultant, director, shareholder or supplier if the work is made under a commission agreement which expressively attributes the ownership of copyright to said legal entity.

A legal entity can become the assignee of the economic rights of the work through an assignment agreement.

It is notable that the scope of a copyright assignment or license shall be as clear as possible since any right not stipulated in the agreement will be presumed to have not been assigned or licensed (Articles 36.3 and 37.1 of the Copyright Act).

Moral rights cannot be transferred or waived. However, it is common in practice to ask the author not to enforce the moral rights against the licensee or assignee of the economic rights. Such covenant not to sue is deemed valid since it is not a waiver of the moral right.

The duration of the economic right is in principle the life of the author and fifty years after the author's death (Article 30.1 of the Copyright Act). The duration of the moral right is during the lifetime of the author and the lifetime of the person designated by the author or the author's legal successor (Articles 18 and 86 of the Copyright Act).

2.3 Enforcement

In Taiwan a work is protected by copyright upon its creation. Absence of a copyright registration, a deposit or a notice will not impede the enforceability of copyright in any aspect.

Industrial designs belong to the work of applied art and can be protected by copyright if they are not purely practical or functional.

In a copyright infringement lawsuit, the plaintiff has to prove that the defendant has access to the plaintiff's work. A substantial similarity between works of both parties will be assessed to establish infringement. It is not necessary for an actual copying.

Copyright can be enforced against a trademark when the device of a trademark is considered as a copyrighted work (IP Court Judgment No. 103-*Ming-Shang-Sue*-24).

Since copyright protection may not extend to technical features of a work, it is not likely to enforce copyright against an invention or a utility model patent.

Copyright can be enforced against a design patent and other IP rights, such as a trade dress protected under the Fair Trade Act, or a design of the integrated circuit layouts regulated by the Integrated Circuits Layout Protection Act.

However, in principle a slogan, common symbol or term is not copyrightable. Copyright cannot be enforced against a domain name, a trade name or a pseudonym if the subject pursuing copyright protection does not satisfy the creativity requirement for copyright protection.

Copyright can be enforced against its unauthorized use in social media when said use constitutes unauthorized reproduction or public transmission of a work.

Copyright can be enforced against an unauthorized use in comparative advertising or in parody, unless such use is considered as a fair use of the work for comments or other legitimate purposes.

Fair use is an available defense to an alleged infringer. There are various categories of fair use in the Copyright Act. For example, within a reasonable scope, a person can quote a published work for reporting, commenting, teaching, research and other legitimate purpose (Article 52 of the Copyright Act). According to Article 65 of the Copyright Act, the following four factors will be considered when determining whether a fair use defense is established:

- the purposes and nature of the exploitation, including whether such exploitation is of a commercial nature or is for non-profit educational purposes;
- the nature of the work;
- the amount and substantiality of the portion exploited in relation to the work as a whole; and
- the effect of the exploitation on the work's current and potential market value.

According to Article 148 of the Civil Act, a right cannot be exercised for the purpose of violating public interests or damaging the others. Therefore, theoretically, copyright can be deemed unenforceable owing to an abusive use of copyright by a copyright holder. However, in practice, so far, the Taiwanese court has not recognized any defense of abuse of copyright.

The statute of limitation for claiming damages for copyright infringement is within two (2) years from the time the copyright holder learns of its right to claim damages and knows the identity of the obligor, or within ten (10) years of the occurrence of infringement, which occurs earlier.

One of the issues that luxury brands face in expanding and protecting their rights in copyright is that the Taiwanese courts have a vague standard of "creativity" when determining whether the products of luxury brands can be protected by copyright. Therefore, luxury brands should not merely rely on the copyright protection at enforcement, but should also take into account other possible rights. It is recommended to simultaneously claim unfair competition based on Articles 22 (infringement of a well-known trade dress) and 25 (substantial plagiarism and free riding upon others' goodwill) of the Fair Trade Act in addition to copyright infringement claims.

3. DESIGN

3.1 Sources of law

In Taiwan, the Patent Act is the exclusive source of law for the protection of designs. Substantive examination is required for a design to be granted and protected as a design patent. Court decisions, though are highly valued, do not have binding effects on subsequent cases with different facts.

3.2 Substantive law

Any creation made in respect of the shape, pattern, color, or any combination thereof, of an article as a whole or in part by visual appeal, as well as computer generated icons and graphic user interface applied to an article can be protected by a registered design patent (Article 121 of the Patent Act). According to the Patent Examination Guidelines amended in 2020, the "article" referred to can be also intangible. That is, an image presentable from a computer program product can be protected as a design patent. Besides, the exterior appearance of a building and interior spaces are also becoming eligible for design patents.

The shape of an article solely dictated by its function, fine arts, the layout of integrated circuits and electronic circuits and an article contrary to public order or morality are excluded from design patent protection. The requirements for a design patent include creativity, novelty and industrial applicability (Articles 122 and 123 of the Patent Act).

If a design is made by an employee of a legal entity in the course of performing the duties, the right to apply for a patent and the patent right thereof shall be vested in said legal entity in the absence of an agreement to the contrary and the legal entity shall pay the employee reasonable remuneration (Article 7.1 of the Patent Act). It is notable that the payment of reasonable remuneration is not a prerequisite to acquire the rights (IP Court Judgment No. 100-*Ming-Zhuan-Sue*-89).

If a design is made by an employee of a legal entity outside the course of duties, the right to apply for a patent and the patent right for such design shall be vested in the employee. However, if such design is made through the utilization of the legal entity's resources or experiences, said legal entity may, after paying the employee a reasonable remuneration, exploit the design concerned in the enterprise (Article 8.1 of the Patent Act).

A legal entity can acquire the ownership of a design patent developed by its consultants, shareholders, directors and suppliers when the development of said design is funded by said legal entity through an agreement which expressively grant the ownership of the patent to said legal entity (Article 7.3 of the Patent Act).

It is notable that if a design assignment is not recorded with the Taiwan Intellectual Property Office (TIPO), such assignment shall have no *locus standi* against a third party (Article 62.1 of the Patent Act).

When drafting a design related assignment agreement with employees, consultants, shareholders, directors and suppliers, there are some precautions to be considered:
- If a design is made outside the scope of employment duties, any agreement precluding the employee from enjoying the rights and interests of the design shall be void (Article 9 of the Patent Act).
- Waiver or assignment of moral rights of a designer in an agreement is a void provision.

The duration of protection for a design patent is within fifteen years from the filing date (Article 135 of the Patent Act).

3.3 Enforcement

When assessing design patent infringement, the court will evaluate whether the overall visual appearance of the assessed product and that of the design patent is substantially identical or similar in the perspective of a general consumer, who is a fictional person familiar with similar prior art.

A design can be enforced against a trademark attached to an article embodied by that design patent by means of a civil action and against a registered design patent through an invalidation proceeding. It is not likely to be enforced against an invention patent or utility model patent since a design patent shall not be functional or technical. It is also not likely to be enforced against a domain name, trade name, any unauthorized use in social media or comparative advertising, since there is not any article to which a design can be embodied.

A design might be enforced against its unauthorized use in parody since parody is not a defense recognized in the Patent Act.

An alleged infringer might raise a "functional" defense arguing that the design is a functional and practical shape. There is not a repair clause under the current Patent Act and "repair part" defense has not yet been recognized as an exemption for infringement by the court (IP Court Judgment No. 106-*Ming-Zuang-Sue*-34).

Although by law the abuse of right can be a defense against a patent infringement claim, so far there is not any case law directly recognizing or confirming such a defense.

The patentee is entitled to file an action claiming damages against the accused infringer within two (2) years from when the patentee became aware of the infringement activities and the accused infringer, or ten (10) years since the infringement occurs. Upon expiration of the periods, an accused infringer may raise statute of limitation defense to avoid liabilities for damages.

In civil actions, a design holder can simultaneously claim design patent infringement, copyright infringement and unfair competition for the same set of facts.

As designs are protected as patents, novelty is a threshold to obtain a design patent. In order not to lose novelty, luxury brands should file for their novel creation in Taiwan within one year from the earliest filing date in one of member states of the WTO.

4. RIGHT OF PRIVACY, PUBLICITY AND PERSONAL ENDORSEMENT

4.1 Sources of law

The law of Taiwan recognizes the right of an individual to control any use of his or her image and likeness as a "portraiture right." Whereas the law also recognizes the right of an individual to control any use of his or her name as the "right of personal name." Although there is not a specific legal concept identical to the right of publicity, the combination of the portraiture right and right of personal name may encompass a similar scope.

Right of publicity can be protected as a right of personality. The context of right of personality includes the right of privacy, freedom, reputation, personal name and portrait and so on. Article 18 of the Civil Act stipulates that an individual has the right to prevent and exclude any infringement of his or her personality. When an individual's right of personality is infringed, he or she is entitled to claim damages (Articles 184 and 195.1 of the Civil Act).

4.2 Substantive law

Right of personality (including the right of publicity) can be enjoyed by any individual without any condition. As a general principle, any right of personality shall expire upon death of an individual, and it cannot be waived, assigned or inherited. However, since the commercial value of personality rights becomes more and more important, the Supreme Court held that inheritance of the economic interest of personality rights is not inadmissible, and the successor of such personality right shall be entitled to exclude any unauthorized use by a third party (Supreme Court Civil Judgment No. 104-Tai-Shang-1407). Accordingly, right of publicity may be inherited and the successor can exclude any unauthorized use by a third party. However, the case law is silent on the duration of the successor's right to exclude unauthorized use.

In practice, right of publicity cannot be assigned by an assignment. However, it is common and valid for an individual to license the right of publicity in an exclusive or non-exclusive way. In addition to general rules for a contract, the law or court opinion does not appear to indicate any special requirement for licensing the right of publicity with respect to the validity, withdrawal or termination of a license. As such, the withdrawal or termination clause should be stipulated in the license agreement.

It is notable that a licensee can exploit the right but is not in the capacity to exclude others' unauthorized use (Taiwan Hualiang District Court Civil Judgment No. 96-*Sue*-200). Therefore, in the license agreement, it is important to obligate the licensor to provide necessary assistance in excluding any unauthorized use.

Following the death of the licensor, a valid license agreement will not be terminated automatically. If the license agreement is still in force, it will bind the successors of the deceased.

Meanwhile, although inheritance of right of publicity is recognized by the Supreme Court, the case law is silent regarding whether the right of publicity can be transferred *mortis causa*.

4.3 Enforcement

The right of publicity can be enforced against any use of that individual's name, image, likeness, or other unequivocal aspects of their identity. It is not necessary to prove the commercial value of the right of publicity.

In practice, freedom of the press can be used as a defense against the claim based on right of publicity. If the unauthorized use is for protecting the societal right to know and does not violate the principle of proportionality, the defense of freedom of the press can be established (Taiwan High Court Judgment No. 101- *Shang*-1308).

The current issue celebrities and others face when exercising their right of publicity when working with luxury brands is that there is no clear rule regarding the duration of the successor's right to exclude unauthorized use and whether the right of publicity can be transferred *mortis causa*.

5. PRODUCT PLACEMENT

Product placement is permitted in Taiwan.

If the product placement is put into a TV program or radio program, there are limitations on product placement in Regulations for the Distinction between Television Programs and Advertisements, Product Placement Marketing, and Sponsorships and Regulations for the Distinction between Radio Programs and Advertisements and Product Placement Marketing and Sponsorships. Said limitations are summarized as follows:

- Product placement is forbidden in news and children's programs.
- Product placement is forbidden for the following products:
    - tobacco;
    - alcohol;
    - international matchmaking;
    - prescription medicine designated by central competent health authorities;
    - illegal commodities and services; and
    - other commodities forbidden from advertising by the law.

If the other party fails to perform the product placement agreement, the brand owner may claim damages for breach of contract. The brand owner may stop the communication if there is an agreement obligating the other party to stop communication upon breach of contract.

Luxury brands do not have unique concerns for product placement since the products of luxury brands do not fall into the scope of products forbidden for product placement in the TV or radio programs as indicated above.

6. PROTECTION OF CORPORATE IMAGE AND REPUTATION

Right of publicity extends to legal entities in a limited way. Right of privacy, however, is exclusive for a natural person; it does not extend to legal entities.

A legal entity can enjoy protection on its name, credit, reputation and goodwill. However, the portrait right, right of privacy and other personality rights cannot be enjoyed by legal entities.

It is generally possible to include specific clauses in agreements aimed at protecting the corporate image/reputation of one of the parties. In principle, it should be legitimate to prohibit a trading counterpart from selling the products to re-sellers whose image is below a certain defined standard for protecting the image and reputation of one of the parties. It should also be legitimate to restrict the trading counterpart from buying non-original spare parts and components for maintaining the quality and safety of the products.

However, if such clauses are imposed for restraining competition, they might be deemed imposing improper restrictions on the trading counterpart's business activity (Article 20.5 of the Fair Trade Act).

It is notable that prohibition to sell below a certain price or to do so outside of specific time periods might constitute restriction of resale price prohibited in Article 19 of the Fair Trade Act unless there is any just cause.

Liquidated damages or stipulated fines clauses for breach of contract are permissible in Taiwan. However, if the court believes the damages or fines are too high, the court may decrease them at their discretion (Article 252 of the Civil Act).

The unique concern of luxury brands in the secondary market is that, in principle, luxury brands cannot exclude third parties from importing or reselling second-hand or parallel imported genuine products. Doctrine of international exhaustion is prescribed in both the Patent Act and the Trademark Act. Notwithstanding the foregoing, since there has not been any repair clause admitted in the Patent Act, luxury brands is recommended to apply for design patents for their spare parts and components.

AUTHOR BIOGRAPHIES

Crystal J Chen

Crystal J Chen is a partner at Tsai, Lee & Chen. Her practices cover all areas of IP law, particularly focused on anti-counterfeiting and infringement solutions relating to patent, trademark and trade dress issues. Her global clientele includes many Global 500 companies in the fashion and luxury industry. Ms Chen is a member of the design committee of the International Association for the Protection of Intellectual Property (AIPPI) and a member of many international IP associations. She has a law degree from Taiwan, and was admitted to the New York State Bar and the China National Bar. She frequently contributes to law journals and IP magazines, as well as speaks at international panels.

Nick J.C. Lan

Nick J.C. Lan is a senior associate at Tsai, Lee & Chen. He specializes in enforcement and litigation of copyright, trademark, and unfair competition. He is fluent in legal research, contract review and due diligence practices. He frequently assists local and foreign clients in contract negotiation and enforcement of rights in various jurisdictions. Nick has a law degree from Taiwan and has acquired the LLM degree from University of Washington in 2013. He was admitted to the New York Bar in 2014.

TURKEY

Özlem Futman & Yasemin Aktas
Ofo Ventura

TURKEY

1. TRADEMARK

1.1 Sources of law

The most pertinent legislation relating to trademarks is the Industrial Property Code no. 6769 (IP Code), which came into force on 10 January 2017. Turkey is a signatory to most of the IP-related international treaties, including:
- the Paris Convention for Protection of Industrial Property;
- the Agreement on Trade-Related Aspects of Intellectual Property Rights; and
- the Protocol relating to the Madrid Agreement Concerning the International Registration of Marks.

Higher court decisions have an influence over the lower courts to ensure uniformity in judicial practice. However, only decisions of a higher chamber of the Court of Appeal (which is responsible for resolving inconsistencies between different judgments of chambers in similar disputes) are binding on lower courts.

According to the IP Code, use can be a source of trademark rights for unregistered marks. If the party using the unregistered mark can prove that it is the creator of the mark and can demonstrate prior use in Turkey, it can seek refusal of the application for the identical or confusingly similar latter mark before the Turkish Patent and Trademark Office (TPTO). Meanwhile, if the latter mark is already registered, the related party can claim invalidation of the disputed registration and termination of the unauthorised use of the mark by filing a civil court action before the Turkish IP courts.

For a registered mark, if, within a period of five years following the registration, the trademark has not been put to use in Turkey without a justifiable reason, or if the use has been suspended during an uninterrupted period of five years, the trademark may be subject to non-use cancellation claims. Plus, the IP Code allows the defendant/applicant (in an infringement and/or invalidation action before the courts or in an opposition action before TPTO) to invite the plaintiff/opponent to prove the use of their marks on which the related actions are based, if the 5 years' use term has passed for them on the date of the filing the infringement action or on the filing/priority date of the conflicting application/registration. If case evidence adequately proving the use of the claimant's trademarks in Turkey cannot be submitted to the file, its claims based on its prior rights arising from the relevant registrations have to be refused without being examined.

1.2 Substantive law

Turkey's trademark practice does not distinguish famous and well-known marks or trademarks with a reputation.

There is no regulation in Turkey providing specific protection for trademarks belonging to the "luxury industry". Yet still, in practice, being a luxury brand could be approached in favor of the brand owner both by the TPTO and IP Courts.

1.3 Enforcement

Turkey grants a broader protection to "well-known" brands registered in Turkey through Article 6(5) of the IP Code which regards dilution. Well-known registered marks are protected for dissimilar goods or services, if there is a possibility that the later mark would take unfair advantage of or be detrimental to the distinctive character or reputation of the well-known mark.

High distinctiveness is another factor widening the protection scope of well-known marks.

The brand owner seeking a broader protection for its registered mark on the basis of Article 6(5) must support the well-known status of its mark through comprehensive evidence (e.g. registration/renewal certificates, invoices showing sales of products/services bearing the related mark, advertising materials, affidavits indicating the history of the brand and geographical area in which the related brand has been used/registered, promotional materials, awards, favorable survey results, customer comments, visibility/follower numbers of their social media accounts and so on).

Oral testimonies are not generally accepted as solid evidence in trademark disputes in Turkey.

Submission of an affidavit helps, and it is advised to submit it as Apostilled.

If needed the Judge in court actions and the Prosecutor in criminal complaints may appoint an official expert(s) for examination as to whether the brand subject to the related conflict could be deemed as "well-known" and could benefit from a broader protection.

A trademark can be enforced against a domain name.

A trademark can be enforced against a trade name, as long as:
- the claimant has an earlier trademark registration for the word(s) of which removal from the conflicting trade name is requested;
- the field of activity of the trade name owner is identical and/or similar with the goods/services within the scope of the claimant's trademark registration(s); and
- the conflicting company name has been used in a sense of trademark rather than a company name in a way to create a likelihood of confusion with the claimant's trademark registration and to cause trademark infringement and unfair competition against the claimant.

A trademark can be enforced against an identical or confusingly similar design as well, if the design consists of the same wordmark in it or identical/similar device to the mark.

A trademark can be enforced against its use as a metatag.

A trademark can be enforced against its unauthorized use in social media as long as:
- the claimant has an earlier trademark registration or use in Turkey; and
- the scope of conflicting use on the social media is identical and/or similar with the goods/services within the scope of the claimant's trademark registration(s)/earlier use or even if the goods/services are not identical/similar when dilution could be claimed.

Use of a third party's trademark in a comparative advertising is currently forbidden in Turkey and the trademark owner can enforce their trademark rights against this kind of usages.

A parody defense against trademark infringement and invalidation claims is not regulated in Turkey and a trademark can be enforced against its unauthorized use in parody if such use causes any unfair advantage to the user in parody due to its association with the trademark under the IP Code and/or unfair competition regulation in Turkish Commercial Code (Commercial Code).

A trademark owner can claim trademark infringement and unfair competition in the same civil or criminal action simultaneously.

Because of the size of its domestic manufacturing industry and its position as an international gateway, Turkey is one of the most crucial and critical territories in the fight against counterfeiting particularly considering that luxury brands are undoubtedly the main target of counterfeiters.

In theory, the most efficient way to tackle counterfeiting is to file a criminal complaint against the counterfeiter and prompt the public prosecutor to start criminal proceedings with a raid for seizure of the counterfeit goods. This should then be followed up by a criminal court action for the punishment of wrongdoers and the destruction of the counterfeit goods. The criminal complaint is submitted to the Public Prosecution Office, but the prosecutor needs approval from the local criminal court of peace to organize a raid on the suspected address. While there are specialized criminal IP courts of first instance applying the IP Code to hear criminal trademark infringement cases, it is unfortunate that criminal courts of peace hear requests for raid orders since, besides not being specialized, they apply the Criminal Procedures Law (the Commercial Law) to all types of crime and that has made getting raid orders very difficult especially in the recent years upon the change in the Criminal Law tightening requirements for issuance of a raid order.

According to the government's 11th National Development Plan, which is due to be fulfilled by the end of 2023, specialised IP chambers will be established under the criminal courts and judges competent in IP law will be appointed to them. Considering that the most challenging part of the battle against counterfeiting is the lack of competence and the strict approach of criminal courts of peace, having specialised IP chambers to handle criminal complaints against counterfeiters is expected to suitably assist brand owners.

Luxury brand owners are not totally safe regarding their preliminary injunction (PI) order requests in civil court actions either, unless some solid evidence is gathered properly before moving on with the PI claim. Plus, IP Courts may sometimes require payment of high guarantee amounts for issuance of a raid order and brand owners may tend not to consider civil proceedings due to this cost, although they would get the related guarantee in case of acceptance of their main claims and finalization of such acceptance.

Finally, luxury brands may be subject to third party applications in different classes which do not fall into their core business. To be able to defend the luxury brand owners' rights against such applications, some brand owners evaluate to keep the scope of their trademark filings broader than their core business. Use of a mark is not required to register it in Turkey and its use cannot be questioned by either authorities or third parties during the first 5 years following its registration. Use of the mark can be questioned upon third parties' requests only upon expiration of 5-year use term. Depending on in which action it was questioned, the related marks may be cancelled due to non-use, or the brand owners may reconsider enforcing their rights arising from such marks for the goods/services on which they cannot prove the use of the brands.

2. COPYRIGHT

2.1 Sources of law

The Law of Literary and Artistic Works No. 5846 (the Law) regulates protection of copyrights.

Turkey has a civil law system based on codified laws. Yet case law is also taken into consideration for the interpretation of laws. Higher court decisions have an influence over the lower courts to ensure uniformity in judicial practice. However, only decisions of a higher chamber of the Court of Appeal (which is responsible for resolving inconsistencies between different judgments of chambers in similar disputes) are binding on lower courts.

2.2 Substantive law

Copyright protection subsists in an intellectual or artistic creation bearing the specialty of its author and being original namely if it is the result of independent, creative effort by the author and being capable of classified as one of the below four (main) categories:
- scientific and literary works;
- musical works;
- artistic works; or
- cinematographic works.

In addition to the above four main categories, the Law recognizes some other sub-categories (e.g. computer software is listed as a sub-category in the Law under "scientific and literary works"). The main four categories listed above are *numerus clausus*, yet, sub-categories are not limited to the ones listed in the Law.

The Law does not exclude any works from copyright protection namely the categories stated above are only indicative. "Crafts and small works of art, miniatures and decorative items, as well as textiles, fashion designs" are also listed under "artistic works" in the above categories in Article 4. Thus, objects of industrial, fashion and accessory design can be copyrightable as long as they meet the requirements listed above.

A copyright holder has the following moral and economical rights:
- adapting the work;
- duplicating/reproducing the work;
- distributing the work;
- performing the work to the public;
- broadcasting or communicating the work to the public by any means of transmission of signs, sounds or images;
- disclosing the work to the public;
- modifying the work;
- integrating the work; and
- having the work attributing to them.

The copyright over works created by an employee, a consultant, a shareholder, a director or a supplier as a part of the duty is regulated under the Article 18(2) of the Law which reads as follows: "Provided that the contrary is not determined by a private contract between the parties or is understood from the nature of the situation, the rights on the works created by officers, servants and employees while they are performing their jobs shall be used by their employers or by the ones who have assigned them to work. The same rule applies in respect of the executive bodies of legal persons".

Thus, all the economic rights over a completed work are assigned to the employer, the consultant, the shareholder, the director, or the supplier once it is created, but the related party remains its author and holds the moral rights in their possession.

However, this provision is not applicable for the works created independently from the job/duty.

The assignment of economic rights on a work - unrestricted or restricted as regards duration, place or scope, with or without consideration - is entirely within the author's discretion.

An assignment of economic rights is valid only if it is in writing and contains the scope of the transferred or waived rights in detail by listing them one by one. Use of general wordings (e.g. all economic rights) in the assignment agreements causes them to be deemed void.

Moral rights are non-transmissible and non-withdrawable by the Law.

Copyright protection starts once the work becomes public, with no requirement for notification or registration. If the author is a real person, the protection lasts during the lifetime of the author, plus 70 years as of their death; this 70 years starts from the first day of the year following the author's death.

In joint authorship, the protection term becomes the life of the last surviving author plus 70 years.

If the author is a legal entity, the protection term lasts 70 years as of the relevant work becomes public.

For orphan works, the publisher would use the rights coming from copyright; if the publisher cannot be identified then the one who makes the reproduction can use the rights. Protection term for orphan works is 70 years from when the work becomes public, unless the author reveals their name before the term expires.

All these 70 years' protection terms in the Law are calculated from the first day of the year following the release of the work to public.

2.3 Enforcement

Under the Law, copyright registration is not mandatory for the purpose of enforcement. Likewise, copyright notice is not required either.

The main way to assess copyright infringement is for the claimant to prove actual copying or unauthorised use of the work. Plagiarism is accepted when there is a substantial similarity between the underlying original themes used in two works.

Copyright can be enforced against a trademark, registered design/design patent, patent or pseudonym. It cannot be enforced against a domain name or a trade name.

Copyright can be enforced against its unauthorized use in social media if the general conditions for enforcement are met. There is no specific provision required for protection against use in social media.

Use of a third party's copyright in a comparative advertising is currently forbidden in Turkey and the copyright owner can enforce it against this kind of usages.

A parody defense against copyright infringement and/or unfair competition claims is not regulated in Turkey and there has been no precedents supporting that a copyright can be used in parody as to our best knowledge.

There are provisions in the Law exempting certain activities from copyright infringement; the main categories are listed below.

Public order: The rights granted to authors shall not prevent a work from being used as evidence in court or before other authorities or from being the subject matter of police or criminal proceedings. Photographs may be reproduced and distributed in any form by official authorities without the author's consent (Article 30).

Public interest:
- The reproduction, distribution, adaptation, exploitation in any other form of officially published laws, by-laws, regulations, notifications, circulars and court decisions that have been officially published or announced is permitted (Article 31).
- The reproduction, public recitation, or broadcasting by radio and distribution by any other means of official speeches is permitted (Article 32).
- Published works may be freely performed in all educational institutions (Article 33).
- It is free to create selected or collected works, which are dedicated to educational purposes (Article 34).
- Quotations of a work are permitted under certain conditions listed under Article 35.
- Daily news and information communicated to the public by the press or radio may be freely quoted (Article 36).
- Recordal of parts of an intellectual or artistic work on devices enabling the transmission of signs, sounds and/or images in relation to current events is permitted provided that this has the nature of news and does not exceed the limits of giving information (Article 37).

Private (personal) use: Reproducing all intellectual and artistic works for personal use without pursuing profit is permitted (Article 38).

And naturally, after expiration of the protection term of a copyright, it enters the public domain and can be used without permission.

The time limit for legal infringement actions is two years as of learning of the infringing act and the infringer. The maximum time limit is 10 years from the date when the cause of action arose. In case the infringing act is also subject to criminal responsibility and if the statutory time limit for criminal responsibility is longer, then the longer period shall apply. It needs to be noted that as long as the infringement is ongoing, the time limit does not start.

As briefly touched above, luxury brands may suffer from identical/similar trademark filings in different sectors and registration of the luxury brand in all classes may of course not be an option in most of the cases. Here, copyright protection may help. In a recent case, the TPTO put copyright protection over well-known trademark protection. An opposition against an application in different classes was based on the well-known status of a registered logo mark and the opponent's copyrights on the logo, but the TPTO accepted it owing to the copyright protection only. Thus, copyright protection can be more advantageous than trademark protection owing to not being limited to any classes and luxury brand owners are advised to also seek copyright protection especially for their marks and designs that can be deemed as a "work" as well.

3. DESIGN

3.1 Sources of law

The most pertinent legislation is the Design chapter of IP Code.

Turkey has a civil law system based on codified laws. Yet case law is also taken into consideration for the interpretation of laws. Higher court decisions have an influence over the lower courts to ensure uniformity in judicial practice. However, only decisions of a higher chamber of the Court of Appeal (which is responsible for resolving inconsistencies between different judgments of chambers in similar disputes) are binding on lower courts.

3.2 Substantive law

In accordance with Article 55 of the IP Code, a product means any industrial or handicraft item, including parts intended to be assembled into a complex product, products like packaging, presentations of more than one object perceived together, graphic symbols and typographic typefaces, but excluding computer programs.

A design can be the appearance of the whole or a part of a product resulting from the features of the line, contour, colour, shape, material or texture of the product itself or its ornamentation.

Complex product shall be a product which is composed of components that can be replaced or renewed by disassembly and reassembly of the product.

The legal conditions for obtaining a registered design right are "Novelty" and "Individual character" according to Article 56 of IP Code. The same conditions are also required for protection of an unregistered designs. Plus, an unregistered design is also required to have been presented to the public for the first time in Turkey.

According to the IP Code, unless otherwise agreed upon due to special contracts made between parties or because of the nature of work, right owners of designs that are made by employees' due to their obligations in a business organization or right owner of designs that are performed by employees based on experiences and operations of business organization shall be the employer.

The right owner of designs that are carried out by employees outside the above scope by means of benefitting from information and tools related to general activity in their business organization shall be the employer, upon request.

TURKEY

If there is a service relationship contract between a legal entity and its consultant or shareholder or director or supplier, then the designs made by them in the frame of this contract would be evaluated under the same conditions with the designs created by its employee.

If the designs made by a legal entity's consultant or shareholder or director or supplier, in the frame of an employment contract not covered by the scope of a service relationship, the right owner shall be determined in the frame of provisions of the contract concluded between the parties.

A design assignment agreement must be in writing and signed by both parties before a Turkish notary or before a foreign notary, as well as apostilled. Where there is a single design, it is possible to transfer the design application entirely, but the partial transfer is not an option, even if more than one person becomes the right owner of that according to Article 70/4 of IP Code. For multiple design applications, both entire and partial assignments are possible.

Designs that can be deemed as "works" within the scope of the Law provide their owners with financial and moral rights within the scope of copyright protection in addition to the design rights recognized by the IP Code. In such a case the designer cannot transfer or waive their moral rights.

For registered designs, the protection term starts with the application or priority date and can be extended up to 25 years by renewal every 5 years as of its registration date. For unregistered rights the protection term starts as of its presentation to public and ends three years later.

The unregistered designs are protected only if they are copied identically or in an indistinguishably similar way in terms of overall expression. It provides protection for 3 years as of the day the design is presented to the public.

3.3 Enforcement

In the Turkish Practice, the overall impressions of the designs in the eye of an "informed user" are considered during infringement assessments. The "informed user" is accepted as the person who is placed between the "average consumer" making a comparison between trademarks without any special knowledge and an expert having technical information as to the relevant sector. In comparison of designs the attention needs to be given to common points of the designs rather than their differences while evaluating similarity. If the informed user evaluates the overall impression of the claimant's design as being identical or indistinguishably similar with each other, then the infringement claims are accepted. There is no difference between registered and unregistered designs in respect of similarity examination.

A design can be enforced against a trademark, a registered design/design patent and patent but not against a domain name or trade name.

A design can be enforced against its unauthorized use in social media if the general conditions for enforcement are met. There is no specific provision required for protection against use in social media.

Use of a third party's design in a comparative advertising is currently forbidden in Turkey and the design owner can enforce it against this kind of usages.

A parody defense against design infringement and/or unfair competition claims is not regulated in Turkey and there has been no precedents supporting that a design can be used in parody as to our best knowledge.

"Repair clause" doctrine and both "must match" and "must fit" approaches are applicable in the IP Code.

Below is the list of main defences:
- Use of the design privately and for non-commercial purposes.
- Use of the design for experimental purposes.
- Use of the design due to the technical function.
- Reproduction for the purposes of making citations or of teaching, provided that such acts are compatible with fair trade practice and do not unduly prejudice the normal exploitation of the design, and that mention shall be made of the source.
- Reproduction of the design in its exact form and dimensions to permit the product in which the design is incorporated or to which it is applied to be mechanically connected to or placed in (must fit defence).
- Training or reference purpose reproductions provided that they comply with good faiths and they don't endanger unnecessarily the normal use of design and they show the sources.
- The equipment on ships and aircraft registered in another country when these temporarily enter the territory of Turkey concerned, and the importation of spare parts and accessories for the purpose of repairing such craft, and the execution of repairs on such craft.
- The use of the design of a component part used for the purpose of the repair of a complex product so as to restore its original appearance within three years after design is released to the market for the first time (must match defence).

According to article 72 of the Code of Obligations, civil actions against wrongful acts must be filed within two years from the day that the doer and the wrongful act is learnt of. In any case, such civil action must be filed within 10 years as of the date the wrongful act occurred. However, if infringement is ongoing, the time limitation would not start.

If a design can be deemed as a "work", the design holder can take action claiming both design infringement and copyright infringement and/or unfair competition for the same set of facts and can filed "one" collective court action with all these claims.

Registration of product designs in a single year period globally may not be an option in most of cases, especially for luxury brands coming up with new designs each season like fashion, home furnishing, accessories industries and so on. Unregistered design protection brought a very practical solution, especially to luxury sectors that need to quickly and frequently orientate themselves in line with the latest trends. Luxury brands in fashion and home furnishing can benefit from unregistered design protection on their designs if they present the design first in Turkey. Although the unregistered design protection is limited to three years as of the first presence of the design, in the example sectors above it will still be beneficial for the right owners.

The other issue is attempts to register luxury brands as a design and the fact that these attempts may sometimes be brought by the luxury brands' own distributors in Turkey. To prevent these types of registration, monitoring design bulletins is essential.

Last, but not least, the IP Code does not implement any criminal sanctions to design infringement, and this makes it difficult for the luxury brand owners to challenge infringing acts without the deterrent impact of criminal sanctions on infringers.

4. RIGHT OF PRIVACY, PUBLICITY AND PERSONAL ENDORSEMENT

4.1 Sources of law

Name, image, likeness or other unequivocal rights have been regulated under one Law in Turkey and are under protection through various regulations, as follows:

- The IP Code (regulating registrability of personal rights as a trademark and protection of name, image etc. against their or their similar versions' use and/or registration as a trademark).
- The Law of Literary and Artistic Works No. 5846 (the Law) (regulating copyright protection over name, nickname, former name, pseudonym, voice, image, portrait, photograph and so on).
- The Commercial Code (forbidding unauthorized commercial use of name, nickname, former name, pseudonym, voice, image, portrait, photograph and so on).
- The Civil Law No. 4721 (protecting personal rights against any infringing attacks).
- The Law on the Protection of Personal Data No. 6698 (protecting fundamental rights and freedoms of people, particularly the right to privacy, with respect to processing of personal data and to set forth obligations, principles and procedures which shall be binding upon natural or legal persons who process personal data).

4.2 Substantive law

Being a living human is enough to own a right of publicity. This applies to all individuals, however, would, from a general perspective, be more relevant with respect to celebrities or well-known individuals who may enjoy a higher degree of protection in this respect

The heirs of a deceased individual have some form of independent rights over that individual's commercially exploitable publicity rights, for example, name, image, likeness or other unequivocal aspects of their identity.

The assignment of the right of publicity in whole is not possible under Turkish law as it contains personality rights which are inseparable from the individual. However, the commercially exploitable elements of publicity rights can be assigned.

An individual can license the commercially exploitable elements of their right of publicity and the licence can be either exclusive or non-exclusive.

An assignment/license agreement should be in writing and contain the scope of the transferred or waived rights in detail by listing them one by one. Specific requirements for this kind of agreements may change depending on which regulation the publicity rights are based.

Turkish law does not specifically regulate the conditions or restrictions of termination of a license agreement. Further, the Turkish Code on Obligations No. 6098 includes provisions on withdrawal from a contract but does not particularize on the termination of a contract. However, in contracts where termed obligations exist, there is consensus in case law and legal theory that *ex-nunc* termination, a right of the parties to end a long-term contract, is possible.

Otherwise, and in principle, the parties to a license agreement can regulate certain events or causes of termination of the license agreement and notice periods under the agreement. A termination that is not in compliance with such termination grounds or notice periods will require the payment of compensation to the counterparty in accordance with general terms. As a general provision of the Law of Contracts, any termination should be made by granting a sufficient notice period to the counterparty. The exact length of such period for license agreements is not determined and should be considered on a case-by-case basis.

The legal consequences of the death of a licensor will depend on the wording of the license agreement. However, as a general rule, the heirs of the licensor will succeed in the deceased's legal position in terms of rights and obligations. Accordingly, a license agreement will remain in force and bind the successors, unless provided otherwise in the license agreement.

The assignment remains valid following the death of the assigner unless the otherwise was agreed on in the assignment agreement.

In the event the heirs have an independent right over the deceased individual's name, image, likeness, or other unequivocal aspects of identity they would have to respect the assignment or license agreement in this respect.

Turkish Law does not provide a fixed period as to when the rights of publicity expire. However, the rights of publicity will expire at some point depending on which regulation it was based. As a rule, the rights of publicity arising from the Copyright Code expire after 70 years after the death of the individual in question, but this period may be longer in the other regulations protecting publicity rights.

4.3 Enforcement

The enforcement of right of publicity is not limited to commercial use and it can be enforced against any infringing use.

It is not a requirement to prove that an individual's name, image, likeness, or other unequivocal aspects of one's identity have a commercial value to obtain an injunction or other remedies for the unauthorized use; however, it would certainly be an important element and would influence the level of damages awarded.

It could be argued that public interest, freedom of the press, and the freedom of speech may allow for *inter alia* a person's picture or name to be used for other purposes than strict commercial purposes.

5. PRODUCT PLACEMENT

According to the Law No. 6112 on the Establishment of Radio and Television Enterprises and Their Media Services (RTUK Law), product placement is permitted in movies made for cinema and television, television series, sports, and general entertainment programs; it is not permitted in news, child programs and religious programs.

Product placement is forbidden for the products and services of which advertising is prohibited such as in the following fields:
- healthcare: pharmaceuticals and medical treatments subject to prescriptions;
- tobacco and alcoholic beverages: tobaccos, cigars, any kind of alcoholic beverage;
- adult content: pornography and resources containing explicit content, prostitution and sex services, massages, stripping and strip clubs, adult erotic and sexual products, and matchmaking services;
- gambling: illegal gambling, casinos, online casinos and all products or services organised similarly to gambling; and
- alternative entertainment: services of psychics, astrologers and seers.

The brand owner can stop the communication and claim damages in the event the other party fails to perform the agreement.

Product placement has always been important for luxury brands, but with Covid-19, its importance has markedly increased with the rise of media and social media platforms used by consumers. In all corners of the Internet or other media channels, conversations about brands are taking place and sometimes those brands may not even become aware of these conversations. As a result of this, luxury brands' one main concern doubtlessly has become "unauthorized product placements" over which they do not have any control. Their valued products are sometimes associated with a miserable or immoral character in shows without their authorizations. Brand owners can enforce their intellectual and industrial property rights against these kinds of usage.

6. PROTECTION OF CORPORATE IMAGE AND REPUTATION

The below laws regarding right of publicity and/or privacy extend to legal entities/corporations:
- The IP Code.
- The Law.
- The Commercial Code.

But the regulations in the Turkish Personal Data Protection Law (n. 6698) are for only natural persons and do not extend to legal entities/corporations.

There is no specific additional condition for corporation to benefit from the rights of publicity/ privacy.

It is possible to include specific clauses in agreements aimed at protecting the corporate image/reputation of one of the parties, such as:
- prohibition to sell the products to re-sellers whose image is below a certain defined standard;
- prohibition to sell below a certain price or to do so outside of specific time periods; and
- prohibition to buy non original – but otherwise legitimate – spare parts and components.

TURKEY

AUTHOR BIOGRAPHIES

Özlem Futman
Founding partner

Özlem Futman is an IP litigator, Turkish trademark and patent attorney and European patent attorney who has more than 20 years' experience practising IP law in Turkey.

Ms Futman has broad experience in effectively managing IP portfolios for national and international companies operating in Turkey. She applies her considerable experience, tenacity and creativity to the handling of more complex matters such as oppositions, dilution claims, domain name issues, copyright matters, negotiating complex licences, customs seizures and anti-counterfeiting matters, as well as non-use and nullification matters.

Ms Futman is an officially appointed expert before the IP Courts in Istanbul. She is also an active member of the MARQUES Geographical Indications Committee, the INTA's Design Committee and the European Communities Trademark Association Geographical Indications Committee.

She has been ranked among the top tier IP professionals in Turkey by *MIP* IP Stars, the *WTR 1000* and the *IAM Patent 1000* and has been ranked as Recommended Lawyer by *LEGAL500*.

Yasemin Aktas
Partner

Yasemin Aktas is an IP litigator and Turkish trademark and patent attorney who has 12 years' experience practising IP law in Turkey.

She advises on a wide range of IP issues and transactions regarding trademarks, designs, domain names, tradenames and copyright, working with foreign and multinational clients from various industries in implementing IP protection, litigation and enforcement strategies and portfolio management.

Ms Aktas has wide experience in building anti-counterfeiting strategies, including customs monitoring, raids, seizures and settlement negotiations.

She is a member of the INTA Anti-counterfeiting Committee, Marques Dispute Resolution Team and ECTA Publication Committee and has been selected as a member of the IP Experts Group to assist the International Anti-counterfeiting Coalition IP Advisory Board.

Ms Aktas has been ranked among the top tier IP professionals in Turkey by the *WTR 1000* and the *IAM Patent 1000* and has been listed as Recommended Lawyer by *LEGAL500*.

UNITED KINGDOM

Rosie Burbidge
Gunnercooke

1. TRADE MARK

1.1 Sources of law

The Trade Marks Act 1994 (TMA) is the main source of law for trade marks in the UK. The TMA is supplemented by secondary legislation such as the Trade Mark Rules 2008. The Manual of Trade Marks Practice sets out useful guidance which is applicable to the UK Intellectual Property Office (UKIPO) working practices.

Prior to the end of the transition period following the UK's departure from the European Union on 31 December 2020 (Brexit), the Trade Mark Directive 2015 (the Directive) and EU Trade Mark Regulation 2017 (the Regulation) also applied to the UK. They remain relevant to the UK because any EU case law that was established prior to the end of the transition period remains a binding precedent.

For the time being EU and UK trade mark law are, to all intents and purposes, consistent. The UK has not diverged from the Directive and there has been no major new trade mark legislation from the EU. This is likely to change over time. At an anecdotal level, it appears that the UK is taking a stricter approach to descriptiveness and distinctive character. There is insufficient data at present to determine whether this is a significant long term change or the product of a large number of new examiners and staffing pressures due to Covid and the impact of Brexit.

The UK is a common law jurisdiction. This means that case law is very important for trade marks in terms of determining the meaning of legislation and a variety of procedural matters.

The UK is a party to the Madrid Protocol. It is also a signatory to the Agreement on Trade-related aspects of Intellectual Property Rights, 1994 (TRIPS). TRIPS is relevant for all IP rights.

Passing off. Passing off is the UK's closest equivalent right to *unregistered trade marks*, unfair competition or related disputes such as parasitic copying.

Passing off is a common law cause of action which offers some protection for business or product names, logos or trade dress (known in the UK as 'get up'). In order to rely on passing off it is necessary to show that:
- there is goodwill in the relevant sign claimed;
- there has been a misrepresentation by a third party who has misused that goodwill; and
- as a result of that misrepresentation there must be damage.

The goodwill must be specific. For example, a famous brand must be able to show goodwill that has been established through trade. Whilst a house brand may be well known, it may be harder to show that a newer sub-brand, packaging or product get up would possess goodwill.

A misrepresentation requires a 'deception'. This is a higher threshold than a 'likelihood of confusion' and requires a level of action on the part of the alleged infringer. Although it is not necessary to prove an intention to deceive, this evidence can be very persuasive. Evidence of actual confusion is not necessary but, again, can be persuasive depending on the type and context.

1.2 Substantive law

Any valid trade mark can be used against the use of an identical or similar sign for identical or similar goods and services. Where there is no double identity, it is necessary to prove that there is a likelihood of confusion.

If the trade mark has a reputation, it is also possible to rely on the mark against the use of an identical or similar sign for identical, similar or dissimilar goods and services provided that it is possible to prove that there has been:
- unfair advantage; or
- detriment to the:
    - distinctive character; or
    - repute of the sign.

This is broadly analogous to free-riding, blurring and tarnishment.

The "aura of luxury" is a particularly relevant consideration when it comes to selective distribution agreements. The key case in this area is *Coty Germany GmbH v Parfümerie Akzente GmbH* (Case C-230/16, ECLI:EU:C:2017:941), an EU case which pre-dates Brexit. Coty builds on another EU case, *Copad SA v Christian Dior Couture SA and others* (Case C-59/08, ECLI:EU:C:2009:260), which established that the quality of luxury goods is not simply their material characteristics but also the "aura of luxury" which comes from luxury goods' allure and prestigious image.

The EU court in Coty found that luxury brands can restrict distributors in selective distribution agreements from selling through third party websites and platforms such as Amazon, provided that this restriction was necessary in order to preserve the aura of luxury.

1.3 Enforcement

The UK consists of three different legal jurisdictions:
- England and Wales;
- Scotland; and
- Northern Ireland.

The same intellectual property rights apply across all through jurisdictions, however the court procedure for enforcement can vary. References to "UK law" are for simplicity but with the warning that there can be local differences in enforcement both in relation to trade marks and other relevant rights.

The limitation period in the UK is six years from the date on which the relevant infringing act occurred. If an infringement is ongoing, the six year period runs from the date that the infringing event ceased. However, it is only possible to claim damages for the six years preceding the date on which the claim form was issued.

The primary evidence is a witness statement which is verified by a statement of truth (think of it as an 'affidavit lite'). The witness statement must be given by someone with personal knowledge of the facts and matters set out in the statement and is commonly supported by documentary evidence in the form of exhibits.

In most cases, any witness who provides a witness statement would be expected to give oral evidence at trial. The court has become more flexible about the way in which this evidence can be delivered. After the pandemic it is expected that evidence will return to being primarily in person but giving evidence via video link remains possible in some circumstances.

There are three main routes for bringing proceedings in the UK. They range from the IP Enterprise Court (IPEC) for smaller claims, to the Shorter Trials Scheme (STS) for cases where tight case management is desirable, to the High Court (for the largest claims). In IPEC, the statements of case, namely the Particulars of Claim, Defence and any Counterclaim or Reply can stand as evidence in chief including the relevant annexes. For this reason, the statements of case must be verified with a statement of truth by someone with first-hand knowledge of the facts detailed in the relevant document.

In some limited circumstances it may be possible to provide survey evidence and/or expert evidence. Both have been discouraged by the courts and have somewhat gone out of fashion but they may be available in a larger case, particularly if there is a potential public policy or precedent setting aspect to the dispute.

A trade mark can theoretically be enforced against use of each of the following:
- a domain name - whether this is possible will depend on the use on the associated website;
- a trade name - again this will depend on the relevant use;
- other distinctive signs such as a product name or packaging; and
- a hashtag or, in some circumstances, a metatag in each case depending on the relevant use.

In most instances, using a third party trade mark as a keyword in online advertising is permitted. The exception to this is if the ad which results from the use of the trade mark as a keyword would create consumer confusion.

Social media enforcement. If a trade mark is used on social media in the course of trade it is likely to be possible to prevent this use. Often infringement on social media is associated with more wide ranging infringement.

Comparative advertising and other procedural issues. The UK allows comparative advertising. The UK law stems from the EU's Comparative Advertising Directive (CAD) (implemented in the UK as the Business Protection from Unfair Trading Regulations 2008). In some circumstances, it is lawful to advertise in comparison to another business and to use that business' trade mark in order to do so. In order for the advert to be lawful, the comparison must be with another product which has the same purpose. It is important to retain evidence to justify why the products are objectively comparable.

Parody is not a defence to trade mark infringement. Whether or not a parody is trade mark infringement depends on the standard criteria for trade mark infringement set out above. In practice, most parodic trade mark use is at a fairly *de minimis* level and it may not be worth taking legal action or the online takedown process may be sufficient.

It is very common to sue for both trade mark infringement and passing off as part of the same case. In practice, if trade mark infringement is established, passing off is usually established as well.

It is important to refrain from threatening trade mark infringement unless there are good grounds. When a threat of infringement is made, it gives rise to a potential counterclaim for 'groundless threats'. This can be an issue particularly

UNITED KINGDOM

if an injunction is threatened or suppliers or customers are also threatened with trade mark infringement resulting in loss of business. For this reason, it is particularly important to seek UK legal advice before making a threat of trade mark infringement which applies, or could apply, to the UK. This issue does not apply to passing off.

In order to be valid, any assignment must be in writing and signed by the assignor (i.e. the person or legal entity who is transferring the trade mark). No other formalities are required but in practice, the assignee usually signs the assignment as well. It is important that the assignment clause is clear and unambiguous. Typically, this is phrased as "X hereby assigns Y". These requirements for assignment of rights apply to all IP rights assignments in the UK.

Luxury brands are currently looking at creative ways to expand their trade mark portfolios including the potential for registering less standard signs such as product shapes or colours. The UK can be a good testing ground for these sorts of applications as it is much less expensive than the European Intellectual Property Office (EUIPO) both in terms of the relevant UKIPO fees and, most significantly, in terms of the evidence of acquired distinctiveness. In the EU, this is required for all 27 member states. Proving acquired distinctiveness in the UK is a more straightforward task.

2. COPYRIGHT

2.1 Sources of law

The Copyright, Designs and Patents Act 1988 (CDPA) is the main source of law for copyright law in the UK. As with trade marks, some EU legislation remains relevant to the extent that it was applied prior to Brexit.

The UK is a signatory to the Berne Convention for the Protection of Literary and Artistic Works (revised, Paris, 24 July 1974).

2.2 Substantive law

The CDPA has a closed list for copyright eligible works. Broadly speaking, the works must be literary, dramatic, musical or artistic. The definition of artistic works under CDPA is very narrow. The only types of three dimensional artistic works that are protected are sculptures and 'works of artistic craftsmanship'.

EU law has a much more expansive approach to the identification of a copyright work. The main criteria is that the work must be the author's own intellectual creation (*Infopaq International A/S v Danske Dagblades Forening,* Case C-5/08, ECLI:EU:C:2009:465).

Prior to Brexit, the EU court handed down a key case, *Cofemel - Sociedade de Vestuário SA v G-Star Raw CV* (Case C-683/17, ECLI:EU:C:2019:721), which established that in order to qualify as a copyright work, there must be an original object and an expression of intellectual creation and a closed list approach is not appropriate. For present purposes, the main takeaway is that protection of three dimensional works using copyright law in the UK is complicated. To the extent that copyright protection is available, it is more likely to be available for a more creative work than an industrial work. This is an important issue for luxury brands, particularly for more heritage designs where design right protection has expired.

A brand name or tagline is very unlikely to be sufficiently original to qualify as a literary work but advertising and marketing copy is more likely to be protected.

Moral rights are automatically protected but can be waived by contract. The main moral rights are the attribution right and the right to object to derogatory treatment. There are very few cases involving moral rights. On the rare occasions where an infringement is proven, the amount of damages at stake is typically very low.

An employer is automatically the first owner of any intellectual property rights, including copyright, which are created in the course of the employee's duties to the business. The line on this can be a bit grey so the statutory position is commonly supplemented in an employment contract.

In all other circumstances such as freelancers, photographers, shareholders, consultants and similar, unless a contract states otherwise, the creator (commonly known as the 'author') of a copyright work is its owner. There will be a licence in place but this will be limited to the purposes for which it was created. In some circumstances, it may be possible to argue that the business owns the equitable title to the copyright work but this is a challenging and expensive argument. It is far better to ensure that the works are assigned by contract and that if there is any doubt about historic copyright ownership that a confirmatory assignment is signed by all relevant parties. It is possible to assign "future copyright" i.e. the rights to copyright works which have not yet been created.

In most instances, copyright protection lasts for the life of the creator (and any joint creator) plus 70 years from the end of the year in which the last author died. This means that on every 1st January a variety of works fall into the public domain.

2.3 Enforcement

Copyright protection in the UK arises automatically on creation. There is no UK copyright register.

A copyright notice is not required in the UK but it is commonly applied. The main benefit of a copyright notice is to identify the copyright owner and deter infringement.

Copyright infringement can be direct or indirect. It is not necessary to prove actual copying. If the copyright work and alleged infringement are sufficiently similar and the infringer would have had access to the work, the burden shifts onto the infringer to prove, on the balance of probabilities that they did not copy the work.

Copyright can be used to invalidate or oppose a trade mark or a registered design. In each case, it is necessary that the relevant work is sufficiently artistic.

Copyright can be used to prevent infringement on social media, provided such use is without the copyright owner's permission. In practice, it is usually only enforced against another someone selling infringing products.

UNITED KINGDOM

The defences to copyright infringement in the UK are very narrow. For example, fair dealing for the purposes of criticism or review would cover a news story about a new fashion collection but would not enable a third party to launch a rival collection and garner PR about the same without running the risk of a copyright infringement claim.

There is a very limited defence to copyright infringement for the purposes of parody, caricature or pastiche. This exception that is designed to facilitate freedom of expression. It does not mean that it is possible to rely on a parody defence to sell clothing or similar products that would otherwise infringe copyright.

In practice, the main defence to copyright infringement is that the work (or at least a substantial part of the work) was not copied.

(See Section 1. Trade Mark for more details on the limitation period and formalities for assignments.)

3. DESIGN

3.1 Sources of law

Designs are one of the most useful and complex areas of law in the UK. As a result of Brexit, there are four different types of design which are potentially applicable in the UK:

- The first are UK registered designs (UK RD) which are governed by the Registered Designs Act 1949 (RDA). The RDA was substantially amended following the Community Designs Regulation 2002. This was the EU regulation that introduced a pan-EU registered design and ensured that all EU member states offered national registered designs which were consistent with EU law.
- The second and third are continuing and supplemental unregistered designs. These unregistered designs concern Community unregistered design right (CUDR). This is a complicated issue - the key takeaway is that to all intents and purposes CUDR continues to apply in the UK, for these purposes, let's call it Continuing CUDR or CCUDR.
- The fourth type is UK unregistered design right (UK UDR). This is a particular type of right which pre-dates CUDR. It is found in the CDPA and has a lot in common with copyright law.

3.2 Substantive law

UK registered designs (UK RD). UK RD protects the shape and appearance of the whole or part of a product which is visible in normal use. An application to register a design must be made within one year of the design first being made available to the public (the 'grace period').

The UK RD must be renewed every five years up to a maximum term of 25 years. There are substantial economies of scale so, broadly speaking, the more designs that are registered in relation to a particular product category, the less expensive each design becomes.

Logos, graphic symbols, user interfaces and similar can all be registered as designs.

The examination process does not consider whether or not the design is valid but simply assesses whether or not the relevant formalities have been complied with. UK RD are typically registered within a couple of weeks. They can be very helpful in infringement proceedings and in online enforcement.

Continuing community unregistered design right (CCUDR). CCUDR protects the shape and appearance of the whole or part of a product. It arises automatically when a CCUDR is first made available to the public and lasts for three years. It is the key IP right for the fashion industry.

The main difficulty with CCUDR is that it depends on the means by which it was first made available to the public. There is an ongoing query as to whether a design being first made available at London fashion week after Brexit might mean that it is not protected in the EU and vice versa for Paris Fashion Week and the UK. For now, the safest solution is to make any new designs simultaneously available online by publishing the collection on a website or social media at shortly before any catwalk show. There was a reference to the EU court on this point in 2019 but the parties appear to have reached a settlement and the reference has been withdrawn (*Beverly Hills Teddy Bear Company v PMS International Group*, Case C-728/19).

UK unregistered design right (UK UDR). UK UDR protects the shape or configuration of the whole or part of a product. Unlike UKRD and CCUDR, it does not protect surface decoration. UK UDR is a very versatile right which lasts for the shorter of 15 years from first creation or 10 years from first marketing.

In order to be eligible for UK UDR, the article made to a particular design or the relevant design document must have been made by a "qualified person". In practice, this means that they must be a national, resident or corporate entity registered in the UK, EU or a limited number of countries which offer the UK reciprocal protection (notably Hong Kong and New Zealand). It is sufficient for a company who meets the relevant criteria to instruct an individual who is not a qualified person to create the UK UDR.

First ownership of CCUDR and UK UDR is governed by the same approach as copyright. In other words, the first owner is the creator unless they are an employee or the rights have been assigned.

3.3 Enforcement

The main defence is that there is no infringement of the relevant design or the design is not valid. The test for infringement for UKRD or CCUDR is that the alleged infringing product produces the 'same overall impression' as the relevant design.

The test for UK UDR is that the infringing product is 'substantially the same' as the relevant design.

It is necessary to prove copying for both types of unregistered design. Copying is not a requirement for registered designs.

It is wise to maintain a list of all registered designs on the main company website via a link at the bottom of each page of the website.

Any type of design can be used to oppose or invalidate a trade mark and to

UNITED KINGDOM

invalidate a registered design. UKRD is particularly useful in online takedowns as they are quickly granted and clearly set out the relevant right claimed. However, when using designs it is important to be careful that a groundless threat is not being made. If this is the case, there is a significant risk of a counterclaim in response to a takedown. There is also the risk of proceedings being commenced to invalidate the design.

The same issues that apply to comparative advertising for trade marks apply to designs. There is no parody defence for designs.

UKRD and CCUDR do not apply in relation to the repair of a component part of a complex product in order to restore a product's original appearance.

It is common to bring proceedings for design infringement together with other rights. This might mean a combination of different designs, such as UK UDR and CCUDR, or could include passing off, copyright infringement and similar rights.

(See Section 1. Trade Mark for more details on the limitation period and formalities for assignments.)

4. RIGHT OF PRIVACY, PUBLICITY AND PERSONAL ENDORSEMENT

4.1 Sources of law

There is no law of image rights in the UK. Protection against use of a person's image is achieved via a patchwork of passing off, privacy law, data protection law (a photograph or other identifying image is personal data) and, less commonly, trade mark infringement.

4.2 Substantive law

Whether a claim for passing off is possible depends on whether the relevant person can claim goodwill in their likeness. This can be very challenging to prove. For example, Rihanna was able to prove that her likeness had goodwill in relation to fashion in a case against Arcadia but the bar for proving a false endorsement remains very high.

It is theoretically possible to assign goodwill to a company that trades under a person's likeness. This might enable a claim for passing off to be brought by a company. In practice, claims for false endorsement are brought by individuals.

Data protection and privacy law are personal rights which cannot be assigned.

A claim for trade mark infringement will be limited to the particular image that has been registered as a sign. It can be challenging to register an image of person as a trade mark in the first place so in practice, this route is rarely relied on. A trade mark may be assigned or licenced and does not need to be owned by the relevant individual.

4.3 Enforcement

Proving goodwill and misrepresentation in a false endorsement case can be challenging. If an image is "doctored" it may be easier to succeed.

See the trade marks section for more details on the requirements for passing off, limitation period and formalities for assignments.

5. PRODUCT PLACEMENT

Product placement in the UK means a company paying a TV channel, producer or distributor to include a product in a TV show. This type of placement is permitted in the UK but remains relatively rare in practice. It is not permitted on the BBC at all due to the rules which govern the BBC licence fee.

If product placement appears in a TV show, a logo must appear at the start and end of a programme and any advertising breaks to alert a viewer that the TV show includes product placement. The script cannot be changed to integrate the product and must be editorially justified.

Use of a product as a prop, without payment, is permitted without a notification being added. It may be possible to prevent the use of a product as a prop if it might imply a false endorsement or, less easily, qualify as a design infringement.

The product placement would be governed by contract. If the TV show failed to follow the product placement laws, they would be obliged to pay any fine that the regulator, Ofcom, decided to levy.

Product placement in film and international TV shows is permitted without any notification being required.

Luxury brands must approach product placement with particular caution as it can damage their "aura of luxury".

6. PROTECTION OF CORPORATE IMAGE AND REPUTATION

Corporations may be able to bring a claim for passing off in response to a false endorsement. It may also be possible to bring a claim for defamation or malicious falsehood in limited circumstances.

It is common to include a non-disparagement clause in sponsorship contracts or with celebrities and influencers. This gives rise to a claim for contract infringement.

As explained in relation to trade marks, it is possible for luxury brands to enter into selective distribution agreements and prohibit the re-sale of their products on specified platforms which might damage their aura of luxury. Broadly speaking, the more that a luxury brand restricts online sale, the easier it is to prevent online resale.

The 'exhaustion' of rights (known in the US as 'first sale doctrine') is currently in a state of flux in the UK. When the UK was part of the EU, it was part of the EU exhaustion regime. This meant that when a right holder first authorised a product to be sold in the European Economic Area (EEA) (the EU plus Norway, Liechtenstein and Iceland), the right holder could not prevent a resale within the EEA unless the goods had fundamentally changed prior to resale (for example, if they had been repackaged). The UK is currently operating on the basis that the rights in goods that were first sold in the EEA are exhausted but there is no such reciprocal relationship in place for rights in goods first sold in the UK. This is one of many issues post Brexit which requires a resolution.

There are many recent developments in successful and scalable business models relating to the resale, rental and repair of luxury goods. The main issues that arise concern ensuring that all goods involved are genuine and that any use of the trade mark or photographs are descriptive. By way of example, issues can arise when bidding on keywords or posting on social media.

There are various exceptions to infringement which can apply to spare parts, this is less of an issue for luxury brands, save for those in the automotive space.

Finally, in a contractual arrangement, liquidated damages are permitted but they must be a genuine pre-estimate of loss. If not, they will be void on the basis that they are a penalty clause.

AUTHOR BIOGRAPHY

Rosie Burbidge
Rosie Burbidge leads the fashion and retail team at Gunnercooke LLP. She is an Intellectual Property law partner and author of the award winning European Fashion Law: A Practical Guide from Start-up to Global Success.

From IP strategy, trademark and design portfolio management to multi jurisdiction litigation, Rosie and her team will identify the optimum strategy and deliver it in a timely manner with clear practical and pragmatic advice.

WIPR's Influential Women in IP identified Rosie as a trailblazer in 2019 – since then she has been identified by Legal 500 and, more recently, Chambers and Partners as one of the top intellectual property partners in the UK.

UNITED STATES

Alan Behr & the Phillips Nizer LLP Team
Phillips Nizer

Tod Melgar, Esq., a partner at Phillips Nizer LLP, authored the section on design patents. Yann Rim provided drafting, research and other support for the section on privacy and publicity (as well as other portions of this chapter) while serving as an intern at Phillips Nizer LLP.

UNITED STATES

THE VERY CURIOUS UNITED STATES LAW OF COPYRIGHT

One of the singular features of the common law method of jurisprudence is that, during key moments when judges have not had available to them the statutory tools to provide what they felt were just solutions, they have reorganized whatever was available to approximate the results they believed to be fair. That is essentially the origin behind the evolution of the United States Copyright Act into an instrument for protecting fashions and other categories of industrial design that inhabit the luxury market. Clothing, accessories, aircraft tailfins and all the rest of it are nowhere directly mentioned in the statute, and protecting designs of those items was never seen as a purpose of copyright law until comparatively recently; but now it is, at least to a point, due to judicial precedent.

The courts have thus filled a statutory gap in that the United States has never adopted EU-style legislation to protect many of the designs, both classic and *au courant*, of the kind familiar to the international market for luxury goods. It is therefore understandable that, in 1980, when *Kieselstein-Cord v. Accessories by Pearl, Inc.*, the first case of consequence protecting a luxury fashion design was won (by this law firm), the appellate court began with "This case is on a razor's edge of copyright law." 632 F.2d 989 (2d. Cir. 1980). The court then found a right of copyright in the ornamental elements of the buckles on two styles of luxury belts. The decision relied heavily on the doctrine of conceptual separability: if you can conceptualize the copyright-protectable decorative elements of an item as separable from its utilitarian elements (the functional parts of a belt buckle, for instance), the decorative elements are protectable if they meet minimal standards of originality.

Thirty-seven years later, the Supreme Court brought order to a developed body of law under which various federal appellate courts had applied different standards in examining whether a particular decorative element in a fashion item was protectable by copyright. In *Star Athletica, LLC v. Varsity Brands, Inc.* (137 S. Ct. 1002 (2017), the court essentially said that, if you could conceptually take a fabric design off a garment and frame it as art, it could be protected by copyright if it met minimum standards of originality. For three-dimensional elements, such as the belt buckle decorations of the *Kieselstein-Cord* case, the test would be whether they could, again conceptually, be put on pedestals as sculpture if they could pass the same minimal standards of originality. That is, the ornamentation on a belt buckle or bracelet clasp might be protectable, but only to the extent that it has nothing to do with keeping the belt or bracelet closed.

That still leaves garment shapes—the core of what is typically considered clothing design—unprotected in any way, a fact that helps explain why companies like Zara have such free reign in the United States to copy luxury designs. There have been several attempts in Congress to provide some legislative protection for clothing designs, albeit for shorter periods of time than for allowed works protectable under the Copyright Act in its current form. All of those efforts have failed. Although what is protectable by copyright in the area of fashion design therefore remains limited, what protection can be had lasts for the same long term of copyright as it applies to a novel or film: the life of the author plus seventy years. (For works-made-for-hire, the term is ninety-five years.)

UNITED STATES

If a work is a statutorily defined "United States work" (17 U.S.C. § 101), registration of the copyright in the work with the federal Copyright Office is a prerequisite for commencing an action for infringement. There are historical reasons for this largely anomalous (by world standards) insistence by the United States that copyrights must be registered, but that requirement has been enforced so strictly that mistakes made in applications that mature into registrations can, in certain cases, cause the registrations to be held invalid and whatever litigation that had been commenced to enforce those registrations to be dismissed. Add to that the cumbersome and often confusing online application process, and it would be hard to fault anyone who did not have to register a copyright in the United States (that is, anyone from outside the country) to consider skipping the registration process entirely. We continue to counsel in most cases not to do so, however. Among other benefits, the registration certificate brings with it a presumption of the validity of the copyright; if the claimed infringer believes otherwise, it is its burden to prove that. Just as important, online retailers and others in US commerce are used to the comfort of seeing a valid registration as an *imprimatur* for protectability, and having a registration certificate to attach to a cease and desist letter or takedown notice is typically a good way to bring potentially decisive firepower to bear.

There are two areas of United States copyright law that often remain, in equal parts, mysterious and frustrating to practitioners from other countries: the concepts of work-made-for-hire (17 U.S.C. § 101) and fair use (17 U.S.C. § 107). Both are statutory and stem in different ways from our core conception of copyright as a property right and not a personal right: a work protected by copyright is legally a commodity, as fungible in the marketplace as a sedan or a lawn mower. Whenever it is asked (as it has been for generations) why the Copyright Act does not recognize *droit moral* (the inalienable moral right of the creator not to see his or her creation altered or disturbed by others) in the protection of works of art or literature, it is in part because assessing artistic or cultural worth is not seen to be the business of the legislature or courts.

Your copyright, in short, is your property — not an extension of your personality or your personal rights — and that is where any legal inquiry into what you can do with it will both start and end. It is therefore possible for an author to divest himself or herself fully of all rights to his or her creation, from the start, as a work-made-for-hire, such as when making contributions to collaborative works or whenever doing anything creative and protectable in the service of an employer.

The work-made-for-hire doctrine was expressly laid out in the Copyright Act in good measure to protect the owners of motion pictures. The products of Hollywood, after all, collectively form a powerful presence in the American cultural experience. It also serves to assure that businesses can confidently use the work product provided by employees without restriction (in the absence of contractual provisions stating otherwise). Due to the work-made-for-hire concept, a frustrated CGI artist, for example, cannot demand that a film be pulled from distribution due to an unresolved creative dispute, and the employee who designed a fabric pattern cannot make a similar claim about a dress with that pattern that found its way into the retail channel over his or her objections.

UNITED STATES

Fair use started as a judge-made concept, but it has been codified in the current Copyright Act, 17 U.S.C. §107. In simple terms, the statute lays out four factors—strictly advisory as enacted but unfailingly applied by federal courts as if they were legislated requirements—to assess whether a copyright-protected work may be used in some form, format or manner by others without permission. Although the provision's terms are simple, clear and flexible, American copyright lawyers make a parlor game of trying to predict how pending fair-use cases will come out. That is because, as applied by the courts, the fair-use doctrine can sometimes appear to slam through copyright law like an errant football.

For instance, beginning in 1962, the artist Andy Warhol became famous in part due to his silkscreen prints and other works that depicted people and things. Although the subject of his first such effort was a one-dollar bill, many later works were based on original images (largely photographs) made by others. During Warhol's lifetime, that practice had sometimes been challenged both legally and ethically, but the works remained central to his artistic canon, the copyrights in much of which passed to a foundation formed after his death in 1987. In 2021, a federal appellate court rejected the defence of fair use raised by the foundation to an infringement claim made by the photographer of the image that formed the basis of a series of Warhol silkscreen prints and pencil drawings of the musician Prince. *Andy Warhol Foundation for the Visual Arts, Inc. v. Goldsmith*, 992 F.3d 99 (2d Cir. 2021), amended by (No. 19-2420-cv), 2021 WL 3742835 (2d Cir. Aug. 24, 2021). The case, which ironically had been initiated by the Warhol Foundation as a declaratory judgment action, is now on appeal before the Supreme Court. Although there are complex issues involving licenses, attribution and other factors arising from a fact pattern spanning decades, whatever its outcome at the Supreme Court, the case will likely add support to the belief, broadly held among United States copyright practitioners, that, when it comes to fair use, you should expect the unexpected.

For the makers and vendors of luxury goods (and that certainly includes works by famous artists), to resolve the question of whether what you are doing is considered fair use, therefore, the sensible course of action is to consult with United States copyright counsel; in doing so, be mindful that the ongoing unpredictability of judicial interpretations of the doctrine will continue to challenge even seasoned practitioners.

THE LUMBERING BUT EFFECTIVE UNITED STATES LAW OF TRADEMARKS
Overview

Although American copyright law has been a slow learner when called into the service of protecting the artistry of fashions, accessories and other fine goods across luxury categories, trademark law has been supportive from the beginning, albeit from a purely commercial perspective.

Our trademark law evolved from the English model of granting exclusive rights to identifiers of sources of goods and, later, services; it therefore incorporates key principles from both English common law and equity. Unlike either copyright or patent protection, which the Constitution says can only be granted by Congress "for limited times," under the use-based United States trademark system, as long as you can prove you are continuously using your mark in commerce among the states or from overseas into any state, your exclusive rights to that mark for your goods or services are theoretically perpetual.

For any non-functional visual element associated with a luxury brand — whether stylized designer initials on a gold bracelet or a hood ornament on a limousine — the key point to consider in determining if it can be claimed and registered as a trademark is if it identifies the brand as the source of the goods. That is why trademark law is sometimes called, without hint of cognitive dissonance, both a right of monopoly and a consumer protection mechanism. Consumers benefit because, if they see a familiar mark, they can trust that it came from the brand (or its licensee) they are seeking to patronize. And what business, caught on the competitive treadmill of a well-functioning market economy, does not secretly pine for the insouciant comfort of even a benign monopoly?

A Short Menu of Steps and Procedures

Following a rough start in the nineteenth century, the core elements for federal trademark protection have remained remarkably consistent.

The mark must be used as a mark, not merely a decorative element. A design spread across the front of a T-shirt is not a mark for the United States Patent and Trademark Office (USPTO) — just a pattern on a shirt. However, the demure Lacoste crocodile or the Ralph Lauren polo player on the top left of the front of a knit shirt is a mark because it is consistently used that way to identify its source. Note that, in the luxury market, usages of that kind — indeed, of all the forms in which "logo" clothing and accessory products are made and sold — have helped expand our notion of where marks can be placed and what does and does not qualify as usage as a mark. Similarly, the marketplace for luxury automobiles is trained to spot devices used as marks on grillwork, at the rear and as hood ornaments; somewhere on the vehicle will likely be the model name — also a mark in most cases.

Moving off the item proper, the hang tag attached to that item is an excellent place to display a trademark, there rarely being any dispute that the mark's purpose is to identify the source of the goods holding the tag. Packaging is the next point on which items can be identified with marks. Indeed, for alcoholic beverages, bottle shapes (as trade dress) and labels (incorporating trademarks) are just about the only reliable ways to identify the source of origin of the contents, and in a market in which a bottle of red wine, for example, can cost a few dollars or thousands of dollars, the distinction (until the bottle is opened) is all about what is on the label. For either consumer goods or services, the use of a mark on a sales site to identify the source of what is being offered is also use as a mark.

Even though registration is not a prerequisite in the United States either to the creation or enforcement of exclusive rights to a mark, except for those style and model marks that are anticipated to last only for a season or two, federal registration of core marks and even secondary marks is nearly always advisable. Filing through the World Intellectual Property Organization (WIPO) under the broadly accepted Madrid System is practical and comparatively quick, but for complicated, multiclass applications for luxury goods or services, doing so is typically more trouble than it is worth. Using the WIPO method, an applicant can file one application for multiple nations at the organization's modernist headquarters near the southern tip of Lake Geneva. It works brilliantly for so many participating nations—just not this one. As one examining attorney of the USPTO once told me, "We are like children. We are very literal." What she meant was that the office expects what, by international standards, are excruciatingly exact lists of goods and services in its applications— something that applicants filing through WIPO routinely fail to provide. To make your WIPO application acceptable to the USPTO, you will need to hire US counsel, but be mindful that, in nearly all cases of which we are aware, fixing the problem that way has proven more expensive than would have been the case had the applicant bypassed WIPO and instructed US counsel to file a national application directly with the USPTO in the first instance.

Although response times vary widely due to workflow and other factors, an applicant can generally expect a turnaround time from the USPTO of between six to eighteen months, from application to registration. Much will depend on how quickly the applicant responds to any office action issued by the examiner for which corrections, clarifications, amendments and responsive arguments will be needed in order to satisfy the office's requirements for registration.

Once granted, registrations must be renewed every ten years. Renewal requires demonstration to the satisfaction of the USPTO that the mark has been in continuous use in interstate commerce in the form substantially in which it was registered. Any goods or services no longer offered under the mark would need to be stricken from the registration at that time. Generally, other than for momentary gaps (which are common in luxury markets, often due to the need to relaunch, rebrand or follow trends), the requirement is for continuous and (this is important) consistent use.

Because luxury rides on a stream of innovation, novelty and change, during the ten years between registration and renewal, it is not uncommon for a mark to have evolved into something different from the form it which it was registered. Again, the USPTO is very literal. Adding a word or even a letter to a mark, as shown in the required specimen of use, could change it enough to prevent renewal of the registration. Similarly, if color was named in the registration as a feature of the mark, or if a particular font or positioning of lettering was also so named, changing any of that may defeat an attempt to renew.

Special Considerations

Given that the United States allows marks to remain unregistered and yet receive full protection under law, a simple examination of the USPTO database (TESS) will not suffice to give a reasonable measure of confidence that a proposed mark can be used without fear of a third-party claim. Consider that in light of the cost to a luxury brand if something goes so wrong that the product has to be pulled at launch (to name just one of several possible nightmare scenarios). That is the reason we strongly encourage our luxury clients, in other than limited and specific circumstances, to authorize us to conduct what is known as a full search of multiple databases.

Another distinction of United States trademark law is the willingness of the USPTO and the courts to reject efforts to claim as marks those terms that, arguably, are merely descriptive of the goods and services they brand. Given the quantity of those marks that come into the USA from other nations, the USPTO has developed its Supplemental Register as a companion to its main trademark register, which is known as its Principal Register. A registration on the Supplemental Register provides modest but authentic advantages, and after five years, the opportunity arises to demonstrate secondary meaning. If the registrant can show that the registered mark has come to be known in the marketplace not as a mere description for the applicable goods and services but as a source identifier, the USPTO will permit the mark to be registered on the Principal Register if a new application is filed with sufficient proof.

In the luxury market, where change is good, styles and models quite purposefully come and go. There are perennials, of course, from Hermès Birkin and Kelly bags to Leica M rangefinder cameras to Mercedes-Benz E-Class sedans. But most models and styles are seasonal, and the question becomes: is it worth the time and expense to apply to register them as trademarks? Although that question is usually answered in the negative, there are exceptions, and a careful examination of marketing objectives in light of cost-effectiveness should be made on a case-by-case basis.

Under precedent that developed in the past few decades, color can be a trademark in the United States. In the luxury area, the classic example is Tiffany, which has even taken the trouble to get its own Pantone shade for its distinctive robin-egg blue (Pantone 1837 Blue). Any jewelry maker with boxes that appear in shades sufficiently close will likely hear from counsel for Tiffany. Successfully claiming color as a mark on products themselves as opposed to their packaging is more challenging, requiring a clear showing of secondary meaning. Rather famously, Christian Louboutin was able to assert trademark rights in its red soles for shoes. Christian Louboutin lost the battle but won the war: the Second Circuit Court of Appeals held that Saint Laurent shoes that were red all over (soles and uppers) did not infringe on the registration held by Christian Louboutin for its red soles (giving the immediate win to Saint Laurent), but the Louboutin registration was held to be valid and enforceable against shoes with uppers in any color other than red because Louboutin was able to sustain its claim that the soles had acquired secondary meaning *Christian Louboutin S.A., et al. v. Yves Saint Laurent America, Inc., et al.*, 695 F.3d 206 (2nd Cir. 2012).

As the foregoing shows, trademark law in the United States offers a range of protection that demonstrably benefits brands in luxury categories, but the process only works when brand owners remain vigilant. Add to it the fact that luxury brands are particularly susceptible to counterfeiting and you can see why, in the USA, much of trademark law as applied to luxury goods and services is about having both a watchful eye and continued attention to detail. Although we all can name exceptions, the general rule is that luxury brands drive markets, not merely with standards of taste and quality, but by turning purchasing into an aspirational pursuit. With so much involved, and with so much at stake, trademark protection and enforcement should therefore remain an absolute priority for any luxury brand seeking to build and protect its reputation in the American marketplace.

DESIGN PATENT LAW FINDS A HOME

Design patent law had, for a long time, an identity crisis. It was drawn up in the nineteenth century to provide protection for ornamental designs in useful articles—in particular ornamental designs in cast iron, but also creative designs of fabrics, rugs and clothing of the era. At the time, there was no means of protecting the ornamental designs because copyright law did not extend to three-dimensional works, and patent protection was only available for the functional and utilitarian aspects of articles of manufacture. Efforts to remedy that deficiency ultimately came to fruition in 1842 in the form of the first design patent law. Act of Aug. 29, 1842, ch. 263, sec. 3, 5 Stat. 543, 543-44. That statue was the foundation for modern United States design patent legislation, through the current law, which provides protection for "original and ornamental design for an article of manufacture..." 35 U.S.C. §171.

Today, all manner of ornamental design in luxury articles can be protected under design patent law, including fabric designs and patterns, articles of clothing, and consumer products, as shown in the examples below:

Fabric Pattern by Louis Vuitton Malletier (U.S. D500,411)	Shoe Design by Fendi S.R.L (U.S. D901,850)	Watch Bezel by Rolex Watch USA (U.S. D695144)

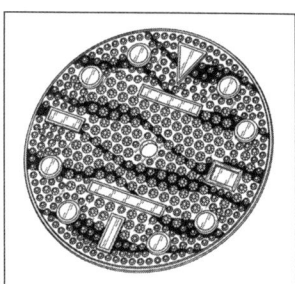

The design must contain novel and non-obvious ornamental features that are not purely functional. The invention must be new and non-obvious. Unlike copyright and trademark law, the inventor's own prior public disclosure and use of the subject design may create a bar to obtaining a design patent. The law does, however, give a one-year grace period during which the inventor may publicly disclose and use the invention without creating a bar to patentability.

In contrast to the procedure in many other countries, a design patent application in the United States must be filed in the name of the inventor. The application can, however, immediately be assigned to an entity. The employer of an inventor whose design was created for the company should have an employment agreement in place that requires employees to make such an assignment and to cooperate in the prosecution of applications.

The USPTO typically takes twelve to eighteen months to grant a patent based on an application. A granted patent lasts for fifteen years. After issuance, a design patent can be enforced against any person or entity that is infringing the patented ornamental design. Determining whether there is infringement is a two-part test: (1) the court must first construe the claim to determine its meanings and scope; and (2) the fact finder (that is, the judge or the jury, as the case may be) must compare the properly construed claim to the accused design.

During claim construction, design patents "typically are claimed as shown in the drawings" contained in the registration, but construction can be helpful to "distinguish between those features of the claimed design that are ornamental and those that are purely functional," because the functional elements of a design cannot be part of the claimed subject matter. *Egyptian Goddess, Inc. v. Swisa Inc.*, 543 F.3d 665, 679-80 (Fed. Cir. 2008). In comparing the claim to the accused design, the "ordinary observer" test is applied, with the fact finder seeking to make the comparison through the eyes of an observer familiar with the prior art, "giving such attention as a purchaser usually gives, two designs are substantially the same, if the resemblance is such as to deceive such an observer, inducing . . . purchase [of] one supposing it to be the other, the first one patented is infringed by the other." Id. at 670, 677.

An action for design patent infringement typically seeks two remedies: (1) an injunction against further sales of the infringing product, and (2) damages to compensate the patent owner for the infringement. A unique feature of the law that has brought more interest to design patents in recent years is that it provides an alternative measure of damages not available for utility patents. Specifically, 35 U.S.C. § 289 states that, whoever "sells or exposes for sale any article of manufacture to which such design or colorable imitation has been applied shall be liable to the owner to the extent of his total profit." A recovery in the event of a previously profitable infringement of the design of a luxury item could therefore be potentially significant — if collectable.

RIGHTS OF PRIVACY AND PUBLICITY FOR THE LIVING AND THE DEAD

Unlike copyright, trademark and design patent law, privacy and publicity are governed largely by state law. Although parental childrearing rights and a woman's reproductive and abortion rights have been grounded in an unwritten constitutional right of privacy, that is a very particular line of cases, one that has not resulted in a universal, federal right of privacy for all purposes. Currently, over thirty states recognize the right of publicity in some form, either under a state statute, state common law or both. Although the privacy side of these twin rights can be said to apply equally to all, the right of publicity is, at its core, largely a benefit to those persons, such as celebrities, who can monetize their personalities. *KNB Enters. v. Matthews*, 92 Cal. Rptr. 2d 713, 717 (Ct. App. 2000). The classic rule was that the right expires on the death of the rights holder, but a majority of the states that recognize the right for their residents now extend it past death. The term and other considerations vary from state to state, with California, the home to many celebrities, recognizing the right for seventy years after death. Cal. Civ Code § 3344.1. Two other states (Oklahoma and Indiana) take it to a full century of protection. New York State is a newcomer to the concept, courtesy of legislation enacted in 2020 that grants post-mortem publicity rights for forty years following death. N.Y. Civ. Rights Law §§ 50 and 51.

Although some states will infer a license of publicity rights from a course of conduct, good practice, as with nearly all important business relationships under the common law, is to have a properly detailed agreement. See *Madrigal Audio Laboratories, Inc. v. Cello, Ltd.*, 799 F.2d 814, 822, 230 U.S.P.Q. 764 (2d Cir. 1986). As with any license, one covering the right to use a celebrity's name, image, voice and other indicia of personality requires a clear grant of rights, performance and payment provisions, but of particular sensitivity these days is the morals clause (also called a moral turpitude clause), which grants the licensee the right to exit the deal, along with other rights, if the celebrity participates in wrongful acts during the contract term.

Celebrities, in the popular definition of people who are well-known for being well-known, can bring great benefits as licensors and endorsers, as many luxury brands have demonstrated over the years. Running in a parallel course now are influencers who, even if self-made, self-taught and free from supervision or editorial oversight, can yet have a powerful effect on brand recognition and acceptance. It has long been the practice, whenever engaging a celebrity, influencer or anyone else to work with a luxury brand, to add a morals clause. It gives a contractual "out" in the event that the person gets into serious trouble, such as criminal activity or the commission of an act that is immoral under generally accepted standards (the definition of which could vary greatly depending on era and circumstances). Only comparatively recently, it has been growing harder to shock or scandalize, making loosely drafted morals clauses more difficult to enforce. However, a magic wand of hyper-sensitivity has now descended, particularly upon young present and future consumers of luxury goods.

In the current environment in the United States, where the #MeToo movement has risen to have such a powerful public presence, and where the recently or habitually famous can be "cancelled" (the electronic-age equivalent of "shunning") for making statements that are potentially dangerous to a brand — even if thoughtfully expressed or factually correct — luxury brands typically insist on morals clauses that give them broad leeway. Being right on a point or having proof that a scandalous allegation is false is no longer enough to assure containment of reputational damage. Was J. K. Rowling cancelled on social media for expressing her opinion on whether a man can be altered into being a woman, and did she then cancel Stephen King for disagreeing with her? They both appear able to ride that wave, but it would not be unreasonable for a luxury brand to elect to steer clear from the entire debate should more equivocal figures be involved. See *www.forbes.com/sites/dawnstaceyennis/2021/05/24/jk-rowling-canceled-stephen-king-for-supporting-transgender-women*.

It is therefore not unreasonable for a brand to seek to include a clause that gives it the right to push the "eject" button immediately and without notice for any reason it deems appropriate for preserving its reputation. The celebrity may insist on exit compensation, whether determined later by arbitration or otherwise, but that can be the subject of negotiation. The main point is that, if the celebrity becomes a potential liability, even under circumstances that, in a more gracious age might have seemed unfair or even unjust, a luxury brand can easily find itself in an incredibly difficult position overnight, and contracts should be drafted with that in mind.

CONCLUSION

An age of interlayered surprises breeds unexpected actions and counteractions. In response, custom and the law may bend, the former in curious ways and the

UNITED STATES

latter in a manner intended to catch up. This is, accordingly, a good moment for luxury brands to pause, reassess their values and priorities—and to check in with counsel. Chances are, something different will need to be done to keep legal practices both creative and vital.

AUTHOR BIOGRAPHIES

Alan Behr

Alan Behr is a partner in the Corporate & Business Law Department and Intellectual Property Practice, and chairman of the Fashion and Luxury Practice Group at Phillips Nizer LLP in New York City. He is also a member of the firm's Executive Committee. Mr. Behr is the chairman of the Enforcement Subcommittee of the Copyright Committee of the International Trademark Association and a member of the Fashion Law Committee of the New York City Bar Association. Mr. Behr concentrates his practice on international intellectual property, fashion and entertainment law and represents established and up-and-coming businesses and individuals in the fields of electronic entertainment, emerging technologies, publishing, fashion, and consumer products. He is a member of the International Trademark Association Panel of Trademark Mediators, the Centre for Effective Dispute Resolution (UK) Exchange Network, has been selected as an International Mediator and a member of the Panel of Distinguished Neutrals for the International Institute for Conflict Prevention & Resolution (CPR). He has been selected by World Trademark Review (WTR) 1000 as one of the leading professionals in trademark law for enforcement and litigation, prosecution and strategy since 2011. He is a frequent author of articles and posts on legal topics and a contributor to books on law and photography.

Tod M. Melgar

Tod M. Melgar is a partner in the Intellectual Property and Litigation Practices and chairman of the Patent Law Practice Group at Phillips Nizer LLP in New York City. Mr. Melgar has been litigating intellectual property cases throughout the United States district and appellate courts for more than twenty years, representing clients in a wide range of patent, trade secret, copyright and trademark disputes, spanning a broad array of leading industries, including fashion, computer hardware and software, medical devices, cellular and digital transmission systems, LEDs and lasers. Mr. Melgar is a registered patent attorney licensed to practice before the United States Patent and Trademark Office (USPTO) and has prepared and prosecuted hundreds of patent and trademark applications. Early in his career, he was also a patent examiner at the USPTO. He has successfully argued and litigated patent validity disputes before the Patent Trial and Appeal Board (PTAB), including appeals, inter partes review (IPR) and reexamination proceedings.

Yann Rim

Yann Rim, a graduate of Loyola Law School in Los Angeles and Paris-Sud University in Paris, France, provided drafting, research and other support for the section on privacy and publicity as well as other portions of this chapter while serving as an intern at Phillips Nizer LLP.

CONTACT DETAILS

CONTACT DETAILS

BELGIUM
Moana Colaneri
Beyond Law Firm
Louizalaan 283/24 Avenue Louise
B-1050 Brussels
Belgium
T: +32 474 40 69 35
E: mco@beyond-lawfirm.com
W: www.beyond-lawfirm.com

BRAZIL
Luiz Edgard Montaury Pimenta & Marianna Furtado de Mendonça
Montaury Pimenta, Machado & Vieira de Mello
Av. Almirante Barroso, 139, 7th Floor
Downtown - Rio de Janeiro
Brazil - 20031.005
T: +55 21 2524 0510
E: montaury@montaury.com.br
     luiz@montaury.com.br
     marianna@montaury.com.br
W: www.montaury.com.br

CHINA
Yunze LIAN & Rebecca LIU
Jadong IP Law Firm
Unit 2705, Full Tower
No. 9 Dongsanhuan Zhong Road
Chaoyang
Beijing 100020
China
T: +86 10 8591 3360
F: +86 10 8591 3350
E: lian@jadong.com.cn
     liu@jadong.com.cn
W: www.jadong.com.cn

CYPRUS
Maria Hinni, George Tashev, Nasos Kafantaris & Ioanna Martidi
A.G. Paphitis & Co
"AGP Chambers"
84 Spyrou Kyprianou Avenue
4004 Limassol
Cyprus
T: +357 25 731000
F: +357 25 761004
E: maria.hinni@agplaw.com
     george.tashev@agplaw.com
     athanasios.kafantaris@agplaw.com
     ioanna.martidi@agplaw.com
W: www.agplaw.com

CZECHIA
Michal Havlík & Michael Feuerstein
Všetečka Zelený Švorčík & Partners
Hálkova 2,
120 00 Praha 2
Czech Republic
T: + 420 224 941 833
F: + 420 224 943 092
E: office@sak-alo.cz
W: www.sak-alo.cz

FRANCE
Sophie Marc
Santarelli
49, avenue des Champs-Elysées
75008 Paris
France
T: +33 1 40 55 43 43
F: +33 1 42 67 56 29
E: sophie.marc@santarelli.com
W: www.santarelli.com

CONTACT DETAILS

GERMANY
Dr. Wiebke Baars
Taylor Wessing
Am Sandtorkai 41
20457 Hamburg, Germany
T: +49 40 36803 220
F: +49 40 36803 280
E: w.baars@taylorwessing.com
W: www.taylorwessing.com

INDIA
Pravin Anand, Dhruv Anand, Udita M. Patro, Kavya Mammen & Sampurnaa Sanyal
Anand and Anand
First Channel Building Plot No. 17A
Sector 16A, Film City
Noida 201301 (UP), India
T: +91 120 4059300
F: +91 120 4243056
E: email@anandandanand.com
W: www.anandandanand.com

ITALY
Fabrizio Jacobacci
Studio Legale Jacobacci & Associati
Via Senato 8
20121 Milan, Italy
T: +39 02 76 02 25 13
F: +39 02 78 16 58
E: fjacobacci@jacobacci-law.com
W: www.jacobacci-law.com

JAPAN
Koichi Nakatani
Momo-o, Matsuo & Namba
Kojimachi Diamond Building
4-1 Kojimachi, Chiyoda-ku
Tokyo 102-0083, Japan
T: + 81 03 3288 2080
E: nakatani@mmn-law.gr.jp
       mmn@mmn-law.gr.jp
W: www.mmn-law.gr.jp

NETHERLANDS
Tjeerd Overdijk, Herwin Roerdink & Nadine Reijnders-Wiersma
Vondst Advocaten
De Lairessestraat 111-115,
1075 HH Amsterdam
Netherlands
T: +31 20 504 20 00
E: tjeerd.overdijk@vondst.com
       herwin.roerdink@vondst.com
       nadine.reijnders@vondst.com
W: www.vondst.com

SOUTH KOREA
Dae Hyun Seo & Won Joong Kim
Kim & Chang
Jeongdong Building, 17F, 21-15
Jeongdong-gil,
Jung-gu, Seoul 04518
South Korea
T: +82 2 2122 3900
F: +82 2 2122 3800 / 741 0328
E: ip-group@kimchang.com
W: www.ip.kimchang.com

SPAIN
Rubén Canales, Eleonora Carrillo, Carolina Montero, Fernando Ortega & Ignacio Temiño
Jacobacci Abril Abogados
C. Zurbano, 76
28010 Madrid
Spain
T: +34 91 7020331
F: +34 91 3083705
E: rcanales@abrilabogados.com
       ecarrillo@jacobacci.com
       cmontero@abrilabogados.com
       fortega@abrilabogados.com
       ignaciot@jacobacci-law.com
W: www.abrilabogados.com

CONTACT DETAILS

TAIWAN
Tsai, Lee & Chen
Crystal J. Chen & Nick J.C. Lan
11th floor
148 Songjiang Road
Taipei 104492
Taiwan
T: +886 2 2571 0150
E: cjchen@tsailee.com.tw
   info@tsailee.com.tw
W: www.tsailee.com

TURKEY
Özlem Futman & Yasemin Aktas
Ofo Ventura
Levent Mah. Cilekli
Caddesi No: 2
34330 Besiktas,
Istanbul
Turkey
T: +90 212 219 67 33
E: ofutman@ofoventura.com.tr
   yaktas@ofoventura.com.tr
   info@ofoventura.com.tr
W: www.ofoventura.com.tr

UNITED KINGDOM
Rosie Burbidge
Gunnercooke
1 Cornhill
London
EC3V 3ND
United Kingdom
T: +44 7708 923 374
E: rosie.burbidge@gunnercooke.com
W: www.gunnercooke.com

UNITED STATES
Alan Behr, Esq. & Tod Melgar, Esq.
Phillips Nizer
485 Lexington Avenue
New York, NY 10017
United States
T: +1 212 977 9700
F: +1 212 262 5152
E: ABehr@PhillipsNizer.com
   TMelgar@PhillipsNizer.com
W: www.phillipsnizer.com